REGIONAL RURAL BANKS AND UPLIFTMENT OF RURAL SOCIETY

CONTENTS

FOREWORD

In India the problem of finance to farmers and other poor sections of the rural society has been very acute since long. The Government of India, after accepting the recommendations of the working group on Rural Bank, set-up five Regional Rural Banks on October 2, 1975 at Gorakhpur and Moradabad in Uttar Pradesh, Bhiwani in Haryana, Jaipur in Rajasthan and Malda in West Bengal. At present, there are 196 Regional Rural Banks in 23 states with more than 14,000 branches. In U.P. the number of these banks and their branches is highest.

The main objectives of these banks are: (i) to grant loans and advances to small and marginal farmers; (ii) to grant loans and advances to co-operative societies, primary agricultural societies and farmers' service societies for agricultural operations; and (iii) to grant loans and advances to artisans, small entrepreneurs and persons of small means engaged in trade, industries and other productive activities. Thus, the main objective of the Regional Rural Banks is to provide financial assistance to weaker sections of the rural society.

These banks have played a very important role in poverty reduction in rural areas and have also mobilised rural savings. Their role in implementing the integrated rural development programme is also commendable. However, there are various problems before them. In view of this, the government of India has taken several steps to improve their viability but still much has to be done in this respect.

The book edited by Dr. Meenu Agrawal by highlighting the ideas and philosophy of learned and eminent scholars, academicians, professors and lecturers in form of research articles, has done a pioneering work in field of the contribution of Regional

Rural Banks in the rural sector in India.

The renowned and reputed scholars from different parts of the country who have contributed their invaluable papers in this volume deserve appreciation.

DR. R.C. AGRAWAL
Formerly: Dean, Faculty of Commerce. & Business Administration, CCS University, Meerut.
Presently: Director, Noida College of Physical Education, Noida (G.B. Nagar).

ACKNOWLEDGEMENTS

A two-day National Seminar on "Role of Rural Banks for Economic Upliftment of Weaker Sections of Rural Society" was held at Ginni Devi Modi Girls' (P.G.) College, Modinagar, UP on 7th and 8th of November, 2008.

I was personally able to examine the quality of the papers at the Seminar. The ever increasing number of papers reflect the rising interest of the authors in academic activities.

For their support and guidance, without whose invaluable contribution the present book could not have turned into reality with such a high standard quality, I am indebted:

To the President, the Manager and all Members of the Management Committee of Ginni Devi Modi Girls (Post-Graduate) College, Modinagar.

To the Principal of Ginni Devi Modi Girls (P.G.) College, Modinagar Prof. Rita Bakshi, for making the provision for necessary facilities to the Department of Economics for organizing the National Seminar.

To my father, Retd. Principal, Ex-Dean, Faculty of Commerce & Business Administration, CCS University, Meerut, Dr. R.C. Agrawal, for his tireless checking of tables, figures, and diagrams and editorial work.

To my mother-in-law, Mrs Gaura Devi, and mother Smt. Kusum Lata who played the key role and whose guidance encouraged me to venture to take on the massive task of writing this volume.

To my husband, Shri Sudhish Aggarwala, for his precious guidance and immense cooperation in this daunting task and my sons Nitish Aggarwala and Kavish Aggarwala, without whose constant and unparalleled support enabled me to keep up the work.

To my sister, Reader & Head, Department of Economics, AKP College, Hapur Dr. Babita Agrawal, for her contribution of precious ideas that concepts that have become a major part of the book.

To my project fellow Ms. Bhawana, Department of Economics, my research scholars Ms. Aditi Tyagi, Ms. Juhi Gupta, Ms. Anita Roy, Department of Economics, Dr. Suman Lata, Lecturer, Department of Economics, Dr. Meenu Agrawal, Ms. Priya Mittal, Ms. Rakhee Mittal, and Ms. Preeti Chhabra, Lecturers, Deptt. of Home-Science, for their kind co-operation in making available the latest information.

To all contributors whose permission was essential to bring out this book in the present form.

To University Grants Commission, New Delhi, for provision of financial assistance for organisation of the National Seminar.

To Deep & Deep Publications Pvt. Ltd., who painstaking edited early drafts of the research papers.

To Dr. K.D. Gaur, Deputy Director, ICSSR, New Delhi; Dr. Sudhansu Shekar Mishra, Reader & Head, Department of Commerce; UNS Mahavidyalya, Mugpal, Jajpur, Orissa; Prof. Prahlad Kumar, Reader & Head, Department of Economics, Allahabad University, Allahabad; Dr. Shobana Nelsco, Reader, Department of Economics; Fatima Post-Graduate College, Madurai; Shri A.K. Loomba, Chairman, Serve UP Gramin Bank, Meerut; Dr. Anil Gupta, Reader & Head, Department of Economics, SDPG College, Muzaffarnagar; Dr. Shyam Sunder Singh Chauhan, Reader and Head, Department of Economics, Government Girls (PG) College, Sirsaganj, Firozabad (U.P.); Dr. A.K. Tomar, Reader & Head, Department of Economics, D.S. College, Aligarh; Prof. R.N. Thakur, Reader & Head, Department of Economics, Samastipur PG College, Samastipur, Bihar; Dr. B.K. Jha, Reader & Head, Department of Economics, DBKN College, Narhan, Samstipur, Bihar.

And to those others whose names cannot all be mentioned here for the sake of brevity.

List of Contributors

Prof. Prahlad Kumar, Reader & Head, Department of Economics, University of Allahabad, Allahabad.

Mr. Vinayak Kant Mishra, Research Scholar, Department of Economics, University of Allahabad, Allahabad.

Mr. Durgesh Kumar Singh, Research Scholar, Department of Economics, University of Allahabad, Allahabad.

Dr. Jai Prakash, Reader and Head, Department of Economics, B.V.R.I., Bichpuri, Agra.

Dr. Meenu Agrawal, Director, Major Research Project and Reader and Head, Deptt. of Economics, Ginni Devi Modi Girls (PG) College, Modinagar.

Dr. Babita Agrawal, Reader and Head, Deptt. of Economics, A.K.P.G. College, Hapur.

Ms. Aditi Tyagi, Research Scholar, Deptt. of Economics, G.D.M. Girls (PG) College, Modinagar.

Mr. Anil Kumar Sharma, Senior Lecturer, Institute of Business Management, Mangalayatan University, Beswan, Aligarh (UP).

Dr. Sidharth Jain, Senior Lecturer, Institute of Business Management, Mangalayatan University, Beswan, Aligarh (UP).

Dr. Shyam Sunder Singh Chauhan, Reader and Head, Deptt. of Economics, Government Girls (PG) College, Sirsaganj, Firozabad (UP).

Mr. Manish Dev, Research Scholar, Deptt. of Economics, Wavair College, Shikohabad, Firozabad (UP).

Dr. Sheelpria Tripathi, Reader and Head, Deptt. of Economic, Government College, Gunnaor, Badaun (UP).

Dr. Nirmal Bindra, Rt. Reader & Head, Deptt. of Economics, M.L. PG College, Saharanpur.

Dr. Sandeep Shandilya, Head of Department, Institute of Business Management, Mangalayatan University, Beswan, Aligarh (UP).

Dr. R.K. Mishra, Lecturer, Institute of Business Management, Mangalayatan University, Beswan, Aligarh (UP).

Dr. Vandana Tyagi, Director, Dr. Ram Manohar Lohia Institute, Modinagar.

Dr. Halima Sadia Rizvi, Associate Professor, Deptt. of Economics, Jamia Millia Islamia University, New Delhi

Ms. Sahna Andrew, Research Scholar, Deptt. of Economics, Jamia Millia Islamia University, New Delhi

Dr. Virendra Kumar, Lecturer, Durga Parsad Baljeet Singh (PG) College, Anoopshahar, Bulandshahar.

Dr. Hari Mohan Mittal, Assistant Professor, University of Rajasthan, Jaipur.

Ms. Bharti Chauhan, LL.M., Advocate, High Court of Rajasthan.

Dr. M.L. Agarwal, Reader & Head, Faculty of Commerce and Business Administration, D.N. College, Meerut (UP).

Ms. Karishna Saraswat

Dr. Anil Gupta, Head, Department of Economics, S.D. College, Muzaffarnagar.

Mr. Atul Gupta, Sr. Lecturer, Statistics, Hindu College, Moradabad.

Dr. Suman Lata, Lecturer, Department of Economics, G.D.M. Girls (P.G.) College, Modinagar.

Ms. Lipi, Research Scholar, Deptt. of Economics, G.D.M. Girls (P.G.) College, Modinagar.

Prof. R.N. Singh, Reader and Head, Deptt. of Economics, Deoghar PG College, Deoghar.

Dr. A. Kumar, Lecturer, Deptt. of Geography, D.A.V. College, Siwan (Bihar).

Ms. Meenakshi Sharma, Research Scholar, Deptt. of Economics, G.D.M. Girls (PG) College, Modinagar.

Mr. Tarun Sharma, Research Scholar, Deptt. of Economics, G.D.M. Girls (PG) College, Modinagar.

Ms. Bhawana Tyagi, Project Fellow, Deptt. of Economics, G.D.M. Girls (PG) College, Modinagar.

Dr. Pratibha Kushwaha, Human Resource Consultant, Faridabad, Haryana.

Ms. Preeti Chhabra, Lecturer, Food and Nutrition, Department of Home Science, G.D.M. Girls (PG) College, Modinagar.

Ms. Priya Mittal, Lecturer, Clothing and Textiles, Department of Home Science, G.D.M. Girls (PG) College, Modinagar.

Mr. Anil Kumar Roy, Research Scholar, Samastipur Post Graduate College, Bihar.

Mr. Prabhat Kumar, Research Scholar, Samastipur Post Graduate College, Bihar

Dr. C.P. Gupta, Lecturer and Head of Department of E.A.F.M., S.P.P.G. College, Bijainagar (Ajmer), Rajasthan.

Ms. Kamlesh Gupta, Teacher, Zinc Vidyalaya, Zinc Colony, Hurda (Bhilwara), Rajasthan.

Mr. Rohit Mehra, Lecturer, Deptt. of Management, Dr. K.N.M.I.E.T., Modinagar.

Ms. Shruti Singh, Head, Deptt. of Management, Dr. K.N.M.I.E.T., Modinagar.

Dr. Prabha Singh, Lecturer in B.Ed. Department, SG Degree College, Lucknow.

Dr. Anju Pal, Lecturer, Deptt. of Pol. Sc., GDM Girls (PG) College, Modinagar.

Dr. Upasna Sharma, Lecturer, Department of Economics, Dr. Susheela Tiwari Degree College, Sitarganj, District Udham Singh Nagar, Uttarakhand.

Dr. Sarita Jain, Lecturer, Department of Economics, G.D.M. Girls (PG) College, Modinagar.

Mrs. Anupa Singh, Lecturer, Department of Economics, D.N. (PG) College, Meerut.

Ms. Shikha Tyagi, Lecturer, Deptt. of Computers, G.D.M. (PG) College, Modinagar.

Ms. Asha Bansal, Lecturer, Deptt. of Economics of Phy. Education, G.D.M. (PG) College, Modinagar.

Ms. Namrata Sharma, Lecturer, Deptt. of Computers, G.D.M. (PG) College, Modinagar.

Ms. Shubhi Goyal, MBA, Research Scholar, MMHPG College, Ghaziabad.

Ms. Chandni Gupta, Computer Department, G.D.M. Girls (PG) College, Modinagar.

Ms. Priyanjana Maurya, Lecturer, Deptt. of Economics, Noida College of Physical Education, Noida.

Dr. Shailendra Bhushan Sharma, Lecturer, Deptt. of Economics, Noida College of Physical Education, Noida.

Dr. Rajeev Tyagi, Unique Institute of Management, Muradnagar.

Dr. Rupesh Tyagi, Lecturer in Economics, G.D.M. Girls (PG) College, Modinagar.

Ms. Neetu Dubey, Research Scholar, D.S. College, Aligarh.

Ms. Renu Dubey, Lecturer, IBM Faculty, Mangalayatan University, Aligarh.

Mr. Mukesh Sharma, Research Scholar, D.S. College, Aligarh.

Regional Rural Banks and their Role Towards Financial Inclusion: Pre- and Post-Merger Scenario

Prof. Prahlad Kumar, Mr. Vinayak Kant Mishra and
Dr. Durgesh Kumar Singh

Regional Rural Banks were established consequent to the acceptance by the Government of India of the recommendations of a working group or rural Banks appointed by the Union Finance Ministry in July 1975, under the Chairmanship of M. Narasimham. The first five RRBs were established on October 2, 1975 following the promulgation of the RRBs ordinance by the Government of India on September 26, 1975. The ordinance was subsequently replaced by the RRB Act, 1976 with an objective to ensure sufficient institutional credit for agriculture and other rural sectors.

RRBs came into existence in 1975 in twelve districts with seventeen branches. The issued and paid up share capital of each RRB is Rs. 25 lakh (subsequently raised to Rs. 100 lakh in March 1996) is held by the GOI, the Sponsor Bank (27 scheduled commercial banks and one state cooperative bank), and the concerned state government in the proportion of 50:35:15

respectively. The management of each RRB is vested in a Board of Directors headed by a Chairman (usually an officer of a sponsor bank and appointed by the Government of India). As in March, 1997, there were 196 RRBs. covering 436 districts, with a network of 14,450 branches in the country.

Since, the establishment of RRBs, there has been a rapid expansion of the number of RRBs, their branches and the district covered until the end of the VIth Five Year Plan. Roughly, the first decade of the establishment of RRBs is a rapid growth. The second decade starting with 1986 to 1996 is a period of consolidation.

The RRBs were established, "with a view to develop the rural economy by providing for the purpose of development of agriculture, trade, commerce, industry and other productive activities in the rural areas, credit and other facilities, particularly to small and marginal farmers, agricultural labourers, artisans and small entrepreneurs and for matters connected therewith and incidental thereto ". (The RRB Act, 1976)

The following Table 1 shows the progress of banking activities of RRBs:

TABLE 1

Progress of Regional Rural Banks

(Rs. in crore)

Sl. No.	*As at the End of*	*No. of RRBs*	*Districts Covered*	*No. of Branches*	*Deposits*	*Outstanding Advances*	*CD Ratio %*
1.	December 1975	6	12	17	0.2	0.1	50
2.	December 1976	40	84	489	8	7	91
3.	December 1980	85	144	3279	200	243	122
4.	December 1985	188	333	12606	1286	1408	109
5.	December 1986	194	351	12838	1715	1785	104
6.	September 1990	196	380	14511	4268	3555	CO
7.	March 1995	196	425	14509	11150	6291	56
8.	March 1996	196	427	14497	14188	7505	53
9.	March 1997	196	427	14461	18032	8718	48
10.	March 1998	196	448	14450	22189	9861	44

Source: NABARD, Statistics on RRBs, Various years.

As is well known deposit mobilization and making advances are the primary functions of modern banking. RRBs are no exception of this rule. This is popularly known as financial intermediation between the saving units and spending units. Financial mobilization by offering a set of incentives and services and allocation on the basis of social priorities underline the activity. CD ratio is a summary measure banking activity of any institution or the set of institutions for any region or nation. We notice from the Table I that except in the first two years of establishment of RRBs the CD ratio was more then 100%, upto 1986. Subsequently, it has intended to decline gradually. It means that in the first phase not only the deposit mobilized by RRBs but also a part of the deposits of sponsoring banks were drawn into the stream of advances. Since the advent of economic reforms a reverse situation is emerging. It implies that there has been an adverse effect on the clientele of RRBs, who are generally poor. The post-reform era, therefore, has a deleterious effect on the rural banking scene and thereby on the rural poor.

Reforms introduced in RRBs by GOI in consultation with RBI and NABARD have yielded positive results in respect of key performance indicators as indicated in Table 2.

TABLE 2

Key Performance Indicators: RRBs

(Amount in Rs. crore)

Sl. No.	*Indicator*	*31st March 2004*	*31st March 2005*	*31st March 2006*
1.	No. of RRBs	196	196	133
2.	No. of Districts Covered	518	523	525
3.	No. of Branches	14446	14484	14494
4.	No. of Staff	69249	68912	68629
5.	Owned Funds	5438	6181	6647
6.	Deposits	56350	62143	71329
7.	Borrowings	4595	5524	7303
8.	Investments	36135	36761	41182
9.	Loans Outstanding	26114	32870	39713
10.	CD ratio	46%	53%	56%
11.	Loans Issued	15579	21082	25427
12.	No. of RRBs having accumulated losses	90	83	58
13.	Accumulated losses	2725	2715	2637

(Contd.)

Sl. No.	*Indicator*	*31st March 2004*	*31st March 2005*	*31st March 2006*
14.	No. of RRBs in Profit	163	166	111
15.	Net NPA (%)	8.55%	4.84%	3.99%
16.	Recovery (% as on 30th June)	73%	78%	80%
17.	Per Branch Productivity	5.71	6.56	7.66
18.	Per Staff Productivity	1.19	1.38	1.62

Source: NABARD.

The following trends can be highlighted:

- 111 RRBs out of total 133 registered profit in the year 2005-06.
- CD ratio has been increasing from 46% on 31st March 2004 to 53% on 31st March 2005 and further to 56% on 31st March 2006.
- Recovery percentage has been improving from 73% during 2003-04 to 80% during 2005-06.
- Consequently, Net NPAs have declined from 8.55% on 31st March 2004 to 3.99% on 31st March 2006.
- Loans disbursement registered an impressive 35% annual growth in 2004-05 and 21% in 2005-06.
- Per branch productivity has increased from Rs. 5.71 crore on 31st March 2004 to Rs. 7.66 crore on 31st March 2006.
- Per staff productivity has increased from Rs. 1.19 crore on 31st March 2004 to Rs. 1.62 crore on 31st March 2006.
- There has been a decline in the total number of staff.

The productivity of the RRBs, both in terms of per branch and per employee increased significantly during 2006-07. The RRBs advance short-term, medium-term and long-term loans for various rural development activities, including crop production, purchase of tractors, setting up of small village industries, village crafts, various artisans' activities, retail trade, consumer durables, house construction, purchase of mini buses, etc. (Table 3)

Initially, RRBs were mandated to cater to the credit needs of the weaker sections of the rural community comprising small and marginal farmers, agricultural labourers, artisans, small entrepreneurs, etc. with effect from December 1993, their mandate has been expanded to include non-target group borrowers also. The RRBs were intended to be low cost small man's banks,

TABLE 3

Business and Financial Indicators of RRBs

Indicator	*2000-01*	*2001-02*	*2002-03*	*2003-04*	*2004-05*	*2005-06*	*20()6-07#*
1	*2*	*3*	*4*	*5*	*6*	*7*	*8*
No. of RRBs	196	196	196	196	196	133	96
Net Profit (Rs. crore)	601	608	519	769	748	617	593
Per Branch Productivity* (Rs. crore)	3.8	4.4	5.0	5.7	6.6	7.7	9.1
Per Employee** Productivity (Rs. crore)	0.8	0.9	1.0	1.2	1.4	1.6	1.9
Accumulated loss as % to Assets	5.6	4.7	4.4	3.9	3.5	2.9	2.9
Salary as % to Assets	2.0	2.2	2.3	2.6	2.0	2.1	1.9
Financial Return*** (%)	9.4	10.6	9.6	8.9	8.2	7.7	7.7
Financial Cost (%)	6.0	6.8	6.1	5.4	4.6	4.1	4.1
Financial margin (%)	3.4	3.8	3.5	3.5	3.6	3.6	3.6
Risk, operational and other cost (%)	2.1	2.6	2.6	2.2	2.3	2.8	2.9
Net margin (%)	1.2	1.8	0.9	1.3	1.3	0.8	0.7

Notes: *Average level of business (in terms of total deposits and gross advances) per branch during the reporting year.
**Average level of business (in terms of total deposits and gross advances) per employee of RRBs during the year.
***% of total income from both advances and investments against average working funds during the year.
# Data is provisional
Source: NABARD.

combining the advantages of cooperatives (close rapport with villagers) and commercial banks (business acumen). To enable RRBs to keep their cost down, the salary and perks of their staff were fixed at par with those of the comparable district level staff of the state government concerned. The SLR was fixed at lower level as compared to commercial banks, and low cost refinance from NABARD and sponsor banks upto prescribed levels were permitted.

The following one and a half decade saw large scale efforts to increase the number of banks, bank branches and disbursement nation-wide.

TABLE 4

Expansion of Regional Banking: 1975 to 1990

	December 1975	*December 1980*	*December 1985*	*March 1990*
Banks	6	85	188	196
Branches	17	3279	12606	14443

Source: NABARD Reports.

By 1991 there were 196 RRBs with cover 14,000 predominantly rural branches in 476 districts with an average coverage of 3 villages per branch. These banks had disbursed over Rs. 3500 crore in credit and mobilized over Rs. 4100 crore in deposits. Perhaps the most significant achievements of RRBs during this period were in enabling the weaker section of the community access to institutional credit. The bulk of the loans from RRBs were to the priority sectors which accounted for over 70% of the total agriculture and allied activities took up more than 50% of the total advances. In addition, the RRBs were instrumental in extending credit for poverty alleviation schemes (for example, IRDP) and disadvantaged area (for example, drought prone regions and desserts) development programmes.

More importantly, the performance of RRBs under GOI's initiatives on doubling of agricultural credit in three years (from base year 2003-04) and greater coverage of small and marginal farmers, have been impressive. They disburse agriculture loans of the order of Rs. 12,404 crore during 2004-05 registering a phenomenal annual growth of 64% against and targeted 30%. During 2005-06 agricultural credit flow stood at Rs. 15223 crore with a growth of 23%. Thus, RRBs financed 18.58 lakh new farmers in 2004-05 and another 17.03 lakh new farmers in 2005-06.

During 2006-07, 96 RRBs extended new loans to the extent of Rs. 32,067 crore as against Rs. 25,427 crore during 2005-06. Of this the share of priority sector was 82.2% as on March, 2007 end, the outstanding advances of RRBs were Rs. 48,494 crore and the share of priority sector was 81.9%. The share of agricultural loans increased to 57.7% on March, 2007 end from 54.2% on March, 2006 end.

TABLE 5

Purpose-wise Outstanding Advances by RRBs (as on March end)

(Amount in Rs. crore)

Purpose		2005	2006	2007 (P)
(1)		(2)	(3)	(4)
I.	Agriculture (i to iii)	16710 (50.8)	21509 (54.2)	27964 (57.7)
(i)	Short-term loans (crop loans)	10980	13877	18813
(ii)	Term loans (for agriculture and allied activities)	5730	7632	9151
(iii)	Indirect advances			
II.	Non-agriculture (iv-vii)	16161 (49.2)	18204 (45.8)	20530 (42.3)
(iv)	Rural Artisians, etc.	713	748	823
(v)	Other Industries	580	757	835
(vi)	Retail Trade, etc.	4364	3452	4152
(vii)	Other Purposes	10504	13264	14720
	Total (I+II)	32,871	39,712	48,494
Memo item				
(a)	Priority Sector	26,077	32,177	39,695
(b)	Non-Priority Sector	6794	7535	8799
(c)	Share of Priority Sector	79.3	81	81.9

P—Provisional

Note: Figures in parentheses are per cent to the total.

Source: NABARD.

TABLE 6

Purpose-wise Advances of RRBs Outstanding (End of September, 1990)

Sl. No.		Amount (in Rs. crore)
1.	Short-term (Crop Loan)	615
2.	Term Loan and Agricultural Activities	669
3.	Allied Activities	555
4.	Rural Artisans, Village and Cottage Industries	277
5.	Retail Trade and Self-employed, etc.	1052
6.	Consumption Loan	54
7.	Other Purposes	290
8.	Indirect Advances	43
	Total	3555

Source: Report on Trends and Progress of Banking in India, 1990-91.

The year 1990 marks the end of the expansion phase of regional banking, beyond which there has been no growth in the number of RRBs (including branches). In 1989, for the first time, the conceptualization of the entire structure of regional rural banks was challenged by the Agricultural Credit Review Committee (Khusro Committee), which argued that these banks have no justifiable case for continuance and recommended their mergers with sponsor banks.

The Committee was of the view that "the weakness of RRBs is endemic to the system and non-viability is build into it, and the only option to merge the RRBs with the sponsor banks. The objective of serving and weaker sections effectively could be achieved only by self-sustaining credit institutions."

At the time such a policy move was politically unthinkable, so the Reserve Bank and GOI quite prudently pushed the Khusro Committee Report under the carpet without a public debate. With the onset of the neo liberal economic reforms and the liberalization of the financial system, the RRBs came under the scanner once again, but this time in a policy regime that was too willing to let the market principles rule. The Narasimham Committee on Financial Sector Reforms, 1991 stressed the poor financial health of the RRBs to the exclusion of every other performance indicator. Out of the 196 RRBs, 172 were recorded unprofitable with an aggregate of loan recovery performance of 40.8%. (June, 1993)

The low equity base of these banks (paid up capital of Rs. 25 lakhs) did not cover for the loan losses of most RRBs. In the case of a few RRBs, there had also been an erosion of public deposits, besides capital. In order to impart viability to the operations of RRBs the Narasimham Committee suggested that RRBs should be permitted to engage in all types of banking business and should not be forced to restrict their operations to the target groups a proposal which was readily accepted. The Vyas Committee (2004) had recommended merger of all RRBs in the same state. Currently, RRBs of the same sponsor bank are merged at state level. By April, 2007, the number of RRBs was reduced to 96. For the time being though, the suggestions of mergers of the RRBs with their sponsor banks, which the Committee on Financial Systems has put forth in a slightly modified from sponsor banks might decide whether to retain the identities of sponsored RRBs or to merge them with rural subsidiaries of commercial banks to be set-up on the recommendations of the Committee was put on hold.

Post-merger RRBs scenario represents a powerful instrument for financial inclusion. Their outreach *vis-a-vis* other scheduled commercial banks particularly in regions and across population groups facing the brunt of financial exclusion is impressive as observed from an analysis of Basic Statistical returns of the RBI. With merger infusing the much needed financial strength in RRBs coupled with the local feel and familiarity they command, RRBs are in a unique position to play a decisive role in financial inclusion.

Outreach

In rural areas, RRBs account for a substantial 37% of total offices of the scheduled commercial banks. In semi-urban areas their shares comes to 15%. It goes without saying that exclusion is more severe in rural areas (see Table 7).

Manpower Deployment

91% of the total workforce in RRBs is posted in rural and semi-urban areas as compared to 38% for other scheduled commercial banks (Table 8). Even in absolute terms, out of a total workforce of 179,423 deployed by all scheduled commercial banks in rural areas, RRBs share is 25% (45,062). This is significant considering that at all India level, manpower of RRBs constitute only 7% of the total manpower of all scheduled commercial banks.

Savings Mobilisation

At all India level, RRBs account for 12% of all deposit accounts of scheduled commercial banks and a meagre 3.5% of deposit amount. However, in rural areas, RRBs share in deposit accounts is a significant 31% and that in deposit amount 19%. This shows that the average deposit amount is lower in RRBs than other commercial banks, thereby implying RRBs better reach to small depositors.

TABLE 7

Offices of Scheduled Commercial Banks—Population Group and Bank Group-wise (March, 2005)

Bank Group	*Rural Offices*		*Semi-Urban Offices*		*Urban Offices*		*Total*	
	No.	*% of Total*	*No.*	*% of Total*	*No.*	*% of Total*	*No.*	*% of Total*
RRBs	11.824	37	2284	15	537	2	14645	21
Scheduled Commercial Banks other than RRBs	20143	63	13335	85	21846	98	55324	79
Total	31967	100	15619	100	22383	100	69969	100

Source: RBI, Basic Statistical Returns, March 2005.

TABLE 8

Distribution of Employees of Scheduled Commercial Banks (March, 2005)

Bank Group	*Total Employees*	*% of Employees Posted in Rural Areas*	*% of Employees Posted in Semi-Urban Areas*	*% of Employees Posted in Urban/ Metro Areas*
RRBs	65599	69	22	9
SCBs other than RRBs	834834	16	22	62
Total	900433	20	22	58

Source: RBI, Basic Statistical Returns, March 2005.

TABLE 9

Deposits of Rural Branches of Scheduled Commercial Banks—Bank Group-wise (March 2005)

Bank Group	*No. of accounts*		*Deposit amount*	
	No. ('000)	*% to total*	*Amount (in Rs. crore)*	*% to total*
RRBs	43540	31	40957	19
SCBs other than RRBs	98368	69	172147	81
Total	141908	100	213104	100

Source: RBI, Basic Statistical Returns, March 2005.

If we include semi-urban areas for both RRBs and scheduled commercial banks, RRBs share in deposit accounts and amount stands at 21% and 11% respectively.

TABLE 10

Deposits of Rural/Semi-Urban Branches of Scheduled Commercial Banks—Bank Group-wise (March 2005)

Bank Group	*No. of accounts*		*Deposit amount*	
	No. ('000)	*% to total*	*Amount (in Rs. crore)*	*% to total*
RRBs	55165	21	56111	1 1
SCBs other than RRBs	211941	79	452678	89
Total	267106	100	508789	100

Source: RBI, Basic Statistical Returns, March 2005.

Credit Disbursed

At all India level, RRBs account for 18% of loan accounts of all scheduled commercial banks and 3% of loans outstanding. However, in rural areas the share of RRBs in loan accounts is an impressive 38%. More significantly despite having 38% of all loan accounts, RRBs account for only 21% of total credit outstanding in rural areas, implying thereby their better reach to small borrowers.

TABLE 11

Credit Disbursed by Rural Branches of Scheduled Commercial Banks—Group-wise (March 2005)

Bank Group	*No. of accounts*		*Deposit amount*	
	No. ('000)	*% to total*	*Amount (in Rs. crore)*	*% to total*
RRBs	10913	38	23017	21
SCBs other than RRBs	18155	62	86959	79
Total	29068	100	109976	100

Source: RBI, Basic Statistical Returns, March 2005.

If semi-urban branches are included, the share of RRBs in credit accounts and amount outstanding is of the order of 29% and 13% respectively.

TABLE 12

Credit Disbursed by Rural and Semi-Urban Branches of Scheduled Commercial Banks-Bank Group-wise (March 2005)

Bank Group	*No. of accounts*		*Deposit amount*	
	No. ('000)	*% to total*	*Amount (in Rs. crore)*	*% to total*
RRBs	13677	29	30546	13
SCBs other than RRBs	33594	71	210071	87
Total	47271	100	240617	100

Source: RBI, Basic Statistical Returns, March 2005.

Both deposit and credit data indicate that RRBs branches in rural areas have performed better in relation to other scheduled commercial bank branches. However, RRBs share comes down significantly and data for both rural and semi-urban areas are considered. This could be due to the fact that branches of other scheduled commercial banks located in semi-urban areas disbursed considerable loans in rural areas also. This is significant from the point of view of financial inclusion as rural branches are closer and more active in extending outreach to remote and interior villages. Viewed from this angle RRBs are particularly well placed to achieve the goal of financial inclusion.

CONCLUSIONS AND SUGGESTIONS

This para conclusively indicate that the RRBs were established as a new set of State sponsored, rural-oriented, region-based, low cost banks, having the ethos of cooperatives and business acumen of commercial banks for providing credit in rural areas, particularly to the relative weaker sections of the society. It would be fair to say that RRBs have succeeded in spreading the banking services to far flung rural areas. mobilizing rural savings, opening up more avenues for rural poor through institutional credit and generating employment opportunities. However, the mandate of financing only their target group borrowers, coupled with an administered interest rate structure, poor recovery performance, increasing establishment cost, and low level of operational efficiency have resulted in RRBs incurring losses and losing their financial viability from their inception.

But RRBs are well positioned to play a major role in financial inclusion particularly in areas/regions with high rates of financial inclusion. RRBs were originally created to cater to neglected sections/areas as they were expected to have sound financial management combined with local feel and familiarities. With the amalgamation of RRBs, they have acquired the critical mass in terms of financial strength to widen and deepen their outreach. With the requisite strength having been developed, RRBs are the best suited vehicles to widen and deepen the process of financial inclusion. However, utmost care must be taken to ensure that in the process of fulfilling the socio-economic objectives of financial inclusion, RRBs do not again fall into the vicious circle of deteriorating financial performance and deviation from their mandate. RRBs may be provided adequate promotional and developmental assistance to contribute substantially to financial inclusion in a way that the business generated out of inclusion efforts add positively to their performance.

RRBs should extend their services into unbanked areas and increased their credit to deposit ratio. As on 31st March, 2006, 37 RRBs had CD ratio of less than 40%, 44 RRBs between 40 and 60% and 52 RRBs above 60%. The CD ratio variation ranged from 20%

to 116% as RRBs operates with branches in remote, interior and tribal dominated areas. They have a special role to play in financial inclusion. The post-merger scenario of RRBs poses a series of challenges for them and needs to be addressed. The following areas would require attention from the point of view of financial inclusion:

1. Setting exclusive targets for micro-finance and financial inclusion,
2. Providing funding support, and
3. Providing technical support.

Keeping the above in view, the following specific suggestions are mentioned:

1. No further merger of RRBs.
2. Recapitalization of RRBs with negative Net Worth.
3. Widening network and expanding coverage.
4. Strategic micro-finance plan with NABARD support.
5. Separate credit plan for excluded regions.
6. Computerization.
7. Strengthening Boards of Management.
8. Tax incentives.
9. NABARD to support HR Development in RRBs.
10. Implementation of RBI initiatives for financial inclusion.

REFERENCES

McCallam, B.T. (1989), "Monetary Economics: Theory and Policy," Macmillan Publishing Co., New York.

Sarap, K. (1991), "Interlinked Credit Market in Rural India," Sage Publication, New Delhi.

Bell, C. (1993), "Introduction between Institutional and Informal Credit Agencies in Rural Areas," in Hoff, A. Braveman and J. Stiglitz (Eds.) "The Economics of Rural Organizations: Theory, Practice and Policy," London, Oxford University Press.

Gordon, David B. and Eric M. Leeper (1994), "The Dynamic Impacts of Monetary Policy: an Exercise in Tentative Identification," *Journal of Political Economy*, Vol. 102, pp. 1128-1247.

Eric M. Leeper, Christopher A. Sims and Tao Zha (1996), "What Does Monetary Policy do? Brooking Papers on Economic Activity, pp. 1-78.

Jain, S. Pankaj (1996), "Managing Credit for the Rural Poor: Lessons from Grameen Bank," *World Development*, Vol. 24, No. 1, pp. 79-89.

Cook, David (1999), "The Liquidity Effect and Money Demand," *Journal of Monetary Economics*, Vol. 41, pp. 377-90.

Mishra, S.N. (2004), "Indian Economy, Socio-Economic Transformation—Emerging Issues and Problems," Deep & Deep Publications Pvt. Ltd., New Delhi.

Reserve Bank of India, Statistical Tables Relating to Banks in India (Various Years).

Reserve Bank of India, Reports on Trend and Progress of Banking in India (Various Years).

Government of India (1998), "Report of the Committee on Banking Sector Reforms" (Chairman Sri M. Narasimham), GOI, New Delhi.

Regional Rural Banks at Crossroads

Dr. Jai Prakash

The banking sector plays a crucial role in the development of any nation. A sound, efficient, effective vibrant and innovative banking system stimulates economic growth by mobilizing savings on a massive scale and efficiently allocating resources for productive purposes and also for consumption which too is a driver of growth. During post-independence era Government of India very aptly initiated bold measures with full commitment and firm determination to conceptualize the policy and operationalise the implementation of various aspects for accelerating the process of developing rural economy.

The role of regional banks is to develop agriculture, small and medium industries, trade and the other productive activities and developing rural economy by providing liberal credit for all the productive activities. The regional rural banks mainly provide various facilities to marginal and small farmers, agricultural labourers, small entrepreneurs and the down-trodden segment of the society.

While Rural Financial Institutions (RFIs), which have been established over a period of time have proved to be catalyst in bringing metamorphic changes in the farm sector till eighties, implementation of financial sector reforms now calls upon to re-orient the role and responsibilities of RFIs to bring about integrated and balanced development of rural economy rather than confining to only farm sector.

Since the beginning of the planning era, one of the main policies has been to streamline and strengthen its rural economy and to uplift the level of living of the people belonging to economically weaker sections of the society as well as down-trodden areas. For supplementing the objective, the financial institutions marched with dynamic innovative programmes and schemes. The banking sector, which is the key instrument of economic development, has undergone a continuous stream of significant structural change and shift in policies over the last six decades.

A number of rural development programmes have been made and implemented since the beginning of our planning, specifically with the start of Community Development Programme in 1952. To suit the requirements of various programmes and schemes, a variety of credit agencies were established which gained varying degree of success. The history of rural credit in India starts with the co-operatives, established in 1904, later on commercial banks and regional rural banks, etc.

INSTITUTIONAL CREDIT

Institutional credit has an effective utility particularly in a rural country like India, where about 78 per cent of the population resides in rural belts and about 66 per cent of the total population is directly or indirectly engaged with agriculture or its allied activities. Therefore, institutional finance has a great significance because without providing proper financial aid it would be quiet impossible to improve the backward economy of rural India.

Extension of credit of small borrowers in the hitherto neglected sectors of the economy has been one of the key tasks assigned to the public sector banks in the post-nationalization period. To achieve this objective, banks have drawn up schemes to extend credit to small borrowers in sectors such as agriculture, small-scale industry, road and water transport, retail trade and small business which traditionally had very little share in the credit extended by the institutional financial agencies. Taking into account the need to provide financial resources through bank credit to weaker sections for specific needs, consumption credit has been included in priority sector.

With a view to augmenting credit flow to small and poor borrowers the commercial banks were advised by the RBI to provide at least 10 per cent of their net bank credit or 25 per cent of their priority sector advances to weaker sections comprising small and marginal farmers, landless labourers, tenant farmers and share croppers, rural artisans, village and cottage industries, where individual credit limits do not exceed Rs. 50,000 and the beneficiaries of various government sponsored schemes.

Institutional credit has an important role in the development of rural economic activities. Banks were initially given a target of extending 15 per cent of the total advances as direct finance to the agriculture sector to be achieved by March 1985. This target was subsequently raised to 18 per cent to be achieved by March 1990. The institutional financial agencies have been given an extra charge of improving the conditions of all the primary activities of the rural areas.

The Regional Rural Banks

The All-India Rural Credit Survey Report (1974) revealed that share of institutional agencies, comprising the government, the cooperatives and the commercial banks in financing the borrowings to the rural households in financing the borrowings to the rural households was marginally low to 18.2 per cent in 1971-72, whereas the corresponding share of Desi moneylenders was 56.6 per cent. This Report also pointed out the real problems of the borrowers and virtual monopoly of Desi bankers in supplying rural credit. The idea of setting up some sort of "Rural banks" was suggested by the Banking Commission in its report in 1972. The Commission recommended the establishment of a new class of "rural banks" in areas where the cooperative and the commercial banks credit structure is generally weak. Ultimately the Regional Rural Banks (RRBs) started their functioning.

By 1987 the number of RRBs increased to 186 with its 13,353 branches covering 363 districts of the country and by 2007 the number of RRBs has been increased to 28,303 branches covering almost all the districts of the country. As on March 31, 2006, the outreach of RRBs in terms of number of deposits and advances was 60.68 million and 18.64 million respectively. The per-employee accounts handled by RRBs were 915 against the national average of 513 in the banking industry. Similarly, the staff and branch network of RRBs, though respectively 7.1 per cent and 23.6 per cent of the national network, served 11.8 per cent of the total deposit accounts and 22.9 per cent of credit accounts of the banking industry. RRBs operate under the regulatory supervision of NABARD, which has the responsibility of laying down the policies for RRBs, to oversee their operations, provide refinance facilities, to monitor their performance and attend to their problems.

The Regional Rural Banks are ailing from a number of maladies as well. While the performance of many RRBs has improved significantly over the years, the performance of some of them remains far from being satisfactory in view of their tardy business growth and lack of operational viability. RRBs which at the outset adopted lower scales of compensation for their staff than their sponsor banks were specially mandated to lend to weaker sections at rates of interest with a concessional element. They could initially manage to lend at concessional rates because of their access to subsidized refinance from their sponsor banks and NABARD. But the RRBs were crippled soon enough by several factors among which was a new compensation policy in pursuance of which they had to pay their employees on par with those of their sponsor banks.

Government has taken several measures for reconstruction/ recapitalization of the RRBs. The performance of RRBs improved in the years immediately following the first phase of recapitalization, i.e., in 1995-96 and 1996-97, but it was overshadowed due to the introduction of prudential norms of Asset classification, Income Recognition and Provisioning of RRBs. The RRBs as a group made a profit of Rs. 73 crore for the first time during 1997-98 and improved the same further to Rs. 601 crore and Rs. 608 crore during 2000-01 and 2001-02. The viability-based categorization of RRBs as on 31 March, 2002 showed that out of 196 RRBs, 86 RRBs have wiped-off their accumulated losses and in a way attained a sustainable viability whereas 89 other RRBs have achieved a turn around and attained a current viability status leaving only 29 RRBs, which continued to incur losses.

The era of economic liberalization has broadly circumvented the RRBs to a large extent. Though a number of initiatives have been taken for RRBs in terms of freedom in interest rate structure, relaxation in target group concept, parity of emoluments to staff with the sponsor bank, etc., albeit these interventions have been inadequate, delayed and tentative. As cardial changes are contemplated in the rural credit delivery system in near future, it is indispensable to synchronize the operations of RRB with the challenges ahead. The opportunities, threats, etc. are to be perceived in context of rapid refinements taking place on financial horizons and there is fundamental necessity for carrying out reforms in RRBs to overcome their limitations.

A big headache of the banking institutions is the low level of recovery performance and the RRBs are also the victims of it. Although the RRBs have shown a consistent improvement in recovery performance from around 40% in 1991-92 to 74% in the year 2005-06. A viability-based review of RRBs shows that the loss-incurring RRBs are concentrated in 3 states, viz. Bihar, Madhya Pradesh and Orissa and in four sponsor Banks, viz., UCO Bank, State Bank of India, BOI and Bank of Baroda. Their common characteristics included low productivity, high transaction costs, lower C-D ratio, negative margins, low recovery rates and high NPAs.

It is high time the RRBs are de-regulated in true sense from the sponsor bank in the matter of designing and marketing of financial products, drawing up of their investment and credit policies, embarking upon the computerization, branch expansion, etc. Even after more than a quarter if RRBs are felt to be incompetent to decide their own business matter, it casts a big question mark on the quality of nurturing and guidance they have been receiving. Hence, the business development should be entirely left to the acumen and experience of the rural banks within the sole criteria of financial viability.

Loaning Priority Sectors

The main function of RRBs was to provide loans to priority sectors and to improve the down-trodden areas. Mostly they collect the rural savings to raise their funds. The saving of rural areas must be used to develop the rural areas, particularly to develop the priority sectors. This theme was virtually started from 1997. By the end of 2005 the total loan amount was 32,870 crore while deposited amount was Rs. 62,143 crore. For improving the position of deposits now the NRI accounts may also be open in the RRBs. The Government of India has started the process of merger of banks. By August 31, 2006, 42 new banks have been organized by the merger of 134 RRBs. This time the number of RRBs has been decreased to 104 from 196. The process of merger is continuously going on.

There is, immediate need for revamping the rural credit delivery system in the light of meeting the estimated supply of credit in an organized manner, particularly for the priority sectors. The level of skill should be improved with the more values. If past experiences were any guide, it has been observed that State Governments have not demonstrated and proved that they have facilitated and supported banks to provide credit by creating climate most congenial for automatic recovery and resource mobilization.

For loaning priority sectors the RRBs have to do some special efforts. It is strongly felt that while multi-agency approach to rural credit delivery system is a must for a country of our size and diversified socio-economic environment. There is immediate need for re-engineering the system through the implementation of well studied and conceived recommendations of the financial committees and bodies. Improving operational efficiency of the Regional Rural Banks may be the best hope of the rural financial system to make the rural financial system vibrant and responding to the changing requirements of the rural areas and removing the regulatory rigidities.

It was the setting up of National Credit Council, which gave the initial indication that serious thinking was taking place in RBI to lay down target for priority sector lending. The Credit Council decided that the RRBs should take up financing of priority sector lending urgently and in a proper way. The Committee also suggested that RBL should take necessary steps for providing liberal finance facilities to the banks and to introduce credit guarantee scheme as support measure to the RRBs for bank lending to the priority sectors.

CONCLUSION

The Regional Rural Banks should be structured in such a way that those have providing gainful employment conditions, create productive assets and achieve integrated rural development. All the programmes and schemes of the government should be interwoven with the RRBs with other banking institutions. Political interference in the functioning of RRBs should be avoided. Bureaucratic attitude should be minimized. These banks should be very liberal in providing loans and advances. Some more activities may also be done by these banking institutions. RRBs should understand the needs of the farmers, traders, entrepreneurs, etc. and should provide all help to them.

It is a known fact that the RRBs have largely achieved the objectives for which those were set-up and those have made significant progress in all the directions. The main reason of it is that the villagers think these banks as their own banks. The RRBs have succeeded to a great extent in the extension of their branch network to the unbanked centers in the interior rural areas. These banks have made a significant progress in deposit mobilization and providing loans, particularly in the backward regions. The high percentage of saving-deposits to the total deposits is indicative to the fact that the RRBs have been able to mop up the savings of the small income group. Thus they can play an important role in mobilizing the rural households' savings in a big way.

The RRBs have made significant progress in the extension of credit to the weaker sections like small farmers, marginal farmers, landless labourers, rural artisans and other weaker sections of the rural society, who had been relatively neglected in the past by the existing banking system at that time.

The reality is that RRBs, by design and operation score over the commercial and cooperative banks for further extension of the banking facilities to the rural areas in view of their comparatively lower cost structure, a great degree of rural orientation due to locally recruited staff, simple form and procedure for advancing loans and advances, having a higher C-D ratio and clearly defined task of meeting most of the credit requirements of the weaker sections of the rural society.

The major problems faced by the RRBs are mounting overdues, accumulated losses, lack of support from other institutional credit institutions and State governments, lack of infrastructure, limited channels of investment, etc. On account of these problems a large number of RRBs have not been able to achieve financial viability. There is, therefore, an urgent need for reorganizing their structure and improve their working in several ways.

If tangible reforms are not infused in RRBs to make them vibrant, these institutions may fail to achieve the very objective for which they were conceived, and decay to oblivion. As is said, "A reform is correction of abuses; a revolution is transfer of power" there is a need for revolution in RRB reforms.

REFERENCES

Economic Survey (2006-07 & 2007-08), Economic Division, Ministry of Finance, Government of India.

Editorial, "The Regional Rural Banks," *Southern Economist*, p. 5, June 10, 2005.

India (2006 & 2007), Published by Ministry of Information and Broadcasting, Government of India.

Main Clippings of Various Newspapers and Magazines.

Malhotra, Rakesh, "Regional Rural Banks—The Forgotten case in Financial Sector Reforms," *Kurukshetra*, August 2002, p. 9.

Patel, A.R., "Integrated Development of Rural Economy—Role of Rural Financial Institutions," *Kurukshetra*, Feb. 2003, p. 12.

Patel, A.R., "Rural Credit System—Need for Revamping," *Kurukshetra*, August 2002, p. 4.

Siddiqui, Badruzzama, "Priority Sector Lending—Some Major Issues," *Kurukshetra*, August 2002, p. 14.

Srinivasa, Lowda, "Manmohan's Dream India—His Vision of Growth," *Southern Economist*, June 15, 2005, p. 33.

Sundaram, S., "Financial Sector Reforms in India," *Southern Economist*, June 15, 2005, p. 36.

Role of Regional Rural Banks for the Upliftment of Weaker Sections

Dr. Meenu Agrawal, Dr. Babita Agrawal and
Ms. Aditi Tyagi

During British rule there was no organized financial institution in rural areas to provide credit to the rural population. During that time most of the rural people were depended on money-lenders. After independence for providing credit to the farmers and rural artisans. Government made efforts through organized financial institutions. That's why: the agricultural co-operative credit societies and Land Development Banks were set-up. These banks provide short-term, medium-term and long-term loans.

Commercial Banks' role was very poor to provide credit for small and marginal farmers. From this point of view, the Central Government persuaded the Private Commercial Banks to set-up their branches in rural areas so that the credit needs of the poor rural people may be fulfilled. The Central Government nationalized 14 Private Commercial Banks in 1969, when all efforts were failed. After taking this step, 53% of their branches were set-up in rural areas. The Commercial Banks have disbursed a high amount in rural areas for various activities.

Hence, Regional Rural Banks were started to provide credit and other facilities, particularly, to the small and marginal farmers, agricultural labourers, artisans and small entrepreneurs so as to develop agriculture, industry, trade, commerce and other productive activities in the rural areas.

Regional Rural Banks started their development process on 2nd October 1975 with the formation of a single bank as Prathama Grameen Bank. Initially, five Regional Rural Banks were set-up on October 2, 1975 at Moradabad, Gorakhpur, Bhiwani, Jaipur, Malda. Authorised capital of each Regional Rural Bank is Rs. 1 crore and issued and paid-up capital is Rs. 25 lakhs. 50% of the share capital of the Regional Rural Banks is subscribed by the Central Government. The State Government has contributed 15% and the sponsoring Commercial Banks 35%. The Regional Rural Banks, though basically scheduled commercial banks, differ from the latter in certain respects:

- The area of Regional Rural Bank is limited to a specified region comprising of one or more districts of a state.
- The Regional Rural Banks grant direct loans and advances only to small and marginal farmers, rural artisans and agricultural labourers and others which have small means for productive purposes.
- The lending rates of the Regional Rural Banks are normally not higher than the prevailing lending rates of co-operative societies. The sponsoring banks and the Reserve Bank of India provide many subsidies and concessions to Regional Rural Banks to enable the latter to function effectively.

From the very beginning, the sponsored banks have continued to provide managerial and financial assistance to Regional Rural Banks and also other concessions such as lower rate of interest on the latter's borrowings from sponsoring banks. Further, the cost of staff deputed to Regional Rural Banks and the training expenses of Regional Rural Banks staff are borne by the sponsoring banks.

The Reserve Bank of India has been granting many concessions to Regional Rural Banks such as:

1. Regional Rural Banks are allowed to maintain a reserve ratio at 3% and statutory liquidity ratio at 25%, and
2. Regional Rural Banks are provided refinance facilities

through National Bank for Agricultural and Rural Development.

It may be stated that there has been a remarkable increase in the deposits of Regional Rural Banks all over India. In the Seventh Five Year Plan more districts were covered as compared to Sixth Five Year Plan. It shows that major thrust is given to rural development through these included in the governmental programmes such as the Integrated Rural Development Programme and National Rural Employment Programme respectively.

In these programmes Regional Rural Banks have been actively participating to extend credit assistance to weaker sections. These banks usually charge interest 11.85% on crop and 10.25% on term loans. Regional Rural Banks have also been playing a major role to provide credit facilities to the people who are below poverty line.

After 1975, the expansion of branches and advancement of loans to weaker sections have taken place. In 1976, there were six Regional Rural Banks having 17 branches in 12 districts of the country. Deposits of these banks are Rs. 772 lakhs. In 1987, there was 196 Regional Rural Banks with 13,532 branches in 363 districts in India. At the end of 2005 there were 196 Regional Rural Banks. But branches and districts increased to 14,446 and 518 respectively in the country. The deposits of banks which were Rs. 8802 crore in 2003 increased to Rs. 17,330 crore in 2005. The bank loans which were Rs. 21,773 crore in 2003 increased to Rs. 31,803 crore in 2005. Fixed deposits of these banks have also increased. In 2003 it was 39,544 crore but in 2005 it increased to Rs. 44,813 crore. As on 31 March 2006, there were 133 Regional Rural Banks (post-merger) covering 525 districts with a network of 14,494 branches. By the end March 2005, there was a remarkable improvement in the financial performance of Regional Rural Banks. The number of banks reporting profit went up 166 of the 196 Regional Rural Banks. As on 31 March 2006, of the total 133 Regional Rural Banks, 111 posted profits and 75 of these Regional Rural Banks were sustainably viable organizations having no accumulated losses as also posting current profits.

REVIEW OF LITERATURE

A number of studies related to Regional Rural Banks and rural economy have been conducted by economists at micro and macro-level.

Chanana, Charanjit (1969), examined the role of commercial banks in financing agricultural credit in rural sectors of India. He emphasized that farmers require credit not only for economic heads of expenditure but also for social and uneconomic ones. He revealed that commercial banks should enter agriculture and small industries by pumping 20% of their credit into these sectors. The supply position would improve only if resources are also raised from within the agricultural sector. This may be done by mobilizing rural savings in view of substantial increase in the rural incomes. He also suggested that for the stamp duty on agricultural credit the farmers should receive the same treatment as he gets in the case of loans from co-operative banks. The bank should charge about 10% interest and stamp duty.

Lal, Chhote (1972), evaluated the roles of institutional and non-institutional credit agencies in eastern U.P. He revealed that only the substantial and well to do farmers benefited from various facilities in the region due to involvement of politics and politicians in the proper dispensing of agricultural credit in the region. The important source of dispensing rural credit was the agency of agriculturist moneylenders who accounted for 45% of the whole borrowings and the percentage of the borrowings from commercial banks was only 0.7% the lowest in the region.

George, P.S., and Srivastava, U.K. (1975), emphasized that the Cattle Development Scheme in Baroda district indicates that such schemes are viable from the point of view of both private cost benefit considerations of various parties involved and from the social cost benefits considerations. This scheme has made some impact on the overall development of the region. The second scheme shows that the farmers with large size of holding were the main beneficiaries.

Desai, D.D. (1977), suggested that commercial banks should provide credit not only to viable but also to potentially viable cultivators and may keep a close watch on utilization of production and development credit.

Sinha, D.P. (1978), said that of the total credit needs, only 22%

in Bhojpur district and 13% in Rohtak district are not by the co-operatives, leaving a credit gap of 78% and 83% respectively. This state of affairs offers a tremendous scope for the rural bank to make brisk business and fill the credit. He suggested that an institution of this nature can make speedy progress only if there is a whole-hearted cooperation of state government's extension machinery and active participation of people.

Reserve Bank of India (1981) examined the financial viability of Regional Rural Banks in India during the period 1975-78. Regional Rural Banks were grouped into two categories, viz., category A and B. Category A consisted Regional Rural Banks having outstanding loan business of Rs. 3 crores and above as on December 31, 1978. Category B consisted Regional Rural Banks having outstanding loan business of less than Rs. 3 crores and completed 3 years of working as on 31 December, 1978.

Kurulka (1983), revealed that the credit provided by non-professionals, i.e non-licensed money-lenders and distant or near relatives generally forms a significant proportion of the total credit provided by all the agencies in the rural areas. He concluded that investment in pump sets (on existing wells) is more profitable than the investments in the construction of new wells in the area.

Hairway (1986), examined the process of penetration of the special programmes in the villages of Gujarat and analyses as to how far these programmes influence the functioning of the village. Hirway revealed that the special programme strategy did not change the basic process of percolation of gains of growth to different sections of the rural society in any significant in the sense, that the strategy tends to leave out the poorest sections from the benefits of special programmes and the strategy is a partial strategy as it takes care of only a limited credit need of the poor.

According to **Khusro Committee** (1989), the financial viability of a large number of Regional Rural Banks has seriously been eroded and as such their ability to provide credit to target groups has been impaired.

Majumdar, N.A. (2002), in order to sustain a high growth rate of 7% with the support of agricultural sector, the rural credit delivery system is a basic necessity. The network of NGOs and SHGs should be expanded in rural areas. In this effort, Reserve Bank of India and National Bank of Rural Development (NABARD) can play an important role.

According to **Amlesh Banarjee** (2003), said the present state of Rural Credit Structure supported by the Regional Rural Banks, Co-operative Banks and Commercial Banks has not sufficiently inspired the agricultural growth, present co-ordination of the structure by the NABARD could arrest neither corruption of the co-operative banks nor growing non-performing assets.

Sahoo, B.B. (2005), observed that acceleration in agricultural growth would not be a distant goal, if it is supported by large flow of rural credit. Necessary legal and institutional changes to governance, regulation and also the attitudinal change of Commercial Banks must be addressed for financing agricultural and rural sector.

Kumar, P. (2005), observed that most of the banks are not paying attention to the credit demands of women entrepreneurs. The banks do not follow the guidelines to provide adequate credit to these women.

Five Year Plans and Regional Rural Banks

Some specified schemes aimed at helping certain specified categories of the weaker sections of rural community were included as part of the five year plans. Further rural credit facilities were also provided to rural masses especially weaker sections, landless labourers, small and marginal farmers, scheduled castes and scheduled tribes with the help of special programmes which have been included five year plans. Main schemes aiming towards the betterment of the weaker sections were financed by Regional Rural Banks during five year plans. These schemes are as follows:

Development

1. Panchayati Raj and Community Development,
2. Twenty-point Economic Programme,
3. Village Adoption Scheme, and
4. Massive Assistance Programme.

Poverty

1. Integrated Rural Development Programme, and
2. Swarojgar Yojna.

Employment

1. Trainning of Rural Youth and Self-Employment Scheme, and
2. National Rural Employment Programme.

Banking

1. Credit Deposit Maintenance Scheme,
2. Differential Interest Rate Scheme,
3. Regional Rural Banks Scheme, and
4. Lead Bank Scheme.

Agriculture

1. Dry Land Farming Projects,
2. Scheme for the Small and Marginal Farmers,
3. Marginal Farmers' Agricultural Labourers Projects,
4. Small Farmers' Development Agency Project,
5. Multiplying Cropping Scheme,
6. Drought Prone Area Programme, and
7. High Yielding Varieties Programme.

Problems Faced by Regional Rural Banks

The Regional Rural Banks are facing more problems in maintaining their working more effectively. Main problems, which they are facing, are as follows:

1. Shortage of the fund is the main problem of these banks. Central Government, Sponsored Banks and State Government arranged the funds for these banks.
2. Due to coverage of the vast area by the Regional Rural Banks, it is very problematic task for banks to work more efficiently and to satisfy all the sections of the society.
3. The bank officials are not properly trained and even they do not understand the needs of the farmers.
4. In rural areas, most of the branches of Regional Rural Banks are facing severe financial strain on account of higher transaction costs involved in handling of large number of small sized loan accounts.
5. The officials do not understand the importance of these banks to the poor people of rural areas.
6. Increasing administrative expenses are also creating various problems.

7. The Sponsoring Banks' branches are also running in rural areas where Regional Rural Banks are already working. This has given to certain anomalies.
8. The low rate of interest on small loans has placed the Regional Rural Banks at a disadvantage in respect of cost of resources.
9. In these banks corruptions are there. That's why influential persons are able to get all benefits which are meant for poor rural people.
10. Regional Rural Banks' viability has been adversely affected on account of increasing amount of over dues.
11. Huge losses have accumulated by these banks. These losses have eroded a part of the deposits of the banks.
12. Another major problem is that there is no proper infrastructure in rural areas.
13. In the working of these banks, local politicians' interference is also creating the problems.
14. Though the area and number of branches have increased but in that ratio number of staff has not increased.
15. The recovering of loans problem is increasing at a faster rate. So this problem has forced the banks to change the system of loans more in favour of urban businessmen and industries.

Conclusion and Suggestions

In rural areas there has always been a great need to set-up organized financial institutions which to increase employment, production, productivity and to reduce the rural poverty.

During the plan period, efforts were made to increase the number of agricultural co-operative societies and the role of Commercial Banks in rural areas. Introduction of Lead Bank Scheme and finally, setting up Regional Rural Banks to meet the credit needs of the small and marginal farmers, agricultural labourers, small traders, and rural artisans have solved the problem to some extent. With the setting up of such institutions, the contribution of organized financial sector in rural credit has increased to 70%.

SUGGESTIONS

1. There are two sectors in rural areas such as farming and non-farming sectors. Banks provided loans to farming sector as well as to non-farm sectors. But more occupations in non-farm sectors have come up in rural areas where financial assistance is very essential. Hence, banks should provide more financial assistance to non-farm sectors.
2. In rural areas, more and more branches of Regional Rural Banks should be set-up to semi-urban and rural areas. These banks should cover more villages so that all weaker sections of the society get the benefits provided by the banks.
3. The State Government should increase the number of these banks and their branches should be set-up in all the villages.
4. To solve the financial needs of small and marginal farmers, small traders, rural artisans and agricultural labourers, the state Government should take more interest.
5. Priority should be given to the selection of families which are really very poor. The objective of Regional Rural Banks is to provide financial assistance to weaker and down-trodden people. Hence, it is very essential to identify such anomalies before giving financial assistance.
6. The job of identification of beneficiaries should be taken up by the Regional Rural Banks. These banks should identify the weaker and down-trodden sections of the society and distribution the assistance to them properly.
7. The Regional Rural Banks should follow the long-term policies in providing loans to the weaker sections and proper measures should be taken to ensure that actual families get the benefits provided by Regional Rural Banks.
8. Over dues problems are increasing day-by-day. This can force the banks to withdraw from the rural areas. Proper plans, schemes and suitable machinery should be set-up for the speedy recovery of over dues.
9. The State and the Sponsoring Banks should provide

adequate financial assistance to Regional Rural Banks so that these may meet the demands of the weaker sections of the society satisfactory.

10. The State Government and Sponsoring Banks should provide proper infrastructure.

REFERENCES

Agrawal, Meenu, *Impact of Economic Reforms on Poverty and Unemployment*, 2008.

All India Rural Credit Survey, 1951-52, All India Rural Debt and Investment Survey, 1961-62, All India Rural Debt and Investment Survey, 1981.

Banerjee, Amalesh, Issues of Financial Reforms—Reforming the Reserve Bank of India, 2003.

Bapna, M.S., *Regional Rural Banks in Rajasthan*, Himalaya Publishing House, New Delhi.

Basu, S.K., *Commercial Banks and Agricultural Credit*, Allied Publishers Private Limited, Regional Rural Banks so that they may carry out their activities more effectively, New Delhi, 1976.

Choubey, B.N., *Agricultural Banking in India*, National Publishing House, New Delhi, 1983.

George, P.S. and Srivastava, U.K., *Planning and Implementation of Rural Development Project* by a Banking Organisation, Indian Institute of Management, Ahmedabad, 1975, p. 140.

Jain, Inu, *Rural Credit and Regional Rural Banks*, Khadi and Gramodyog, 28 Sept. 1981.

Krishan, C., Regional Rural Banks and Rural Development, *Yojana*, January 1-15, 1990.

Kumar, Pawan, *Indian Banking Today—Impact of Reforms*, 2005.

Kumar, V. Anand, *Performance of Regional Rural Banks*, Rural Economy of India, Mittal Publications, Delhi, 1989.

Majumdar, N.A., *Financial Sector Reforms*, Vol. 11, 2002.

Majumdar, N.A., *Issues of Financial Reforms, Banking Sector Reforms*, 2003.

Mehta, Basant, *The Organisation and Working of Lead Bank Scheme in India*, Vohra Publishers and Distributors, Allahabad, 1989.

Memoria, C.B., *Rural Credit in India*, Kitab Mahal, Allahabad, 1982.

Mohanan, N., *Development Finance for Small Farmers*, University of Pune, Pune, Regional Rural Banks, 1977, p. 350.

Mukherjee, Pranab, Regional Rural Banks: The Task Ahead Supplement to Capital, 24th Feb. 1977, pp. 21-24.

Regional Rural Banks come into their Own, *Eastern Economist*, 1978, pp. 184-85.

Report of Bhandari Committee on Regional Rural Banks, 1989.

Report of Khusro Committee on Regional Rural Banks, 1989.

Reserve Bank of India, Viability of Regional Rural Banks, *Reserve Bank of India Bulletin*, Mumbai, March 1981.

Sahoo, B.B., Primary Lending Institutions and Rural Credit, *Kurukshetra*, Dec. 2005.

Selvakumar, A. Subbiah, M., Regional Rural Banks and Agricultural Credit, *Kurukshetra*, Dec. 2005.

Sen, Manab, *Issues of Financial Reforms—Current Trends in Rural Banking in India*, 2003.

Sethi, T.T., *Progress of Nationalised Commercial Banks in India*, Agra University, Agra, 1982.

Sharma, D.K., *New Horizons of Rural Development Planning for the Poor*, Institute of Regional Analysis, Bhopal, 1978, p. 139.

Singh, Ajit, *Rural Development and Banking in India*, Deep & Deep Publications, New Delhi, 1985.

Sinha, D.P., Role of Regional Rural Banks in Rural Development, *Khadi and Gramodyog*, Vol. 24, 1978, pp. 464-67.

Vaishnaw, B.L., *Regional Rural Banks in India—An Appraisal with Special Reference to Rajasthan*, University of Jodhpur, 1985, Indian Dissertation Abstract, January-March, 1988, Vol. XVIII, No. l.

Verma, M.L., *Rural Banking in India*, Rawat Publications, Jaipur, 1988.

Impact of Rural Banks on Poverty Index

Mr. Anil Kr. Sharma and Dr. Sidharth Jain

1. Introduction

The rural banks are playing important role in improving the poverty Index. This paper cover various such aspects which project rural banks as social entrepreneur. These banks advance money to the business and help in meeting their requirement of short, medium and long-term. The satisfaction levels of rural public increase by these kinds of activities. As a fact, financial intermediaries are passing through significant changes all over the world under the impact of deregulation, technology upgradation and financial innovations. The traditional face of banking is no longer as it was few years back. The provision of formal financial services in rural India was traditionally under the domain before the beginning of the first phase of economic reforms in 1991-92, almost the entire banking sector institutions owned over 90% of the assets of the entire banking sector (Deolalkar, 1999). India's principal commercial banks were taken over in 1969 and 1980 by the government through successive phases of nationalisation. The rural coverage of public sector banks was augmented through the introduction of two other types of institutions—the Regional Rural Banks (RRBs) and the Cooperative Banks (CBs)—the former through an act of the central government in 1975 and the later through central and state acts in the 1980. Together, these three (PSBs, RRBs and CBs) categories of institutions carry out almost the entire formal sector financial activity in rural India.[1]

The National Bank for Agriculture and Rural Development (NABARD) started its operation with effect from 15th July, 1982 as the apex bank for financing agriculture operations. The NABARD took the entire undertaking of ARDC (Agricultural Refinance and Development Corporation), the refinancing functions from the ACD (Agriculture Credit Department) of the Reserve Bank in relation to State Cooperative Banks (SCBs) and Regional Rural Banks (RRBs). The NABARD is authorised to give loans and advances to state governments for periods not exceeding 20 years to enable them to subscribe directly or indirectly to the share capital of Cooperative Banks. It can give long-term loans directly to any institution set-up by the Central Government. It can also contribute to the share capital or invest in the securities of any institution concerned with agricultural and rural development. It may be noted that short-term farm credit repayable over periods not exceeding 18 months will be provided by state co-operative banks and Regional Rural Banks. These loans could be converted into medium-term loans for periods not exceeding seven years under specific conditions. Medium-term loans not exceeding seven years and not less then 18 months will be provided to state cooperative banks and regional rural banks as determined by NABARD. The NABARD provides long-term loans and advances by way of refinance to Land Development Banks, RRBs, and SCBs and other financial institutions.[2]

1.1 Co-operative Banks

The principle of cooperative banks is to extend credit facilities to farmers and small scale industrial concerns and promote in general the habit of thrift and self-help among the low and middle income groups of the society. The distinguishing feature of a co-operative bank is the absence of profit motive. Co-operative banks are very helpful to meet the requirements of small farmers, artisans, etc. In India cooperative banks have been the pioneers in mobilizing rural deposit. Today, however the cooperative banks have been putting more weight on their lending activities than on deposit mobilisalion.

1.2 Regional Rural Banks (RRBs)

Cooperative banking has a three-tier structure. At the top-there is State Cooperative Bank at the state level. This is the apex bank which governs all the cooperative banks in the state. At the intermediaries level, there are Central Cooperative Banks. There is generally one central cooperative bank in each district. At the base of the pyramid, there are primary Agricultural Credit Societies at the village level. Each higher level institution is a federation of those below with membership and loan operations restricted to the affiliated units

1.3 Land Development Banks (LDBs)

Land Development Banks provide long-term credit to agriculturists against security of their land for purchasing tools and implements, etc. and for permanent improvements of land. In India, these banks were set to provide loans to agriculturists on easy terms against mortgage of land for the purpose of repayment of loans to village moneylenders and indigenous bankers.

2. An Overview of Rural Banking

Indian banking sector is an agglomeration of banks dimensionally poles apart, functionally different and structurally non-comparable. They are operating at various levels of efficiency. Their percentage and patronage make some of them distinctly different from others. Before any thought was bestowed on realigning them, new banks were licensed while the other banks continue to operate parts in rural areas with their brick and mortar branches, the new banks have chosen to expand in urban areas with their IT-supported banking transactions.

Rural banking has emerged as a significant development in Indian banking sector over last three decades. Efforts made to reach out to the villages have resulted in a growing number of rural customers availing the services of banks, even in remote villages. The available data provide an impressive picture of the rural outreach of the banking sector. A qualitative assessment of the rural credit cannot be readily made because of the paucity of relevant data classified separately for rural and urban business. Delinquency ratio of agricultural advances is not a good surrogate for an analysis of the quality of rural credit management. The available data pertaining to the NPA ratios of priority and non-priority sector would lead to an inference that the contaminated advances are relatively lower in size in rural credit.

3. Regional Rural Banks (RRBs)

Regional Rural Banks have been set-up in backward rural areas where the coverage of the commercial and cooperative banks is poor. The purpose of these banks is to finance agricultural operations and provide employment to rural educated youth who possess the requisite orientation to look after needs of rural folk. RRBs have been conceived to combine the strong point of both the co-operative and commercial banks eliminating the weaknesses of both. The RRBs have been included in the second schedule to the RBI act and therefore they enjoy the same privileges and facilities as the scheduled banks, including access to the Reserve Bank for financial accommodation. The depositors with these banks also enjoy the insurance facility granted by the deposit insurance and credit guarantee corporation.[3]

3.1 Restructuring of Regional Rural Banks (RRBs)

The growth of rural banking in India has not been the result of a consistent long-term plan. It was more of a hurdle race sponsored by the state, after the nationalisation of the major commercial banks in 1960, banks were directed to go to village. The Regional rural banks were set-up in India on the lines of peoples' banks in Cylon. The first commission (BCR, 1972) recommended the establishment of rural banks to meet the credit needs of the rural people. The government did not implement the recommendation of the commission. A study group was appointed under the chairmanship of M. Narsimham in July 1975, by Government of India. The RRBs were established on 2nd Oct. 1975 on the basis of recommendation made by Narsimham Committee. An ordinance was promulgated in Sept. 1975 which was subsequently replaced by Regional Rural Banks Act of 1976. The objectives of the banks are to provide facilities to the rural areas for the development of agriculture, trade, commence, industry and other activities in rural areas, credit and other facilities particularly to small and marginal farmers, agricultural laboures, artisans and small entrepreneurs and for matters connected with or incidental thereto. Recently the objective has been extended to meet the credit needs of the non-target groups to make the banks economically viable.

Various studies conducted by Committee/Commissions (RBI, 1975 and 1977) show that there is a credit gap in the rural areas of the country. Commercial Banks have not got success in meeting the credit needs of the disparate groups. The regional banks were set-up to bridge up the credit flows to rural areas. The banker thus finds himself in rural banking, not due to his initiative and continues to be there so long as he is asked to remain there. Participating in some of the populist lending schemes he has created non-performing assets of small sizes in large numbers.

Regional Rural Banks, which were super-imposed on the rural scene since, 1975, also have the similar story, with one major difference, they are in rural banking not by compulsion but by design. Their problem was that they were prevented from expanding their need business because of the restrictions imposed on them in selecting their customers. Operations confined to limited geographic area and customer base restricted to the target groups these banks were operating in suffocating environment. The need for restructuring the banking sector was recognized by the Narsimham Committee on the financial system in 1991. It's recommendations were, however, vague and inconclusive. The formation of a Reconstruction Commission was hinted at. But the roadmap of financial sector reforms has virtually bypassed rural banking. For the first time the attention of banks and the regulators was drawn to profitability and viability of rural operation. The suitability of regional rural banks as an effective rural credit agency was doubted; the propriety of directed lending was also questioned. But precious little has been done so far in drawing a long-term strategy for restructuring.[4]

A Plea is made for functional specialization and structural reorganization of rural banking business with a view to strengthen the competitive edge scenario, while the new banks prefer to flourish in cities, gramin banks are directed to operate in rural areas and public sector banks struggle to remain in both the world. They have done this balancing act for over three decades.

4. Problems of Regional Rural Banks

The institution of RRB was designed to provide a low cost alternative to the operation of commercial bank branches and provide much more under range of services to priority sector in rural areas but the functioning of RRBs gives much cause for concern due to the following problems:

- **Organisational Problems**—Each RRB is sponsored by a commercial bank. The central government and the concerned state government also contribute to its capital thus there is a multi-agency control of RRBs. Due to this there is lack of uniformity in their functioning, lack of proper monitoring by the sponsor bank, lack of proper system and procedure and constraint of restricted clientele.
- **Problems of recovery**—Recovery position of RRBs is very poor. As on June, 1986, the recovery of RRBs was 49 per cent of demand. Wilful defaults, misuse of loans, lack of follow-up, wrong, Identification of borrowers, expansion of benami loans, staff agitations contributed to poor recovery of RRBs.
- **Mounting Losses leading to non-viability**—Sustainability and viability implies that a credit programme is to be so directed so as to continuously increase the capital base of intermediaries to sustain further expansion of their leading business on a long basis. In order to be sustainable, the credit institutions are required to have sufficient margin between leading rates and the cost of funds raised for leading. In 1994-95, out of 196 RRBs as many as 150 had shown losses in each of the previous five years. Average net margin in the case of RRBs deteriorated from 2.54 to 3.72 per cent in 1997-98.

  A number of factors had contributed to the problem of mounting losses. RRBs are confined to lending to weaker sections where margin is low and cost is high. Opening branches year by year and non-availability of competent and trained staff also posed serious problem.

- **Management Problems:** Since the RRBs are district level small institutions, the sponsor banks depute only middle management staff to run them. Such staff fails to take independent decisions. Moreover, meetings of the board of director of the RRB are also not held regularly. RRB have emerged as the only surviving rural financial institutions with the professional management culture to meet rural credit needs. Therefore, it is essential to revitalize RRBs so that they play critical role in achieving the developmental targets in rural sector under 10th Plan and emerge stronger.

5. Conclusion and Suggestion

Because of the 'built in non-viability' of the RRBs a suggestion was made by the Khusro Committee that there can be no place for RRBs and they should be merged with the sponsor banks. According to committee such merge will not only be able to strengthen their delivery system but will also enhance their deposit of RRBs with the sponsor banks will not solve problem of losses it will only conceal these losses on loans to weaker sections will continue to occur unless interest rates on these loans are hiked but in the post-merger scenario the very concept of poor man's banking would vanish. The fact of the matter is that RRBs have an important role to play as a part of the multi-agency approach to rural credit and as an instrument of income distribution in rural areas. In the former role as noted by Kelkar Committee RRBs are eminently suitable to do the job envisaged for them and they can exit side by side with cooperative and commercial banks. In the later role RRBs can keep on doing the good work of providing resources to the weaker sections.

To solve the problem of losses of RRBs and improve their viability, efforts have been made in recent years to restructure their operations and infuse fresh capital into them. RRBs have been granted greater flexibility in their lending operations.They can lend to target groups issue drafts, get into non-fund business, etc. Interest rates have also been deregulated. The most important move taken for rehabilitation of RRBs is that whereas previously they were mandatorily required to extend credit to the priority sector only, the monetary policy of April 1997 allowed them to target just 40 per cent advances to priority sector. This places them on par with the commercial banks. However, the critics point that this has defeated the very purpose of establishing them. Out of 196 RRBs, 187 have been taken up for recapitalization under phases of restructuring. 158 of these have been fully recapitalized. Total recapitalization support provided to RRBs amounts to Rs. 2188 crores.

Credit flow of agriculture can also be increased by facilitating credit through non-banking intermediaries who can get refinance from RRBs and can give loan to agriculture and bear the risk of default. Such arrangement would reduce transaction costs and ensure good recovery.

Mechanism should be worked out under which the RRBs could place surplus funds with either NABARD or with a special federal type of agency that might be set-up for this purpose. Similarly, instead of RRBs Investing in government and government securities for purposes of SLR compliance, they could keep cash balance with NABARD or special agency which could pay interest on such balances by investing or deploying these funds to the best advantage on their behalf and thus help augment the income of RRBs.

There should by greater coordination between district planning authorities, Panchayati Raj Institutions and the banks operating is rural areas. RRBs should be encouraged to develop more sophisticated methods of credit delivery to meet the changing needs of farming, only then the RRBs will fulfil the promise that is essential for rural development.

Notes and References

1. Minakshi Garg, 'Indian Banking Industry in 2020', editor R.K. Uppal and Rumpi Kaur, Chapter: Regional Rural Banks (A Backbone of Indian Economy), Mahamaya Publication, Delhi.
2. Falguni C. Shastri, 'Restructuring of Indian Banks', Book Enclave, Jaipur, Year 2007.
3. B.L. Mathur, 'Banking Facing the Facts', Wide Vision, Jaipur, Year 2008.
4. R.K. Uppal and Rumpi Kaur, Banks is New Millennium Issues, Challenges and Strategies, Mahamaya Publication, Delhi.

The Social Concern of Regional Rural Banks: A Drive Towards Financial Inclusion

Dr. Shyam Sunder Singh Chauhan, Mr. Manish Dev and Dr. Sheelpria Tripathi

Developmental aspect of the economy treats the access to safe, and affordable credit and other financial services by the poor and vulnerable groups, disadvantaged areas and lagging sectors, as a pre-condition for accelerating growth and reducing income disparities and poverty. A well functioning financial system provides equal opportunities to economically and socially excluded people who can integrate themselves with the economy with fall of their potential and thus help them to contribute to development and protect themselves against economic shocks. Despite the broad international consensus regarding the importance of easy and timely access to financial institutions as a crucial tool to alleviate the poverty and increase employment opportunities, it is estimated that more than two billion people globally are currently excluded from the ambit of financial system (UNO, 2006). In India only 44.9 percent of income earners had an account in a bank. Just 38 per cent of income earners in rural areas had a bank accounts compared to 62 per cent of their counter-parts in urban areas. As for the disbursal of institutional credit is concerned, the situation is quite grim. About 75 per cent of the bottom half of Indian households still depend on informed sources, such as moneylenders and less than 15 per cent have access to bank credit (Naik, 2008). Of the 89 million farmer households in India, 73 per cent had no access to the formal credit market. The credit market is regionally skewed with the under-developed states and the North-East suffering the worst consequences of under-banking. The so called bottom of pyramid still remain largely deprived of institutional credit and other financial services despite the growth of a fairly robust banking system over the decades.

Ever since India adopted planned economic development, Government as well as Reserve Bank of India, have adopted several measures to provide credit and financial services to the wider sections of the population, through a wide network of financial institutions established over the years. The organized financial system comprises the Commercial Banks, Regional Rural Banks (RRBs), Co-operative Banks, Post-offices, and several developmental Banks such as IDBI, SIDBI, NABARD, NHB, Ex-IM Banks, etc. Besides, MFIs, SHGs, NGOs, etc. also meets financial requirements of the people. Out of these organized institutions ***Regional Rural Banks*** have been created in 1975 with the explicit objective of bridging the credit gap in rural areas, and bring that section of population to the ambit of financial services, which were hitherto remained outside the financial system.

The RRBs, called by different names in different states, such as Grameena Banks, Gramin Banks, Grama Banks, Gramya Banks, Elaquai Dehati Banks, Gaonlia Banks, etc. were started in 1975, i.e. during the Emergency days, with the aim of providing credit to small and marginal farmers, agricultural labourers, rural artisans, street vendors and all those living below the poverty line as the preamble of the Regional Rural Banks Act, 1976 proclaimed in unequivocal terms. The need for the new genre of banks was felt as then existing institutions — commercial banks and cooperatives — were found to be suffering from some weaknesses *vis-a-vis* rural credit, particularly for the weaker sections. Based on the recommendations of a working group, hurriedly set-up under the chairmanship of M. Narasimham, the experiment of these new banks, tiny scheduled commercial banks in the central sector with one or two districts as their areas of operation, was started in 1975. Their share capital was apportioned by the central government, the respective state government and another commercial bank, called the sponsor bank, in the ratio of 50:15:35. (Rao, 2008)

If the nationalization of 20 leading commercial banks was the first measure step towards financial inclusion in India, then the creation of RRBs was a specific step towards this direction.

The broad strategy for financial inclusion in Indian has following elements:

- encouraging penetration into unbanked and backward areas and encouraging agents and intermediaries such as NGOs, MFIs, CSOs and business correspondents (BCs);
- focusing on a decentralized strategy by using existing arrangements such as State Level Bankers' Committee (SLBC) and District Consultative Committee (DCC) and strengthening local institutions such as co-operatives and RRBs;
- using technology for furthering financial inclusion;
- advising banks to open a basic banking 'no frills' account;
- emphasis on financial literacy and credit counseling; and
- creating synergies between the formal and informal segments.

Despite their several weaknesses in terms of profitability, efficiency and economic viability, RRBs have done a commendable job in proving banking services to rural people, especially small and marginal farmers, weaker sections, SMEs, landless agricultural labourers, better traders, etc.

As these banks were designed to exclusively cater to the credit needs of the poor in the rural and far-flung areas it was presumed that they would incur some losses. The framers of the RRB policy spelt this out in the very beginning, not as if they were discovered subsequently. These losses were supposed to be treated as the necessary social cost for the social benefit of covering the rural poor.

In fact, the RRBs lived up to this expectation; as many as 196 RRBs were established by 1990 with more than 14,400 branches across the length and breadth of the country, taking banking services to the unbanked rural, tribal and other interior areas. About 123 million persons, belonging to the weaker sections, benefited from these banks.

The RRB's performance in respect of some important indicators was certainly better than that of commercial banks or even cooperatives. As of March 31, 2004, the credit-deposit ratio of all the RRBs taken together was more than 46 per cent, and the recovery of loans was 74 per cent. Despite the widespread perception that most RRBs are struggling with losses owing to bad loans in fact most RRBs have been profitable - out of 196 RRBs, 165 earned profit and only 31 incurred losses, and the group as a whole showed a net profit of Rs. 754 crores in 2003-04. Non-Performing Assets (or bad loans) amounted to only 16 per cent of gross advances in 2003-04.

Further, priority sectors have accounted for over 70 per cent of RRBs' lending, with loans specifically to agriculture amounting to 46 per cent. RRBs have also performed better in terms of providing loans to small and retail traders and petty non-farm rural activities. In recent years, they have taken a leading role in financing Self-Help Groups (SHGs) and other micro-credit institutions and linking such groups with the formal credit sector. (Ghosh, 2006)

In the about scenario, the present paper analyses the performance of RRB in relation to their role in financial inclusion. The paper is divided into four sections, namely: (i) The concept of financial inclusion, (ii) Initiatives for financial inclusion in India, (iii) Role of RRBs in financial inclusion, and (iv) Conclusion.

I. Financial Inclusion: Conceptual Framework

Each and every person or household has some financial requirements which are fulfilled either by own resources or by borrowing. Financial resources can be borrowed from institutional sources—banks, co-operative credit societies, etc. and non-institutional sources—friends, relatives, moneylenders (Sahukars/ Mahajans). But, when we talk about financial inclusion, our concerns is with the access of a household with an institutional source of finance. Financial inclusion has become an issue of worldwide concern, relevant equally in economies of the under-developed, developing and developed nations. Building an inclusive financial sector has gained growing global recognition brining to the fore the need for development strategies that touch all lines, instead of a select few. (UN, 2006). The essence of financial inclusion is in trying to ensure that a range of appropriate financial services is available to every individual and enabling them to understand and access those services. Financial inclusion, thus, includes:

- A basic no frills banking account for making and receiving payments;
- Regular form of financial intermediation;
- A saving product suited the pattern of cash flows of a poor household;
- Money transfer facilities; and
- Several loans and overdrafts for productive, personal and other purposes.

Committee on financial inclusion defined financial inclusion as the process of ensuring access to financial services and timely and adequate credit where needed by vulnerable groups such as weaker sections and low income groups at an affordable cost (CFI, 2008). Holding a bank account itself confers a sense of identity, status and empowerment and provides access to the national payment system. Two foremost issues are addressed through the promotion of financial inclusion:

(i) The issue of financial inclusion of those people who desire the use of financial services, but are unable to do so because of their lower level of education, high incidence of poverty and lower level of collateral assets.

(ii) The issue of *social inclusion* is also of greater significance. Social inclusion means bringing those sections of society to mainstream of banking services which are out of the banking system through the series of generation.

The financial inclusion has also been defined in terms of financial exclusion which has several dimensions such as 'breadth', 'focus' and 'degree' of exclusion. 'Breadth' dimension links financial exclusion to social exclusion which defines financial exclusion as the process that prevent poor and disadvantaged social groups from gaining access to the financial system (Leyshon and Thrifty, 1995). 'Focus' dimension defines financial exclusion as the potential difficulties faced by some segments of population in accessing mainstream financial services such as bank accounts/ house insurance (Meadows *et al.*, 2004). This dimension also include various segments of population such as individuals, households, communities, and businesses. The 'degree' dimension, a very narrow concept, defines financial exclusion as exclusion from particular source of credit and other financial services including insurance, bill payment services and accessible and appropriate deposit accounts (Rogaly, *et al.*, 1999).

So far the vast segments of rural India is concerned, the financial exclusion covers all the above three dimensions. Majority of small and marginal farmers, landless agricultural labourers, petty traders, small businessmen do not have any linkages with institutional finances.

There are various indicators which can be used to assess the level of financial exclusion in a society. These are—

The access to finance could be divided into four segments: (i) the proportion of the population that uses a bank or bank like institution; (ii) the population which uses service from non-bank 'other formal' financial institutions, but does not use bank services; (iii) the population which only uses services from informal financial service providers; (iv) percentage of population transacting regularly through formal financial instruments; and (v) the population which uses to financial services. (RBI, 2008).

Financial exclusion, in India, is a result of century old process of exploitation of down-trodden class by landlords and Sahukars/ Mahajans of rural areas. The story is the same in other countries, World Bank (2008), Asian Development Bank (2007) and Kampson *et al.* (2004) identified following factors affecting access to financial services:

- **Gender issue:** Access to credit is often limited for women who do not have, or cannot hold title to assets such as land and property or must seek male guarantees to borrow.
- **Age factor:** Financial service providers usually target the middle of the economically active population, often

overlooking the design of appropriate products for older or younger potential customers.

- **Legal identity:** Lack of legal identities like identity cards, birth certificates or written records often exclude women, ethnic minorities, economic and political refugees and migrant workers from accessing financial services.
- **Limited literacy:** Limited literacy, particularly financial literacy, i.e., basic mathematics, business finance skills as well as lack of understanding often constrain demand for financial services.
- **Place of living:** Although effective distance is as much about transportation infrastructure as physical distance, factors like density of population, rural and remote areas, mobility of the population (i.e., highly mobile people with no fixed or formal address), insurgency in a location, etc., also affect access to financial services.
- **Psychological and cultural barriers:** The feeling that banks are not interested to look into their cause has led to self-exclusion for many of the low income groups. However, cultural and religious barriers to banking have also been observed in some of the countries.
- **Social security payments:** In those countries where the social security payment system is not linked to the banking system, banking exclusion has been higher.
- **Bank charges:** In most of the countries, transaction is free as long as the account has sufficient funds to cover the cost of transactions made. However, there are a range of other charges that have a disproportionate effect on people with low income.
- **Terms and conditions:** Terms and conditions attached to products such as minimum balance requirements and conditions relating to the use of accounts often dissuade people from using such products/services.
- **Level of income:** Financial status of people is always important in gaining access to financial services. Extremely poor people find it difficult to access financial services even when the services are tailored for them. Perception barriers and income discrimination among potential members in group-lending programmes may exclude the poorer members of the community.

- **Type of occupation:** Many banks have not developed the capacity to evaluate loan applications of small borrowers and unorganized enterprises and hence tend to deny such loan requests.
- **Attractiveness of the product:** Both the financial services/ products (saving accounts, credit products, payment services and insurance) and how their availability is marketed are crucial in financial inclusion.

Access to a well functioned financial system now widely regarded as essential supports for personal financial management and for undertaking transactions in modern societies (Speak and Graham, 1999). According to the Treasury Committee, UK (2006), financial exclusion can impose significant costs on individuals, families and society as a whole. These include: (i) barriers to employment as employers may require wages to be paid into a bank account; (ii) opportunities to save and borrow can be difficult to access; (iii) owning or obtaining assets can be difficult; (iv) difficulty in smoothening income to cope with shocks; and (v) exclusion from mainstream society.

Thus, financial exclusion can be regarded a symptom as well as a cause of poverty. It is unevenly distributed throughout society, especially in rural areas; it is concentrated among the most disadvantaged groups and communities and, as a revolt contributes to a much wider problem of social exclusion.

II. Initiatives for Financial Inclusion in India

Process of financial inclusion in India started in 1967 with the announcement of the policy of social control over banks in 1967. Subsequently the National Credit Council was set-up in 1968 mainly to assess the credit needs of the various segments of the society. Nationalization of 14 large commercial banks in July 1969, Lead Bank Scheme (1969) created a plateform for the implementation of the two-fold objectives of deposit mobilization on an extensive scale and stepping up of credit flow to weaker sections of the society. RBI issued guidelines to all the public sector banks to step up the flow of bank credit to agriculture, small-scale industries, self-employed, small business and weaker sections, within these sectors. Banks were director to earmark at least 40 per cent of their advances (32 per cent, inclusive of export credit, in case of foreign banks) for specified priority sectors. The Differential Rate of Interest (DR) scheme was started in 1972 to provide credit at concessional rate to low income groups in the country.

Pace of financial inclusion, in real sense, got momentum with the establishment of Regional Rural Banks in 1975. The Narasimham Committee (1974) conceptualized the creation of RRBs as a new set of regionally-oriented rural banks, which would combine the local feel and familiarity of rural problems characteristics of cooperatives with the professionalism and large resource base of commercial banks.

RRBs, often viewed as the small man's bank, have done a remarkable job in the field of financial inclusion. These banks have taken deep roots and have become a sort of inseparable part of the rural credit structure. RRBs have played a key role in rural institutional financing in terms of geographical coverage, clientele outreach and business volume as also contribution to development of the rural economy.

A remarkable feature of their performance over the past three decades has been the massive expansion of their retail network in rural areas. From a modest beginning of 6 RRBs with 17 branches covering 12 districts in December 1975, the numbers have grown into 196 RRBs with 14,446 branches working in 518 districts across the country in March 2004. RRBs have a large branch network in the rural area forming around 43 per cent of the total rural branches of commercial banks. The rural orientation of RRBs is formidable with rural and semi-urban branches constituting over 96 per cent of their branch network. The growth in the branch network has enabled the RRBs to expand banking activities in the unbanked areas and mobilise rural savings.

RRBs alone have organized roughly 12 lakh self-help groups, 45 per cent of the total self-help groups in the country. RRBs have also issued over 40 lakh Kisan Credit Cards to the farmers and organized over 5,000 out of 11,000 farmers' clubs under NABARD scheme.

The RRBs, over the years have made impressive strides on various business indicators. Deposits of RRBs have grown by 18 times and advances by 13 times between 1980 and 1990. Between 1990 and 2004, deposits and advances grew by 14 times and 7

TABLE 1

Evolution of RRBs: Select Indicators

(Rs. crore)

Parameter	*1980*	*1985*	*1990*	*1995*	*1996*	*1997*	*1998*	*1999*	*2000*	*2001*	*2002*	*2003*	*2004*	*2005*	*2006*
No. of RRBs	85	188	196	196	196	196	196	196	196	196	196	196	196	196	133
Capital	21	46	91	166	358	705	1,118	1,380	1,959	2,049	2,143	2,141	2,221	NA	NA
Deposits	222	1,315	4,023	11,141	14,171	17,976	22,191	27,059	32,226	38,294	44,539	49,582	56,295	62,143	71,329
Investments	20	164	60	1,348	2,879	3,891	5,280	6,680	7,760	8,800	9,471	17,138	21,286	36,761	41,182
Advances	262	1,405	3,384	5,987	7,057	7,908	9,021	10,559	12,427	15,050	17,710	20,934	25,038	32,870	39,713
Total Assets	426	2,320	6,081	14,886	18,969	24,376	29,468	35,820	42,236	49,596	56,802	62,500	70,193	NA	NA
Interest earned	NA	NA	480	1,158	1,421	2,033	2,624	3,281	3,938	4,619	5,191	5,391	5,535	NA	NA
Other income	NA	NA	113	72	89	103	136	151	207	240	370	430	697	NA	NA
Total income	NA	NA	593	1,230	1,511	2,136	2,760	3,432	4,145	4,859	5,561	5,821	6,231	NA	NA
Interest expended	NA	NA	326	851	1,065	1,462	1,773	2,131	2,565	2,966	3,329	3,440	3,363	NA	NA
Operating expenses	NA	NA	254	657	726	804	845	982	1,056	1,165	1,459	1,667	1,825	NA	NA
Provisions and contingencies	NA	NA	NA	120	171	673	72	99	96	128	163	132	289	NA	NA
Total expenses	NA	NA	581	1,509	1,791	2,265	2,617	3,113	3,621	4,130	4,787	5,107	5,187	NA	NA
Operating Profit	NA	NA	12	-279	-280	-129	143	319	524	729	774	714	1,044	NA	NA

Note: Total expenses are excluding provisions and contingencies.
Source: Reserve Bank of India.

times, respectively (Table 1). Between the year 2000 and 2004, loans disbursed by RRBs more than doubled reflecting the efforts taken by the banks to improve credit flow to the rural sector. The average per branch advances also increased from Rs. 25 lakh in March 1990 to Rs. 154 lakh in March 2003. When one considers the deployment of credit relative to the mobilization of resources, the credit-deposit (C-D) ratio of RRBs were more than 100 per cent during the first decade of their operations up to 1987. Though the C-D ratio subsequently became lower, of late, it has shown an improvement and went up from around 39 per cent in March 2000 to 44.5 per cent in March 2004.

The network of RRBs is spread over 26 States. Uttar Pradesh has highest number of RRBs as well as their branches, followed by Madhya Pradesh, Bihar, Andhra Pradesh, Rajasthan and Karnataka. Arunachal Pradesh, Manipur, Meghalaya, Mizoram, Nagaland and Tripura have only one RRB. Bank-wise, highest number of RRBs has been sponsored by SBI (30), followed by Central Bank of India (23), PNB (19), BOB (19), Bank of India (10), United Bank of India (11), UCO Bank (11) and Syndicate Bank (10). Other Commercial Banks have little presence (Table 2). It is worth mentioning here that more than half of loss-making RRBs are found to be operating in four States, i.e., Bihar, Madhya Pradesh Maharashtra and Orissa. Seen at the level of sponsor banks, three banks, i.e., Bank of India, Central Bank of India and State Bank of India accounted for more than half of the loss-making RRBs.

TABLE 2

Key Performance Indicators of RRBs

(Rs. crore)

Sl. No.	*Indicator*	*31.3.2004*	*31.3.2005*	*31.3.2006*
1	2	3	4	5
1.	No. of RRBs	196	196	133
2.	No. of Districts covered	518	523	525
3.	No. of Branches	14446	14484	14494
4.	No. of Staff	69249	68912	68629
5.	Owned Funds	5438	6181	6647
6.	Deposits	56350	62143	71329

(Contd.)

1	2	3	4	5
7.	Borrowings	4595	5524	7303
8.	Investments	36135	36761	41182
9.	Loans outstanding	26114	32870	39713
10.	Credit-Deposit Ratio	46%	53%	56%
11.	Loans issued	15579	21082	25427
12.	No. of RRBs having accumulated losses	90	83	58
13.	Accumulated Losses	2725	2715	2637
14.	No. of RRBs in Profit	163	166	111
15.	Net NPAs (%)	8.55%	4.84%	3.99%
16.	Recovery (%)	73%	78%	80%
17.	Per Branch Productivity	5.71	6.56	7.66
18.	Per Staff Productivity	1.19	1.38	1.62

Source: Rangarajan Committee on Financial Inclusion, 2008, p. 59.

III. Role of RRBs Financial Inclusion

RRBs have potential and capacity to play a key role in financial inclusion in rural India because of their vast branch network and expertise in micro-finance. An analyses of Basic Statistical Returns of RBI by the committee on Financial Reforms substantiate this view (NABARD, 2008): RRBs account for a substantial 37% of total offices of all scheduled commercial banks. In semi-urban areas their share comes to 15%. Out of the total 31967 branches in rural areas of all the scheduled commercial banks, 11824 branches are of RRBs. As on March 2006, 69% of the work force of RRBs is posted exclusively in rural areas against only 16% of workforce of scheduled commercial banks (other than RRBs). In absolute terms, out of a total banking work-force of 170,423 working in rural areas, RRBs share is 25% (45,062).

At all India level, RRBs account for 12% of all deposit accounts of scheduled commercial banks and a meagre 3.5% of deposit amount. However, in rural areas, RRBs share in deposit accounts is a significant 31% and that in deposit amount 19%. This shows that the average deposit amount is lower in RRBs than other commercial banks, thereby implying RRBs' better reach to small depositors. If semi-urban areas are included than RRBs' share in deposits accounts and amount stands at 21% and 11% respectively.

RRBs' contribution in credit distribution in rural and semi-urban areas is more significant. As on March 2005, RRBs account for 18% of loan accounts Self-Help Group—bank linkage is regarded as the most successful financial inclusion because of its higher reach to weaker-sections through micro-finance activities. Of the total 22.38 lakh SHGs credit linked by all scheduled commercial banks as on 31 March 2006, 33% linkages were done by RRBs. This is impressive by any standard. More significantly, the more backward a region is, the greater is the presence of RRBs. In North-Eastern Region, the share is 56%, in Central Region it is 48% and in Eastern Region it reaches 40%.

Also in terms of bank loans provided cumulatively until March 2006 to SHGs, the share of RRBs is an impressive 29% with higher shares in North-Eastern, Eastern and Central Regions.

TABLE 3

SHG-Bank Linkage : Cumulative No. of Groups Linked—Region-wise Participation by RRBs Versus Other Banks (March 2006)

Region	*No. of SHGs credit linked*		
	by RRBs	*by all banks (including coop.)*	*% by RRBs*
Northern	45772	133097	34
North-Eastern	35108	62517	56
Eastern	159652	394351	40
Central	128390	267915	48
Western	34424	166254	21
Southern	336678	1214431	28
Total	740024	2238565	33

RRBs role in financial inclusion is of great importance because of their better performance in SHG - bank linkage programme and their contribution at Self Help Promotion Institutions (SHPIs). As on March 2006, 104 RRBs were functioning as SHPIs with financial assistance from NABARD, RRBs has a crucial role as SHPIs in those areas, particularly in NE Region, Eastern Region and Central Region, where NGOs presence is minimal.

TABLE 4

SHG-Bank Linkage : Cumulative Bank Loans—Region-wise Participation by RRBs Versus Other Banks (March 2006)

Region	*Cumulative bank loans (Rs. in crore)*		
	by RRBs	*by all banks*	*% by RRBs*
Northern	125.64	398.58	32
North-Eastern	57.09	165.70	34
Eastern	367.72	935.42	39
Central	352.14	805.00	44
Western	116.11	525.14	22
Southern	2303.44	8567.69	27
Total	3322.14	11397.53	29

Source: NABARD (2008): Report of Committee on Financial Inclusion, New Delhi, p. 64.

Thus, it is an established fact that irrespective of their poor performance in commercial terms (Profitability and economic viability), RRBs have proved their effectiveness in the field of financial inclusion. In true sense, they are poor-men's bank. RRBs have proved their worth as an effective tool of mobilizing savings in rural areas and providing credit to those sectors/regions of the country which were a neglected lot in relation to financial activities. Thus, they have achieved their basic objective of providing financial services in neglected areas. With the amalgamation of RRBs, they have acquired the critical mass in terms of financial strength to widen and deepen their reach.

TABLE 5

Bank Credit to Agriculture

Year	*Commercial Banks*	*Cooperative Banks*	*RRBs*	*Total*
2005-06	125477	39786	25223 (13.97)	180486
2006-07	166485	42480	20435 (8.91)	229400
2007-08	175072	43684	24814 (10.18)	243570

Source: *The Business Line*, 6th November, 2008.

IV. Conclusion

From the perspective of institutional development, the role of RRBs, which were established to expand the delivery of financial services in the unbanked sectors/segments, suffered a setback due to their poor financial health. With the recent initiatives to strengthen them, it is expected that they would play a greater role in promoting financial inclusion. RRBs can serve, with the support of NABARD, GOI, RBI and the sponsor banks, as active player in financial inclusion specially in areas with high degree of financial exclusion. RRBs have the potential and capability to emerge as niche operators in the field of micro-finance. Restracturing of RRBs have given greater financial strength to widen and deepen their reach. Thus, they have become best suited vehicles to widen and deepen the process of financial inclusion. However, utmost care must be taken to ensure that RRBs do not again fall into the vicious circle of deteriorating financial performance in achieving socio-economic objective of financial inclusion.

The Role of RRBs in Rural Development (With Special Reference to the Credit Requirement and Problem of the Borrowers of the Weaker Sections of the Rural Societies in India)

Dr. Nirmal Bindra

After about sixty-one years of independence, we find a sea-change in the economic situation of India. The country is self-reliant in the supply of food-grains, infra-structural facilities in terms of power, irrigation, health and education have been strengthened during the plan period. But even today we are not completely out of woods. The main reason is that Indian economy was predominantly an agricultural economy. About 80% people lived in rural areas. There is a big gulf between urban and rural people regarding wealth, wages, education and employment.

Indian farmer was exploited by money-lenders and traders. The role of institutional credit in financing Indian agriculture was very poor. The availability of credit is the most important determinant in the process of rural development. Gunnar Myrdal has termed—"Credit as an accelerator of development. For sustainable development in rural areas in consonance with rural people's wishes and aspirations, huge investments are being made by the Ministry of Rural Development through different programmes. Such as—CDP, IRDP, SGSY, JRY, TRYSEM, DPAP, DDP, CADP, and DWCRA.

Inspite of them, the primary emphasis at this juncture was on making banking facilities available in a large number of unbanked centers in rural and semi-urban areas both from the point of resources mobilization and extention of credit facilities. At this point the co-operatives were not able to meet the need for credit which had increased considerably with Green Revolution and the boost which it had provided to agricultural production and productivity. The nationalization of banks enable them to supplement the efforts of the co-operatives. As there were still spatial gaps in rural lending the Regional Rural Banks were introduced in 26 September 1975 the ordinance was replaced by the Regional Rural Bank Act, 1976. The RRBs were established with a view to developing the rural economy by providing, for the purpose of development of agriculture, trade, commerce, industry and the productive activities in the rural areas.

Over the years, the RRBs which are often viewed as the small man's bank have taken deep root and have become a sort of a inseparable part of the rural credit structure. They have played a key role in rural institutional financing in terms of geographical coverage, clientele out-reach and business volume as also contribution to development of the rural economy.

According to the NABARD Reports and the Reserve Bank of India occasional report—From a modest beginning of 6 RRBs with 17 branches covering 12 districts in December 1975, the numbers have grown into 196 RRBs with 14,446 branches working in 518 districts across the country in March 2004. The rural orientation of RRBs is formidable with rural and semi-urban branches constituting over 97% of their branch network.

The main objectives of setting up of RRBs were to provide larger volume of institutional credit to agricultural sector for rapid development and thereby helping in reduction of regional imbalance in the availabilities of credit in rural areas. Farmer needs finance for making permanent improvement in land for production purposes and consumption also. The problem of the small farmers is also acute. So the second aim of RRBs to provide credit and other facilities especially to the small/marginal farmers' agricultural labours, rural artisan and small entrepreneur in rural areas. RRBs also supplement various credit institutions working in the field of agriculture to achieve adequate credit planning. All those working of RRBs are very important for rural development in India.

Our economy is largely agrarian keeping in view the crucial importance of agriculture and in the context of the strategy adopted for increasing foodgrains production so as to ensure food security and the need for greater involvement of banks in supporting these efforts. Banks were asked to step up the direct finance extending to agriculture so as to reach a level of atleast 18 per cent of the total outstanding credit by March 1990. This was done as credit support from the banks was considered necessary for increasing agricultural production in the country. Perhaps the most significant achievement of RRBs during this period was in enabling the weaker sections of the rural community access to institutional credit. The bulk of the loans from RRBs were to the priority sections, which accounted for over 70% of the total. Agriculture and allied activities took up more than 50% of the total advance (see Table 1).

TABLE 1

Purpose-wise Advances of RRBs Outstanding (September 1990)

(Rs. crore)

1.	Short-term (crop loan)	615
2.	Term Loan and Agriculture Activities	669
3.	Allied Activities	555
4.	Rural Artisans—Village and Cottage Industries	277
5.	Retail trade and Self-employment, etc.	1052
6.	Consumption Loan	54
7.	Other Purpose	290
8.	Indirect Advance	43
	Total	3555

Source: Report on Trend and Progress of Banking in India, 1990.

RBI has granted certain relaxation to the RRBs as far as the cash and liquidity requirements. RRBs are authorized to refinancing facilities from the RBI. The Central Government has also prescribed that the rate of interest changed by the RRBs on it direct loans to the person belonging to the specified categories of the rural society would be at par with the rate of interest charged by the primary credit society from their clients.

The other peculiarity of the RRB is that they are meant to provide banking Service to a particular class of borrowers namely small/marginal farmers and other weaker sections of rural society to whom institutional credit was hitherto not available. These areas of operation is specified and their beneficiaries are also particularized. Almost all the resources at their disposal are used only for weaker section of the rural population.

RRBs were instrumental in extending credit for poverty alleviation scheme (e.g. IRDP) and disadvantaged area (drought-prone regions and deserts) development programme. The role of credit institution is important in poverty alleviation because of relation between assetlessness and poverty. RRB was the major programme for families below poverty line in the rural area of the country.

RRBs and co-operative banks extended micro credit to 1,49,050 news SHGs during the year 2000-01. In terms of volumes, micro-credit extended by banks aggregated Rs. 287.9 crore during the year. Commulative micro-credit from banks to SHGs stood at Rs. 480.8 crores as at the end of March 2002. (*Source*: *Yojana*, 2002 January-September.)

RRBs have also been extending finance to small scale industries including the tiny sector of rural artisans, Cottage and Village Industries. Banks are required to lend 60% of their SSI advances to the tiny sector within the small scale industries.

The RRBs, over the years have made impressive strides on various business indicators. For instance, deposits of RRBs have grown by 18 items and advance by 13 times between 1980 and 1990. Between 1990 and 2004, deposits and advances grew by 14 times and 7 times, respectively (Table 2) between the year 2000 and 2004, loans disbursed by RRBs more than doubled rejected the efforts taken by the banks to improve credit flow to the rural sector.

The subject of consolidation of the RRBs as a way of raising their viability and profitability has recurred several times since the beginning of the reform process but without any policy outcome. Various working groups and committees have prescribed different measures for restructing the RRBs. Lastly, it decided that it could not consider "The option of merger with the sponsor bank, as it would go against the rationable of this channel for rural credit with a clear rural focus and regional orientation."

TABLE 2

Evolution of RRBs: Select Indicators

Parameter	*1990*	*1995*	*1996*	*1997*	*1998*	*1999*	*2000*	*2001*	*2002*	*2003*	*2004*
No. of RRBs	196	196	196	196	196	196	196	196	196	196	196
Capital	91	166	391	766	1358	1905	1118	1380	1959	2149	2221
Deposits	4223	11141	14171	17976	22191	27059	32226	38294	44538	49582	56295
Investments	60	1348	2879	3891	5280	6680	7760	8800	92171	17138	21286
Advances	3384	5984	7057	7908	9021	10559	12427	15050	17710	20934	25038
Total Assets	6081	14886	18969	24376	29468	35820	42236	49576	56802	62500	70195
Interest Earned	480	1158	1421	2033	2624	3281	3938	4619	5191	5391	5535
Other Income	113	72	89	103	136	151	207	240	370	430	697
Total Income	593	1230	1511	2136	2760	3432	4145	4859	5561	5820	6231
Interest expended	326	851	1065	1462	1773	2131	2565	2966	3329	3440	3363
Operating expenses	254	657	726	804	845	982	1056	1165	1459	1667	1825
Provisions contingencies	NA	120	171	673	72	99	36	128	163	132	289
Total expenses	581	1509	1791	2265	2617	3113	3621	4130	4787	5107	5187
Operating Profit	12	.279	.280	.129	143	319	524	729	774	714	1044

Source: Reserve Bank of India, Occasional Paper, Vol. 27, 2006.

Instead, it recommended merger of RRBs so as to create a Zonal Bank for RRBs in the North-East and rural banks at State level for the rest of the country. These banks would work on a stand alone basis and the sponsor banks plus NABARD would contribute to the equity.

We have briefly reviewed the three phases of Regional Rural Banking in India—The inception and expansion phase (1976-90) which saw rapid growth of RRBs activities; the reform phase (1991-2003) which raised the profitability of these banks at the cost of massive rural disintermediation, particularly of the targeted borrower categories; and the most recent phase of stock taking and perhaps some repositioning to strike a balance in the condrum of viability *versus* outreach. At present the mergers of RRBs are taking place entirely with a view to improve profitability. The purpose of the ownership reform of the RRBs must be the same as for other aspects of RRB policy to foster a bank-led equitable rural growth. It is no doubt, in its two phases (in the beginning) RRBs have become an integral part of the rural banking system of the country and have been playing a commandable role providing credit and banking services to the rural areas by opening a large network of branches.

References

Bikker, J.A. Hu, H. (2002), Cyclical Pattern.

Bose, Sukanya (2005), "Regional Rural Bank: The Past and the Present Debate".

Consideration of Regional Rural Banks (Amendment) Bill, 2004.

Demisgue-Kunt, A. Huizinga H. (2000), *Financial Structure and Bank Profitability*.

Kannan, R. (2004), RRBs URL: http://www.geocities.com/leasing/banking 2 urbhtml.

Malhotra, Rakesh (2002), "Performance of India's Regional Rural Banks, Effect of the Umbilical Cord".

Narain's Series : Simple Indian Economics by H.S. Agarwal.

Rural Development in India, Dr. R.K. Verma.

Yojana, Vol. 46, January 2002, A development monthly.

Reserve Bank of India, Occasional Papers.

RRB Act, 1976 stipulates that only on request of a sponsor Bank, Central Government would consider the establishment of RRB.

DPAP = Drought Prone Area Programme.

CADP = Command Area Development Programme.

DWCRA = Development of Women and Children in Rural Areas.

Socio-economic Significance of RRBs for Rural Economy of India

Dr. Sandeep Shandilya and Mr. R.K. Mishra

1. Introduction

Indian banking system is not uniform when it comes to the working of banks in rural and urban areas. Agriculture still continues to be the occupation of a large proportion of Indian population. Commercial banking system in India mostly caters to the needs of urban society. Though, commercial banks were assigned the duty to take care of the agriculture which is a priority sector but due to various constraints, they have failed to do justice to rural sector. It is because of all these reasons that working group on rural banks (1975) recommended the establishment of RRBs to supplement the efforts of commercial banks and co-operatives in extending credit to weaker sections of the rural community. Various beneficiaries from RRBs include small and marginal farmers, landless labourers and artisans, etc. RRBs were established to give new lease of life to rural credit system. RRBs can play significant role in socio-economic fabric of India. These banks are concerned with the poorest among the poors belonging to rural economy. Proper management of these banks can help in eradicating poverty from rural sector. Such eradication of poverty from rural sector will definitely reflect in the overall poverty index of the nation.

2. RRBs: Their Socio-Economic Worth

Regional Rural banks are valuable for India from both aspects, i.e. social as well as economic. It will not be an exaggeration to say that RRBs are economic agents which can play wonderful role in social transformation. In peculiar Indian circumstances, social face of RRBs perhaps over showdown their economic face. Indian economy is a mixed economy. On one hand, we have big Multinational Companies (MNCs) and on other hand, we have micro, small and medium enterprises starving for funds. MNCs are known to concentrate wealth at a point but in order to give a fitting reply to the disease called poverty, India needs equitable distribution of income to all sections of society. In this context socio-economic worth of RRBs becomes self-explanatory. RRBs are aimed to provide credit to small and marginal farmers, landless labourers and artisans, etc. They are true agents of Indian banking system who can inculcate the spirit of democratisation in Indian economy. RRBs have the potential to convert idle resources and manpower of rural economy into active participates of socio-economic revaluation in India particularly in rural sector. To see to it that above mentioned fact becomes a reality, we need to improve the reach as well as influence of RRBs spread all over the country.

3. Amalgamation of RRBs: Pros and Cons from Socio-Economic Angle

Seeds of amalgamation of RRBs were sawn with the constitution of Khusro Committee which suggested that RRBs were of no use for rural economy of India. At present the number of RRBs has been reduced from 196 to just 96. Here is an excerpt from project monitor, India's first news paper on projects mentioning the formation of 'Neelanchal Gramya Bank' with its head office at Bhubaneswar, whereas the central government, after consultation with the National Bank for Agriculture and Rural

Development (NABARD), Government of Orissa and Indian Overseas Bank being the sponsor bank of Puri Gramya Bank and Dhenkanal Gramya Bank (regional rural banks), is of the opinion that it is necessary in the public interest and in the interest of the development of the area served by the aforesaid regional rural banks and also in the interest of the said banks themselves, that the said regional rural banks should be amalgamated into a single regional rural bank. Now, therefore, in exercise of the powers conferred by sub-section (1) of section 23A of Regional Rural Banks Act, 1976 (21 of 1976), the central government hereby provides for the amalgamation of the said regional rural banks into a single regional rural bank, which shall be called as "Neelanchat Gramya Bank" with its head office at Bhubaneshwar.[1] Though above information is concerned with the case of amalgamation of regional rural banks in Orissa but the reasons sighted above behind such an eventuality can be uniformly associated with the cases of amalgamation of RRBs in the other states of the country.

Now the question arises that what would be the possible socio-economic repercussions of such amalgamations of regional rural banks and thus an overall reduction in the number of such regional rural banks to just 96 from the earlier figure of 196. In other words, there has been a decrease of around 100 regional rural banks in numerical terms. The most important aspect which needs to be analysed is the effect of geogrphical spread of these banks and reach to far flung areas of rural sector. It needs to be seen that with such an amalgamation of regional rural banks will the reach of these banks (both geographic as well as socio-economic) suffer a severe jolt. It remains to be analysed sincere that in order to achieve administrative advantage, are we going to jeopardize other characteristic features of regional rural banks. A large number of rural banks would have facilitated the uniform demographic spread of such banks over entire rural sector of Indian economy thus facilitating equitable distribution of rural credit to rural sector of Indian economy.

4. Labour-Intensive Character of Agriculture: RRBs and Employment Generation

Agriculture is a labour-intensive industry. It has a high

potential of employment generation. This peculiar feature of agriculture can help in addressing the problem of unemployment to a considerable extent. "Agriculture is the mainstay of Indian economy because of its high share in employment and livelihood creation not withstanding its reduced share of contribution to the nation's GDP. The share of agriculture in the Gross Domestic Product has registered a steady decline from 36.4 per cent in 1982-83 to 18.5 per cent in 2006-07. Yet this sector continues to support more than half a billion people providing employment to 52 per cent of the workforce. It is also an important source of raw material and demand for many industrial products, particularly fertilizers, pesticides, agricultural implements and a variety of consumer goods."[2] This information taken from economic survey, 2007-08 of India amply reflects on the employment generating capacity of agriculture. It is worthwhile to note that agriculture sector gives employment to 52 per cent of the work force of India.

As regional rural banks provide loans to marginal farmers, they can act as an agent of transformation in rural economy of India. Moreover, their 'outreach' is one of the most significant feature, they possess. An overall improvement in the management and efficiency of RRBs will go a long way in revamping rural economy of India. In economic planning of India care must be taken to develop a balanced plan for the growth and development of both capital intensive as well as labour-intensive industries. In present circumstances, both types of industries are significant from India's point of view. Capital-intensive industries provide an impedes to the application as well as growth of the modern technologies but they provide employment to considerably lesser number of people. India's emergence as a global player in the field of Information Technology and Software reflects her huge potential in these sectors. This fact is a welcome sign and every Indian should feel pride of it. However, rampant unemployment alongwith disguised labour are certain crucial issues which need to be addressed with true zeal and vigour. Agriculture still continues to be the occupation of the sizeable chunk of the population of India. Effective use of information technology in this sector will serve dual purpose. On one hand it will help in modernizing Indian economy and on the other hand it will generate employment in rural sector. Regional Rural Banks and policies concerning them must be framed in such a manner that their ability and feature of 'outreach' gets fully capitalized.

5. Ownership Pattern of RRBs with Reference to Its Socio-Economic Weight

Ownership pattern of Regional Rural Banks in India is quite interesting. An analysis of this ownership pattern will reflect on the socio-economic worth of RRBs. It will also suggest certain changes in ownership pattern if needed. "With partnership with the Central Government (50 per cent) State Government (15 per cent) and Commercial banks (15 per cent), the number of RRBs rose from just fix in 1975 to 196 by 1987, coming 476 districts. They financed only the weaker sections of the rural community small and marginal farmers, agricultural labourers, small traders and so on.[3]

We find that half of the partnership is of central government alone whereas state governments constitute only 15% and sponsoring bank has 35% partnership.

The story of birth of Regional Rural Banks is an interesting one. Co-operations working in rural areas are at an advantageous position due to valuable local familarity and outlook they posses. Their local feel is of vital concern which can be utilized for upliftment of local people. However, this valuable aspect and character of co-operatives goes in vain due to lack of modernised of these co-operatives. Though co-operatives working in these rural continue to be less modernised and efficient, Indian banking sector has been sufficiently modernized due to advancement in information technology and use of other modern technologies. The zeal to establish institutional framework for rural credit which has been a local know how as possessed by co-operatives and modernisation content of commercial banks, ended in formation of Regional Rural Banks. However, our RRBs[4] are plagued with several deficiencies which range from organizational problems to management problems. Problem of bed debts and losses is a severe one. Perhaps the 35 per cent stake of sponsoring bank which is a scheduled commercial bank motivates it to make RRBs function in the same manner as commercial banks do. However, there is big difference when we analyse the nature and pattern of customers in both the cases. In case of RRBs mostly the customers are marginal farmers. There is an urgent need to sensitise RRBs towards the credit needs of these poor farmers and artisans. Too much emphasis on commercial aspect may dilute their social worth. Social aspect of RRBs is no less than their economic worth for Indian economy.

6. Philosophy of RRBs is Closer to the Sentiments of Gandhian Economy

The vary concept and idea of RRBs has its roots in Gandhian philosophy. RRBs are meant to provide funds to marginal farmers, landless labourers and artisans, etc. These are the people who were very close to the heart of Mahatma Gandhi. It was not just a coincidence that very first RRBs came into existence on Gandhi's birth anniversary. "Initially five Regional Rural Banks were set-up on October 2, 1975 at Moradabad and Gorakhpur in Uttar Pradesh, Bhiwani in Haryana, Jaipur in Rajasthan and Malda in West Bengal. Each regional rural bank has an authorized capital of Rs. 1 crore and issued and paidup capital of Rs. 25 lakhs. The share capital of the regional rural bank was subscribed by the central government (50%), the state government concerned (15%) and the sponsoring commercial bank (35%). The regional rural banks, though basically scheduled commercial banks, differ from the later in certain respects."

Individual occupies the central space in Gandhian economy. Well-being of an individual decides the welfare of entire society and entire nation in Gandhian economy. Regional rural banks caters to the needs of those individuals of Indian society who have had a long history of sufferings and apathetic treatment given to them. Mahatma Gandhi had a deep understanding of Indian society particularly rural India. With this understanding he could guide Indian freedom struggle in a manner which entire world recognizes and salutes even today. His words: "True India lives in villages" are not mere world but an entire thesis and school of thought which can abily guide economic planners of India to formulate and develop effective economic plans for India. It will not be an exaggeration to say that RRBs are true torch bearers of Gandhian economy. When wisdom and guidance of Mahatma Gandhi could take us to long awaited independence why cant today we guide ourselves by his words of wisdom: "True India lives in villages."

7. Suggestions and Conclusion

India still continues to be predominantly an agrarian economy. Industrialisation is also on the rise and share of agriculture in India's GDP is also declining. Even after all these changes, the fact that a huge proportion of Indian population lives on agriculture, still holds good. With the advent of globalisation, different economies of the world are undergoing drastic changes in their structure. Agriculture sector has also been greatly affected by the implementation of the Agreement on Agriculture (AoA) under World Trade Organization (WTO). Demand for food is increasing at more than 2 per cent per annum. World population is also increasing at a rapid pace. This population needs food for survival. The outcome of this is that the financial, land and water resources in the rural sector have come under severe strain. Agriculture sector is turning out to be a crucial sector of world economy and India is not exception. Enhancement in productivity, expansion of rural credit, infrastructural development and export competitiveness are certain vital areas of concern for agricultural sector. Poverty eradication is also a socio-economic agenda which is intimately connected with agricultural sector at least in case of India.

RRBs are considered by some economists as the only surviving rural financial institutions with a professional management culture to meet small value, large-volume rural credit needs. RRBs can serve dual purpose, i.e. they can improve the conditions of agriculture sector in the country and also contribute in the eradication of poverty by improving rural per capita income. Moreover, we know that by nature agriculture is a labour-intensive sector and thus investment in agriculture can generate considerable employment opportunities in rural sector. Overall efficiency of agriculture sector can be improved by introducing a feel and touch of modernization to it while keeping its labour-intensive character intact. In this regards, it becomes imperative that use of Information Technology and other modern technology be permitted in the functioning of RRBs. RRBs must be permitted to recruit specialists in the technology and agriculture fields. A provision of soft loans must be there so that RRBs may have an access to new technologies. It will help RRBs to compete with commercial banks that invest heavily in technology projects. The induction of new and modern technologies in RRBs will infuse a sense of confidence among them and facilitate the handling of low-value and high-volume business in cost effective manner.

Various other issues need to be addressed in the context of the socio-economic worth of RRBs. One such issue is the amalgamation of RRBs and thus overall reduction in their numerical figures. Such amalgamation of RRBs must be thoroughly analysed from their socio-economic perspective and effect on their feature of 'outreach'. Gandhian spirit which effect from his words: "True India lives in villages" must remain a guiding force for overall functioning of RRBs in India.

Notes and References

1. "Amalgamation of Regional Rural Banks," *Project Monitor*, India's first newspaper on projects, Nov. 5, 2008.
2. "Economic Survey of India: 2007-08."
3. V. Jagan Mohan, 'Regional Rural Banks need a shot in the arm', *Business Line*, The Hindu group of publications, Delhi, March 19, 2004.
4. Dutt and Sundram, "Indian Economy," S. Chand & Company Ltd., Delhi, 2007, p. 584.

Role of Regional Rural Banks in Indian Economy and Rural Development

Dr. Vandana Tyagi

Introduction

Regional Rural Banks were established under the provisions of an ordinance promulgated on the 26th September 1975 and the RRB Act, 1976 with an objective to ensure sufficient institutional credit for agriculture and other rural sectors. The RRBs mobilize financial resources from rural/semi-urban areas and grant loans and advances mostly to small and marginal farmers, agricultural labourers and rural artisans.

RRBs are jointly owned by Government of India, the concerned State Government and sponnsor Banks (27 Scheduled Commercial Banks and one State Cooperative Bank) the issued capital of a RRB is shared by the owners in the proportion of 50%, 15% and 35% respectively.

Reform Process

RRBs started their development process on 2nd Oct. 1975 with the formation of a single bank (Frathana Grameen Bank). As on 31st March 2006 there were 133 RRBs (Post-Merger) covering 525 districts with a network of 14,494 branches. RRBs were originally conceived as low cost intitutions having a rural ethos. Local feel and pro-poor focus. However within a very short time most banks were making losses.

When the reform process in the banking sector was initiated, RRBs were taken up for a close look. The GOI consultation with RBI and NABARD started the reform process through a comprehensive package for RRBs including cleansing their balance sheets and recapitalising them. Extent lending restrictions were removed and space and variety available for investment of their surplus funds was expended. Simultaneously a number of human resources development and organisational development initatives (ODI) were taken up by NABARD with funding support of the Swiss Development Corporation (SDC) and with the tools, of trainning and exposure visits (ODI) technology support computerization and use of IT system development, etc. for business development and productivity improvement. By end March 2005 there was a remarkable improvement in the financial performance of RRBs as compared to the position prevailing in 1994-95. The Number of Banks reporting profits went up to 166 of the 196 RRBs. As on 31st March 2006 of the total 133 RBSs (Post-Merger) 111 Posted profits and 75 of these RRBs were sustainably viable organisations having no accumulated looses as also posting current profits.

Government of India initiated the process of structural consolidation RRBs by amalgamating RRBs sponsored by the same bank within a state as per the recommendations of the Vyas Committee (2004). The amalgamated RRBs were expected to provide better customer service due to better infrastructure computerization of branches pooling of experienced work force common publicity/marketing effrots, etc. and also derive the benefits of a large area of operation enhanced credit exposure limit and more diverse banking activities. As a result of the amalgamation the number of RRBs was reduced from 196 to 133 as on 31 March 2006 and to 96 as on 30 April 2007.

Coverage of Rural Markets by Banks

	PSBs	*RRBs*	*CBs*	*Private, foreign and others*
Number	27	196	397	76
Total Branches	46118	14473	N.A.	5595
% Rural Branches	42%	83%	N.A.	20%
Total Deposit Balance (Rs. billion)	9688	432	944	2340
Total Credit outstanding (Rs. billion)	5094	184	823	1716
Credit in rural area % of total credit	10%	72%	~100%	2%
Credit in small rural accounts % of total outstanding credit	6%	65%	>90%	1%

*Author's estimate.
CBs = Cooperative Banks; PSBs = Public Scector Bannks.
Source: RBI (2002a; 2001)

Key Performance Indicators

Reforms introduced in RRBs by GOI in consultation with RBI and NABARD have yielded positive results in respect of key performance indicators as indicated under:

(Amount Rs. Crore)

S. No.	*Indicator*	*31.03.2004*	*31.03.2005*	*31.03.2006*
1	*2*	*3*	*4*	*5*
1.	No. of RRBs	196	196	133
2.	No. of districts covered	518	523	525
3.	No. of Branches	14446	14484	14494
4.	No. of Staff	69249	68912	68629
5.	Owned funds	5458	6181	6647
6.	Deposits	56350	62143	71329
7.	Borrowings	4595	5524	7303
8.	Investments	36135	36761	41182
9.	Loans Outstanding	26114	32870	39713
10.	Credit-deposit ratio	46%	53%	56%
11.	Loans Issued	15579	21082	25427

(Contd.)

1	2	3	4	5
12.	No. of RRBs having	90	83	58
13.	Accumulated losses	2725	2715	2637
14.	No. of RRBs in profit	163	166	111
15.	Recovery %	73%	78%	80%
16.	Per Branch Productivity	5.71	6.56	7.66
17.	Per Staff Productivity	1.19	1.38	1.62

Source: NABARD.

The following trends can be highlights.

"Performance under Doubling of Agriculture Credit" RRBs

More Importantly the performance of RRBs under GOIs Initiative on doubling of agriculture credit in three years (from base year 2003-04) and greater coverage of small and marginal farmers have been impressive. They disbursed agriculture loans of the order of Rs. 12,404 crore during 2004-05 registering a phenomenal annnual growth of 64% against the targeted 30%. During 2005-06 Agricultural credit targeted 30%. During 2005-06 Agriculture credit flow stood at Rs. 15,223 crore with a growth of 23%. Thus RRBs have achieved the target of doubling of agriculture credit in 2 years. RRBs financed 18.58 lakh new farmers in 2004-05 and another 17.03 lakh new farmers in 2005-06.

Post-Merger RRBs represent a powerful instrument for financial inclusion. Their outreach *vis-a-vis* other scheduled commercial banks particularly in regions and across population groups facing the brunt of financial exclusion is impressive, as observed from an analysis of Basic Statistical Returns of the RBI and indicated in the following paragraphs. With merger infusing the much needed financial strength in RRBs coupled with the local feel and familarity they command, RRBs are in a unique position to play a decisive role in financial inclusion.

In rural areas, RRBs account for a substantial 37% of total offices of all scheduled commercial banks. In semi-urban areas, their share comes to 15%. It goes without saying that exclusion is more severe in rural areas.

At all India level, RRBs account for 12% of all deposit account of scheduled commercial banks and a meagre 3.5% of deposit amount. However, in rural areas, RRBs share in deposit accounts is a significant 31% and that in deposit amount 19%. This shows that the average deposit amount is lower in RRBs than other commercial banks, thereby implying RRBs' better reach to small depositors.

Offices of Scheduled Commercial Banks Population Group and Bank Group-wise (March 2005)

Bank group	Rural Office		Semi-urban offices		Urban/metro-offices		Total	
	No.	% to total	No.	% to total	No.	% to total	No.	% to total
RRBs	11824	37	2284	15	537	2	14645	21
SCBs other than RRBs	20143	63	13335	85	21846	98	55324	79
Total	31967	100	15619	100	22383	100	69969	100

Deposits of Rural Branches of Scheduled Commercial Banks—Bank Group-wise (March 2005)

Bank group	No. of Accounts		Deposit Amount	
	No. ('000)	% to total	Amount (Rs. crore)	% to total
RRBs	43540	31	40957	19
SCBs other than RRBs	98368	69	172147	81
Total	141908	100	213104	100

If we include semi-urban areas for both RRBs and schedule commercial banks, RRBs' share in deposit accounts and amount stands at 21% and 11% respectively.

Deposits of Rural/Semi-urban Branches of Scheduled Commercial Banks—Bank Group-wise (March 2005)

Bank group	No. of Accounts		Deposit Amount	
	No. ('000)	% to total	Amount (Rs. crore)	% to total
RRBs	55165	21	56111	11
SCBs other than RRBs	211941	79	452678	89
Total	267106	100	508789	100

At all India level, RRBs account for 18% of loan accounts of all scheduled commercial banks and 3% of loans outstanding. However, in rural areas the share of RRBs in loan accounts is an impressive 38%. More significantly, despite having 38% of all loan accounts, RRBs account for only 21% of total credit outstanding in rural areas, implying thereby their better reach to small borrowers.

Credit Disbursed by Rural Branches of Scheduled Commercial Banks—Bank Group-wise (March 2005)

Bank group	*No. of Accounts*		*Deposit Amount*	
	No. ('000)	*% to total*	*Amount (Rs. crore)*	*% to total*
RRBs	10913	38	23017	21
SCBs other than RRBs	18155	62	86959	79
Total	29068	100	109976	100

If semi-urban branches are included, the share of RRBs in credit accounts and amounts outstanding is of the order of 29% and 13% respectively.

Credit Disbursed by Rural and Semi-urban Branches of Scheduled Commercial Banks—Bank Group-wise (March 2005)

Bank group	*No. of Accounts*		*Deposit Amount*	
	No. ('000)	*% to total*	*Amount (Rs. crore)*	*% to total*
RRBs	13677	29	30546	13
SCBs other than RRBs	33594	71	210071	87
Total	47271	100	240617	100

Both deposit and credit data indicate that RRB branches in rural areas have performed better in relation to other scheduled commercial bank branches. However, RRBs' share comes down significantly when data for both rural and semi-urban areas are considered. This could be due to the fact that branches of other scheduled commercial banks located in semi-urban areas disburse considerable loans in rural areas also. This is significant from the point of view of financial inclusion as rural branches are closer and more active in extending outreach to remote and interior villages. Viewed from this angles RRBs are particularly well placed to achieve the goal of financial inclusion.

Outreach across Regions

The table below point to RRB's significant presence in North-Eastern, Eastern and Central Regions which manifest financial exclusion of a high order. Of all the scheduled commercial banks, RRBs account for 34% of branches in North-Eastern, 30% in Eastern and 32% in Central Regions whereas their presence is significantly lower (9% to 17%) in other regions. The data points to the fact that as an institutional group, RRBs are best suited to take up the leadership role in financial inclusion across priority areas in States of North-Eastern, Eastern and Central Region featuring high levels of exclusion.

Offices of Scheduled Commercial Banks—Region and Bank Group-wise (March 2005)

Regions	*RRBs*		*Other SCBs*		*Total*
Northern	1937	17	9627	83	11564
North-Eastern	659	34	1283	66	1942
Eastern	3617	30	8594	70	12211
Central	4545	32	9451	68	13996
Western	982	9	9912	91	10894
Southern	2905	15	16457	85	19362
Total	14645	21	55324	79	69969

Source: RBI Database.

Although RRBs account for only 12% of total number of deposit accounts at all India level, share is significantly higher (18% to 29%) in the North-Eastern, Eastern and Central Regions where major interventions are required for financial inclusion. Further, the share of RRBs in a region in terms of no. of accounts is significantly higher than in terms of amount of deposit in the same region. This points to the fact that they basically cater to small depositors or the small depositors are more inclined towards RRBs.

Deposits of Scheduled Commercial Banks—Region and Bank Group-wise (March 2005)

Regions	*No. of Accounts ('000)*		*Amount (Rs. crore)*	
	RRBs	*Other SCBs*	*RRBs*	*Other SCBs*
Northern	5570 (7%)	75157 (93%)	8225.26 (2%)	402179.85 (98%)
North-Eastern	3015 (29%)	7327 (71%)	2950.09 (11%)	24850.91 (89%)
Eastern	13085(18%)	60868 (82%)	14400.73 (7%)	194611.28 (93%)
Central	20528 (22%)	71782 (78%)	20651.99 (8%)	198854.37 (91%)
Western	3271 (4%)	76390 (96%)	3348.75 (1%)	489284.78 (99%)
Southern	12219 (9%)	117581 (91%)	11870.08 (3%)	375585.96 (97%)
Total	57688 (12%)	409105 (88%)	61446.90 (4%)	1685367.15 (96%)

Source: RBI Database.

RRBs account for about one-third of total number of credit accounts in North-Eastern, Eastern and Central Regions as against only 18% at all India level as detailed in the Table below. Further, the average loan amount disbursed by RRBs is significantly less than by other scheduled commercial banks. In North-Eastern Region, RRBs account for 36% of loan accounts but only 13% of the outstanding loan amount. For Eastern Region, the respective shares are 35% and 6% and for Central Region they are 31% and 10%. It is obvious, RRBs command better outreach and level of comfort for small borrowers.

Credit of Scheduled Commercial Banks—Region and Bank Group-wise (March 2005)

Regions	*No. of Accounts ('000)*		*Amount (Rs. crore)*	
	RRBs	*Other SCBs*	*RRBs*	*Other SCBs*
Northern	967 (12%)	7043 (88%)	4091.03 (2%)	240118.72 (98%)
North-Eastern	489 (36%)	886 (64%)	1218.26 (13%)	8514.40 (87%)
Eastern	3590 (35%)	6575 (65%)	6147.17 (6%)	88943.56 (94%)
Central	3617 (31%)	8086 (69%)	8577.20 (10%)	808969.11 (90%)
Western	659 (6%)	11233 (94%)	1696.19 (-)	409595.05 (100%)
Southern	4845 (14%)	29160 (86%)	10958.97 (4%)	291638.27 (96%)
Total	14167 (18%)	62983 (82%)	32688.82 (3%)	1119779.11 (97%)

Self Help Groups—Bank Linkage

The microfinance services provided through SHG-bank linkage has so far been the most successful initiative in financial inclusion. Therefore, an analysis of RRB's involement in the SHG movement will be an important indicator of the kind of mandate which RRBs could be given for further widening and deepening of financial inclusion.

Of the total 22.38 lakh SHGs credit linked by the banking industry as on 31 March 2006, 33% linkages were done by RRBs as detailed in the Table below. This is impressive by any standard. More significantly, the more backward a region is, the greater is the share of RRBs. In North-Eastern Region, the share is 56% in Central Region it is 48% and in Eastern Region it reaches 40%.

Also in terms of bank loans provided cummulatively until March 2006 to SHGs, the share of RRBs is an impressive 29% with higher shares in North-Eastern, Eastern and Central Regions. State-wise particulars are indicated in Annexure II.

SHG-Bank Linkage: Cumulative No. of Groups Linked—Region-wise Participation by RRBs Versus other Banks (March 2006)

Region	*No. of SHGs credit linked*		
	by RRBs	*by all banks (including coop.)*	*% by RRBs*
Northern	45772	133097	34
North-Eastern	35108	62517	56
Eastern	159652	394351	40
Central	128390	267915	48
Western	34424	166254	21
Southern	336678	1214431	28
Total	740024	2238565	33

RRBs as Self Help Promotion Institutions (SHPI)

RRBs have not only provided financial services to the SHG-Bank Linnkage Programme, but have also played a significant role as SHPIs. As many as 104 RRBs (31 March 2006) are also functioning as SHPIs with grant assistance from NABARD. Non-availabiliy of good NGOs is a matter of concern especially in

North-Eastern, Central and Eastern Regions. RRBs can play a vital role as SHPIs in such areas.

SHG-Bank Linkage: Cumulative Bank Loans—Region-wise Participation by RRBs Versus other Banks (March 2006)

Region	*No. of SHGs credit linked*		
	by RRBs	*by all banks (including coop.)*	*% by RRBs*
Northern	125.64	398.58	32
North-Eastern	57.09	165.70	34
Eastern	367.72	935.42	39
Central	352.14	805.99	44
Western	116.11	525.14	22
Southern	2303.44	8567.69	27
Total	3322.14	11397.53	29

The foregoing paragraphs conclusively indicate that RRBs are well positioned to play a major role in financial inclusion particularly in areas/regions with high rates of financial exclusion. RRBs were originally created to cater to neglected section/areas as they were expected to have sound financial management combined with local feel and familiarity. With the amalgamation of RRBs, they have acquired the critical mass in terms of financial strength to widen and deepen their outreach. With the requisite strength having been developed, RRBs are the best suited vehicles to widen and deepen the process of financial performance and deviation from their mandate. RRBs may be provided adequate promotional and development assistance to contribute substantially to financial inclusion in a way that the business generated out of inclusion efforts add positively to their performance.

Recommendations

RRBs should extend their services into unbanked areas and increase their credit-debit (CD) ratio. As on 31 March 2006, 37 RRBs had CD ratio of less than 40%, 44 RRBs between 40% and 60% and 52 RRBs above 60%. The CD ratio variations ranged from 20% to 116%. As RRBs operate with branches in remote, interior and tribal-dominated areas, they have a special role to play in financial inclusion. The following areas would require attentionn from the point of view of financial inclusion.

- Setting exclusive targets for microfinance and financial inclusion,
- Providing funding support, and
- Providing technology support.

Keeping the above in view, the following specific recommendations are made:

No Further Merger of RRBs

There is a need for policy refinement regarding further merger of RRBs. The Vyas Committee had recommended merger of all RRBs in the same state. Currently RRBs of the same sponsor bank are merged at State-level. By April 2007, the number of RRBs was reduced to 96. If sponsor banks are to have the requisite initiative to support their RRBs fully, they would need assurance that there will be no further mergers. The Committee is of the view that further merger of all RRBs at State-level is not required. It may also not be desirable if there has to be a firm reinforcement of the rural orientation of these institutions with a specific mandata on financial inclusion. The committee, therefore, recommends that the process of merger should not proceed beyond the level of sponsor bank in each State.

Recapitalisation of RRBs with Negative Net Worth

Recapitalisation of RRBs with negative net worth has to be given a serious consideration as it would facilitate their growth, provide lenders a level of comfort and enable their achieving standard capital adequacy ratios. As on March 2004, 98 RRBs were in need of Rs. 3,050 crore for making the net worth positive. The position, as on 31 March 2006, is that 40 RRBs would require Rs. 1,718 crore.

Widening Network and Expanding Coverage

As on 1 April 2007, RRBs were covering 535 districts. They may be directed to cover all unbanked areas in these districts, taking the village as a unit, either by opening a branch (wherever feasible) or through the BF/BC model in a time bound manner.

As on 01 April 2007, 87 districts in the country were not covered by RRBs and their area of operation may be extended to cover these districts.

Strategic Microfinance Plan with NABARD Support

RRBs have the potential and capability to emerge as niche operators in microfinance They are playing a major role in the SHG-Bank Linkage Programme especially also as SHPIs. It is significant that as an institution they have the expertise and potential to fulfil both the requirements of SHGs—formation plus nurturing and financial service provisions (credit plus). Their dual role has special meaning in areas which face severe financial exclusion and which do not have a sufficient presence of well performing NGOs. However, to upscale the programme to a level where it can really make a visible impact, RRBs need handholding particularly in the areas of training, promotion and development. NABARD may provide required assistance.

NABARD should prepare a strategic action plan RRB-wise, for promotion and credit linkage of SHOs. RRBs may be asked to form, nurture and credit link at least 3,000 SHGs in all districts covered by them in North-Eastern, Eastern and Central Regions. A Memorandum of Understanding (MoU) may be signed by RRBs with NABARD for a period of 5 years—with NABARD providing the promotional and development assistance out of the "Financial Inclusion Promotion and Development Fund" and RRBs forming, nurturing and providing financial services to SHGs. RRBs may accomplish the task with the support of individual rural volunteers, BFs, their staff members, etc. NABARD may closely monitor the programme—with focus on qualitative aspects.

NRFIP for RRBs

The strategy recommended earlier in the Report for NRFIP for commercial banks would be equally applicable for RRBs. The process of undertaking a survey, identification of excluded households, dissemination of the information, setting of bank-wise/branch-wise targets, etc., could be followed. RRBs will have certain handicaps in executing the Plan. They would require promotional, funding and technology support in different areas as outlined below. RRBs may endeavour to cover a large part of their incremental lending through the group mode (SHGs/JLGs) as it will enhance their outreach to the financially excluded. Lending through group mode would also keep NPAs at low level.

Pilot testing of BF/BC Model by RRBs

RRBs should adopt the BF and BC models as a major strategy of financial inclusion. NABARD should extend the required support including running pilots in selected banks. The proposal for a technology-based intervention under the BF/BC model would be equally relevant for RRBs. However, RRBs would require some handholding in implementing the proposal. NABARD may indentify 10 RRBs across the country, giving greater weightage to regions manifesting higher levels of financial exclusion and work in strategic alliance with these RRBs and their sponsor banks in implementing the proposal.

The RRBs identified by NABARD for the project will require to develop a core banking software for proper integration of the technology model proposed. NABARD should enter into a MoU with identified sponsor banks and RRBs and provide initial funding and technology support.

Separate Credit Plan for Excluded Regions

The Committee recommends that RRBs operating in predominantly tribal areas and having high levels of exclusion may prepare annual credit plans having a separate component for excluded groups, which would integrate credit provision with promotional assistance such as agricultural services and BDSs for the farm and non-farm sectors respectively including entrepreneurship development and formation and strengthening of producer's organisations like dairy cooperatives. Refinance and promotional support may be provided by NABARD to RRBs on a large scale for implementation of these credit plans.

Computerisation

With a view to facilitate the seamless integration of RRBs with the main payment system, there is a need to provide computerisation support to them. Banks will be eligible for support from the Financial Inclusion Funds on a matching contribution of 50% in regard to districts other than tribal districts and 75% in case of branches located in tribal districts under the Tribal Sub-Plan.

Strengthening Boards of Management

Further, now that RRBs are being merged and are becoming large size entities, it is necessary that their Boards of Management are strengthened and powers delegated to them on policy and business operations, viz. introduction of new liability and credit products, investment decisions, improving market orientation in raising and deployment of resources, non-fund-based business, career progression, transfer policy, etc.

Tax Incentives

From 2006-07, RRBs are liable to pay income tax. To further strengthen the RRBs, profits transferred to reserves could be exempted from tax till they achieve standard capital adequacy ratios. Alternately, RRBs may be allowed tax concessions to the extent of 40% of their profits, as per provisions under Sec. 36(1)(viii) of the Income Tax Act.

REFERENCES

Challenge: A study of Financial Markets, Volume 5: INDIA. Manila: Asian Development Bank. IES (2002), Economic Survey, 2002, New Delhi Ministry of Finance of India.

NABARD (2002), 'Review of the Performance of RRBs as on 31 March 2002', Mumbai: National Bank for Agriculture and Rural Development.

NABARD (2001), 'Regional Rural Banks—Key Statistics, 31 March 2001,' Mumbai: National Bank for Agriculture and Rural Development.

RBI (2002), Report on Trends in the Indian Banking Sector, November 2002, Mumbai: Reserve Bank of India.

RBI (2002b), 'Master Circular. Rural Planning and Credit Department, 11 November 2002', Mumbai: Reserve Bank of India.

RBI (2001), 'Basic Statistical Returns, March 2001', Mumbai: Reserve Bank of India.

Ruthven, O. and Kumar, S. (2002), "Fine-grain Finance: Financial Choice and Strategy among the poor in Rural North India." Working Paper 57, Manchester Institute of Development Policy and Management, University of Manchester.

Sinha, S. and Patole, M. (2002), 'Microfinance and the Poverty of Financial Services. How the Poor in India could be Better Served', Working paper 56, Manchester: Institute of Development Policy and Management, University of Manchester.

Regional Rural Banks—A Case Study of Washim, Vidarbha

Dr. Halima Sadia Rizvi and Ms. Sahna Andrew

Introduction

India is the home for nearly one-sixth of the world's population. Due to its large size and population of 1.1 billion in 2007, the country ranks among the upcoming super-powers of the world. However, according to Indian Planning Commission, about 27.5% are living below poverty line. From among these, 75% of the poor reside in the rural areas of the country. According to the International Poverty Line of income $1.25, 41.6% of the population is below poverty. Regional Rural Banks were an attempt to provide credit and economic opportunity for these rural poor to uplift themselves.

The lack of access to credit is often cited as the main reason why poor people remain poor. Rohini Pande and Robin Burgess[1] used the Regional Rural network in India to prove it empirically. According to the study, the main thrust to rural branch expansion was the imposition of the 1:4 license rule in 1977. The rule stated that a bank could open a branch in a location with one or more branches only if it opened four in unbanked locations. The rule was abandoned in 1990. The study shows that between 1977 and

1990, the license rule caused banks to open more rural branches in states with lower initial financial development. Beyond the period the trend was reversed.

FUNCTIONING OF RRB

The genesis of the Regional Rural Bank's (RRB) can be traced to the need for a stronger institutional arrangement for providing rural credit. The Narasimham Committee conceptualized the creation of RRB's in 1975 as a new set of regionally-oriented rural banks. These banks would combine the loçal feel and familiarity of rural problems with the professionalism and large resource base of the commercial banks. As the RRB Act, 1976 clearly puts it, "The RRB's were established with the view to developing the rural economy by providing, for the purpose of development of agriculture, trade, commerce, industry and other productive activities in the rural areas, credit and other facilities to the small and marginal farmers, agricultural labourers, artisans and small entrepreneurs." This Act officially established these banks. The equity is held by the Central Government, the concerned state government and the sponsor bank in the proportion of 50:15:35. According to the NABARD report, from a modest beginning of six RRB's with 17 branches covering 12 districts in December 1975 to covering 535 districts by April 2007, the RRB's have covered almost the entire nation. There are 196 RRB's presently with 14,446 branches across the country.

India's commercial banks were taken over by the government through successive phases of nationalization in 1969 and 1980. These banks referred to, as Public Sector Banks constitute the mainframe of the Indian financial sector. The Bank Acquisition Act, 1969 empowered the State to nationalize commercial banks. It makes the intentions of the government very clear. "The Banking system touches the lives of millions and has to be inspired by a larger social purpose and has to sub-serve national priorities and objectives such as rapid growth of agriculture, small industries and exports, raising employment levels, encouragement of new entrepreneurs and development of backward areas". This statement thus clearly brings out the welfare aspect of these rural banks.

The rural coverage is augmented through the introduction of

two other types of financial institutions—the Regional Rural Banks and the Cooperative Banks. Together these three institutions carry out almost the entire formal banking sector activity in rural India. During the 1990's however private and foreign banks have also gained importance.

Regional Rural Banks play an important role in rural financial sector. Since its inception, they are seen as a vital means of dispensing credit to low income families in rural areas. Traditionally they have been assigned the primary responsibility for the outreach of government sponsored lending schemes that are intended for the poor rural families. Historically, however, the Rural Banks have incurred losses that are accentuated by politically motivated decision-making and an overall welfare orientation that is expected of these institutions. A study by Biswa Swarup Misra[3] examined the link between loss-making Regional Rural Banks and their sponsor Banks. It was found that the problem of loss-making is neither confined to some specific states or group of sponsor banks. The sponsor bank contributes positively to the financial health of a profit-making rural bank. It acts as a drag on the performance of the loss-making ones. Loan management is a major concern of the loss-making rural banks.

Although the RRB's are spread across twenty-six states, they have a strong presence in seven states—Andhra Pradesh, Bihar, Karnataka, Madhya Pradesh, Rajasthan and Uttar Pradesh. Uttar Pradesh has the highest number of rural banks—36 and Kerala has only two amongst the major states. The North-eastern states like Manipur, Meghalaya, Mizoram and Nagaland have each one RRB only. (Table 1)

The National Sample Survey Organisation (59th Round) estimated that 60.4% of the rural households were farmers and 48.6% of them are indebted. The survey also found farmers took loans for farming—current and capital expenditures. At the all India level for every Rs. 1000 borrowed, Rs. 584 had been borrowed for these two purposes. Marriage expenses, health and education came next. However, the fact remains that farmers borrow heavily from indigenous moneylenders. On an average, 29 out of 100 indebted borrow from indigenous moneylenders.

TABLE 1

State-wise Distribution of Regional Rural Banks

State	*Regional Rural Banks*	*Profit-making Rural Banks*
Andhra Pradesh	16	15
Bihar	16	8
Karnataka	13	12
Madhya Pradesh	19	14
Maharashtra	10	5
Manipur	1	0
Meghalaya	1	1
Nagaland	1	0
Rajasthan	14	10
Tripura	1	0
Uttar Pradesh	36	34
Kerala	2	2
Mizoram	1	1

Source: Statistical tables, RBI documents. Based on three consecutive years performance beginning with the year 2000-01.

CASE STUDY

Even though there is such a widespread network of rural banks, almost everyday one can read about farmers' committing suicides in the newspaper. The case in point is Vidarbha. Vidarbha is located in eastern Maharashtra. The major city 'Nagpur' is the second capital of the state and hosts the winter sessions of the state assembly. The region has earned its nickname 'The California of India' as it is famous for its oranges. It is also famous for cotton. However the name Vidarbha now conjures up images of death and desperation. The region came into national headlines when a spate of suicides by the farmers caught the nation's attention. Pradeep Mitra was quoted saying in Mid-day that three debt-ridden farmers commit suicides everyday in Vidarbha. The toll has crossed 1000. In August 31, 2008, nine more farmers have taken the extreme step. On September 1, on the eve of Pola, the year's biggest festival for the farmers, four farmers took their lives. All of them were debt-ridden and found no other way to escape.

All the 11 districts of Vidarbha have good banking network

consisting of 823 commercial banks, about 200 RRB's and about 60 other banks according to RBI records. There are thus 1790 bank branches in the 11 districts of Vidarbha. The direct finances to agriculture are Rs. 2449.76 crore as on March 2005. About 80% however are defaulters which mean that they are not eligible for fresh loans. Access to institutional credit thus becomes difficult for them. A study by the Planning Commission[4] found that 3.2 million cotton farmers in Vidarbha are defaulters. For every Rs. 100 they borrow, about Rs. 80 goes into servicing of old loans. The team found that the current outflow of credit was very insufficient. Unless the existing loan burden is eased, the farmer cannot get fresh loans.

The Government of India has announced relief packages for the farmers from time to time. However, according to the Comptroller and Auditor General's audit (CAG) of the relief package for Vidarbha farmers, 2008, the packages are tardy in implementation, mindless in conceptualization and inconsistent with local needs. The money did not help mitigate the agrarian crisis or even reduce suicides. Evaluation of the implementation of the package in terms of the reduction in agrarian distress was also not conducted. In CAG's evaluation, agrarian crisis is essentially caused by un-remunerative agriculture and it is possible that the crisis would start rising again in the closing phase of the relief programmes. The report stated that there was no reliable data relating to the expenditure under the different components of the package. Recently in the budget for the financial year 2008-09, the government announced the waiver of farmers' loans to the tune of Rs. 71,860 crore. This write-off will benefit 43 million farmers nationwide. The spin-off of this gesture by the government is that banks feel that farmers who have been prompt in paying back their loans may now start defaulting on them in the hope of benefiting from a similar scheme in future. Many farmers who were making regular payments have criticized the government's debt waiver, saying that it would have been better if the government had raised the minimum support price that state agencies pay for farm output or offered subsidies on seeds, fertilizers and pesticides. Such measures would have been easy to implement and would have ensured uniform benefits, unlike the complex waiver package.

As Jaideep Hardikar[2] rightly points out, it is easier to get an automobile loan than to get credit for agriculture. According to Jaideep, the problem of Vidarbha or any other rural area is not just about unscrupulous moneylenders and farmers. It is about the anti-farmer policies followed by the government. It is also about the lack of access to credit. It is easier to buy a Maruti car than to buy seeds in India. The availability and utilization of credit is under severe strain, with a gap of 50% in agricultural requirement for credit. The government's response of putting all private money-lenders in Maharashtra behind bars in 2006 is not the solution.

In order to get a better picture of the situation, let us focus on one district in Vidarbha—Washim. According to the Fact-Finding Committee, Planning Commission, a total of Rs. 84.41 crore worth of loans was distributed to 49,000 farmers in 2006 in Washim. However, it was a little over 50% of the requirement of Rs.150 crore. Nearly 45% of the farmers therefore have no access to institutional credit. Most of the money handed out would return to the banks for servicing of outstanding loans. The study shows that in Washim, there was a gap of Rs. 75 crore between the credit required and credit available. If the household requirements are also added, the amount doubles to Rs. 150 crore. Illegal money-lenders provide close to Rs. 30 crore, input dealers give credit of Rs. 21.5 crore—grain merchants gave 10.7 crore and other sources pay Rs. 0.2 crore. These informal providers of credit also charge whopping rates of interests on the principal amount.

Withdrawal of low interest loans has been a key element in World Bank economic reforms. As rural banks and co-operatives close down and nationalized banks get privatized, institutional credit available to farmers gets reduced and they are forced to seek the help of the moneylenders. An area-wise classification of banks show an increase in the concentration of banks in the urban metropolitan areas and a complete absence of foreign banks in the rural regions.

The district of Washim is divided into six talukas. Table 2 shows that the average loan of farmers who committed suicides was between Rs. 3,000 to Rs. 31,000. The maximum number of suicides occurred in Manora, which had an average debt of only

13,650. Risod with the highest average of debt, Rs. 31,808 accounts for 19 suicides between 2001 and 2006.

TABLE 2

Taluka-wise Average Indebtedness of Farmers who Committed Suicides

Name of Talukas	*Total amount*	*No. of farmers committed suicides between 2001 and 28.02.06*	*Average loan*
Washim	1,28,735	6	21,455
Malegaon	22,090	6	3,681
Risod	6,04,353	19	31,808
Mangrulpir	97,166	15	6,477
Manora	4,36,829	32	13,650
Karanja	3,61,248	22	16,420

Source: Report of Fact Finding Team, Planning Commission, Government of India, 2006.

In Washim, out of the total 5,15,266 hectares of land, 3,92,501 hectares are under cultivation. Cotton is grown in 82,245 hectares yielding a productivity of 120 cotton bales of 170 kg each. Cereals take up 1,17,493 ha. of land, oilseeds 1,08,982 ha. and other crops take up 11,680 ha. As Table 3 shows clearly, there is a supply shortage of credit in all the crops requirements. Soybean faces the highest shortage of Rs. 35.38 crore. Wheat does not receive any loan and so wheat growers have to depend on private moneylenders. The gap in the needed credit and the loans that are available has been the main cause for distress among the farmers. Due to the gap, they are forced to borrow from other private sources that charge exorbitant rates of interest. The table clearly shows that there is a gap of Rs. 72.45 crore and this contributes to the dominance of moneylenders in Washim district. Manora, the taluka with highest number of suicides also has high number of farmers borrowing from private hands.

The lowest rate of recovery is from Mangrulpir. Of Rs. 7,14,000 lent by the private lenders, only Rs. 46,412 have been recovered.

TABLE 3

Gap in Availability of Credit

(in Rupees crores)

Name of crop	*Actual need of credit*	*Loans disbursed*	*Shortage in supply of credit*
Cotton	57.57	39.64	17.93
Soyabean	68.38	30.00	35.38
Wheat	8.06	—	8.06
Jowar	26.85	15.77	11.08
Total	157.86	85.41	72.45

Source: Report of Fact-Finding Team, Planning Commission, Government of India, 2006.

TABLE 4

Position of Moneylenders

(Amount in Rs.)

Talukas	*No. of money-lenders*	*Total No. of borrowers*	*Amount*	*Current recovery*
Washim	2	230	1,56,650	1,22,460
Malegaon	—	—	—	—
Risod	2	209	2,64,000	2,12,327
Mangrulpir	1	25	7,14,000	46,412
Manora	2	1024	255,15,200	18,822,556
Karanja	1	1127	45,39,765	2,812,321
Total	8	2615	311,89,615	220,16,076

Source: Report of Fact-Finding Team, Planning Commission, Government of India, 2006.

TABLE 5

Outlay Allocation for Irrigation and Expenditure Incurred in Vidarbha Region

Annual plan years	*Outlay in Irrigation*	*Actual expenditure*	*Shortfall*
2002-03	932.70	353.63	579.07
2003-04	1151.82	501.48	650.34
2004-05	1835.27	536.47	1298.80

Source: Report of Fact Finding Team, Planning Commission, Government of India, 2006.

Table 5 points out that there have been shortfalls in the actual expenditure incurred with the outlay given. Farmers are allocated fund for irrigation facilities although the actual expenditure incurred always fall short. Without proper irrigation, the crops depend on the vagaries of the monsoons and incur further losses. Unable to repay the loans undertaken last season, the farmer is denied institutional credit. He is thus forced to approach the moneylender for help to plant the next crop. The vicious cycle of debt thus begins with death seemingly the only option.

CONCLUSION

Thousands of farmers have already taken their lives. The individual act of suicide has turned into a social phenomenon. Social suicides are wreaking chaos in the lives of the rural people. Farmers competing with the global markets are forced to borrow more and are lead to despair.

The problem of the farmers in Vidarbha or any other part of the country is not one that has a single solution. It is a multiple facet problem that requires a solution at different levels. Improving the access to credit of the farmers is the step in the right direction. Regional Rural Banks have a very important role in providing the credit requirements of the farmers. According to P. Sainath[5] of the Vidarbha Jan Andolan Samiti, 4,750 rural banks have closed in the past 15 years. The country has witnessed an average of one Rural Bank branch of a scheduled commercial bank being closed every single working day for the past 15 years. The Reserve Bank officials argue that these are not all closures but mergers and consolidation. Merging banks that are 200 kms apart is however not beneficial for farmers. Banks claim ATMs have been opened to fill the need. The fact remains that loans are not given at ATMs.

The Regional Rural Banks need to rise up to the challenge of providing the much-needed credit to the farmers when they need them. Timing is very important for the farmer. If the farmer is not able to secure the loan in time, he has no choice but to go to the moneylender so that the seeds can be sown in time.

According to the All India Regional Rural Bank Employee Association, the Rural Banks must be given full autonomy and fully delinked from the corporate culture of the sponsor banks. It must be restructured into zonal and state level RRB's with any public sector apex-banking institute. This would ensure unity of command and cross-subsidization. The central balance sheet prepared at the apex level could then easily take care of the losses of the few RRB's that occur due to infrastructural deficiencies.

Although the banking sector is open to foreign banks, their presence in the rural areas is nil. It is a combination of co-operative banks and Regional Rural Banks that serve the rural people of our country. They also have the local advantage as about 95% of the staff in RRB's is from the same region and 90% of them are posted in rural branches. Availability of cheaper credit and better implementation of the various schemes and packages for the farmers is urgently required. Regional banks need to be more sensitive to the cause of farmers' distress.

References

1. Burgess, Robin and Rohini Pande (2003), "Do Rural Banks Matter? Evidence from the Indian Social Experiment" in series STICERD Development Economics Papers No. 40, Suntory and Toyota International Centers for Economic and Related Disciplines.
2. Hardikar, Jaideep (2006), "Rise of the Moneylender" in www.indiatogether.org.
3. Misra, Biswa Swarup (2006), "The Performance of Regional Rural Banks in India: Has Past Anything to Suggest for the Future?" RBI Occasional papers, Vol. 27, Nos. 1 and 2.
4. Report of Fact-Finding Team on Vidarbha: Regional disparities and rural distress in Maharashtra with particular reference to Vidarbha, Planning Commission, Government of India.
5. Sainath, P., (2008), "4,750 Rural Banks Closed in 15 years," *The Hindu*, March 28.
6. Sinha, Sanjay, Tanmay Chetan, Orlanda Ruthven and Nilotpal Pathak (2003), "The Outreach/Viability Conundrum: Can Regional Rural Banks really serve the Low-Income Clients?" Working paper No. 229, Overseas Development Institute, London.

The Performance of Regional Rural Banks of India

Dr. Virendra Kumar

Introduction

The establishment of the regional rural bank is the outcome of the various recommendations by the banking commission, which was set-up in 1972. Regional Rural Banks have been in existence for around three decades in the Indian financial scene. Inception of regional rural banks can be seen as a unique experiment as well as experience in improving the efficacy of rural credit delivery mechanism in India. In Government and the sponsoring bank, an effort was made to integrate commercial banking within the broad policy thrust towards social banking keeping in view the local peculiarities. The genesis of the regional rural bank can be traced to the need for a stronger institutional arrangement for providing rural credit. The Narsimham Committee conceptualized the creation of regional rural bank in 1975 as a new set of regionally-oriented rural banks, which would combine the local feel and familiarity of rural problems characteristic of cooperatives with the professionalism and large resource base of commercial banks. Subsequently, the regional rural bank was set-up through the promulgation of Regional Rural Banks Act of 1976. Their equity is held by the Central Government, concerned State Government and the Sponsor Bank in the proportion of 50:15:35. Regional rural banks were supposed to evolve as specialized rural financial institutions for developing the rural economy by providing credit to small and marginal farmers, agricultural laborers, artisans and small industries.

Over the years, the regional rural banks, which are often viewed as the small man's bank, have taken deep roots and have become a sort of inseparable part of the rural credit structure. They have played a key role in rural institutional financing in terms of geographical coverage, clientele outreach and business volume as also contribution to development of the rural economy. A remarkable feature of their performance over the past three decades has been the massive expansion of their retail network in rural areas. From a modest beginning of 6 regional rural banks with 17 branches covering 12 districts in December 1975, the numbers have grown into 196 regional rural banks with 16,500 branches working in 618 districts across the country in March 2008. Regional rural banks have a large branch network in the rural area forming around 43 per cent of the total rural branches of commercial banks. The rural orientation of regional rural banks is formidable with rural and semi-urban branches constituting over 97 per cent of their branch network. The growth in the branch network has enabled the regional rural banks to expand. Banking activities in the unbanked areas and mobilize rural savings. The mandate of promoting banking with a rural focus, however, would be an enduring phenomenon only when the financial health of the regional rural banks is sound. With built-in restrictions on their operations, it is common to expect that the financial health of the regional rural banks itself would be a matter of concern. As regards their financial status, during the year 2003-04, 163 regional rural banks earned profits amounting to Rs. 953 crore while 33 regional rural banks incurred losses to the tune of Rs. 184 crore. Ninety regional rural banks had accumulated losses as on March 31, 2004. Aggregate accumulated loss of RRBs amounted to Rs. 2,725 crore during the year 2003-04. Of the 90 regional rural banks having accumulated loss, 53 regional rural banks had eroded their entire owned funds as also a part of their deposits.

Furthermore, non-performing assets of the regional rural banks in absolute terms stood at Rs. 3,299 crore as on March 31, 2004. The percentage of gross non-performing assets was 12.6 during the year ending March 31, 2004. While 103 regional rural banks had gross non-performing assets less than the national average, 93 had non-performing assets more than it. Given the multi-agency share-holding, this study makes an attempt to enquire into such factors that influence the performance of the regional rural banks and the role played by sponsor bank in a broader scenario. The problem has been approached in a deductive pattern. First, an attempt is made to identify the extent of the problem of loss-making regional rural banks and see if they are confined to some particular sponsor banks or States. If the problem banks and States could be identified that would help in focusing the attention for an enduring solution. Subsequently, a model-based approach has been pursued to identify the factors that are responsible for the problems faced by the regional rural banks. This study contributes to the literature on regional rural banks primarily in two ways. First, the issues concerning regional rural banks are an area that is less visited empirically (econometrically) compared to the vast literature on commercial banks. Whatever studies have emerged on the topic, they have primarily relied on exploratory analysis done for a particular year or on a group of regional rural banks to draw inferences. This kind of an approach has a serious limitation in that the findings are guided by the choice of the year of analysis or the particular regional rural banks in question. To overcome this problem, one needs to consider, as attempted in this paper, a reasonably long period for analysis where extreme observations would be evened out so that one gets results that are more dependable. This study is an attempt in that direction. The present study considers the entire population rather than a few regional rural banks and a ten-year period for empirical analysis so that results are broad-based and robust. Second, given the attention at the policy level to restructure the regional rural banks, it is necessary that the behavior of regional rural banks be analyses separately for the profit and loss-making ones, than all regional rural banks bunched together so that it helps in policy formulation. Such an approach has been followed in this study.

RESTRUCTURING STRATEGIES

The financial viability of RRBs has engaged the attention of the policy-makers from time to time. In fact, as early as 1981, the Committee to Review Arrangements for Institutional Credit for Agriculture and Rural Development (CRAFICARD) addressed the issue of financial viability of the RRBs. The CRAFICARD recommended that 'the loss incurred by a RRB should be made good annually by the shareholders in the same proportion of their shareholdings'. Though this recommendation was not accepted under a scheme of recapitalization, financial support was provided by the shareholders in the proportion of their shareholdings. Subsequently, a number of committees have come out with different suggestions to address the financial non-viability of RRBs. For instance, the Working Group on RRBs (Kelkar Committee) in 1984 recommended that small and uneconomic RRBs should be merged in the interest of economic viability. Five years down the line, in a similar vein, the Agricultural Credit Review Committee (Khusro Committee), 1989 pointed out that 'the weaknesses of RRBs are endemic to the system and non-viability is built into it, and the only option was to merge the RRBs with the sponsor banks. The objective of serving the weaker sections effectively could be achieved only by self-sustaining credit institutions'. The Committee on Restructuring of RRBs, 1994 (Bhandari Committee) identified 49 RRBs for comprehensive restructuring. It recommended greater devolution of decision-making powers to the Boards of RRBs in the matters of business development and staff matters. The option of liquidation again was mooted by the Committee on Revamping of RRBs, 1996 (Basu Committee). The Expert Group on RRBs in 1997 (Thingalaya Committee) held that very weak RRBs should be viewed separately and possibility of their liquidation be recognized. They might be merged with neighbouring RRBs. The Expert Committee on Rural Credit, 2001 (Vyas Committee I) was of the view that the sponsor bank should ensure necessary autonomy for RRBs in their credit and other portfolio management system. Subsequently, another committee under the Chairmanship of Chalapathy Rao in 2003 (Chalapathy Rao Committee) recommended that the entire system of RRBs may be consolidated while retaining the advantages of regional character of these Institutions. As part of the process, some sponsor banks may be eased out. The sponsoring institutions may include other approved financial institutions as well, in addition to commercial banks. The Group of CMDs of Select Public Sector Banks, 2004 (Purwar Committee) recommended the amalgamation of RRBs on regional basis into six commercial banks—one each for the Northern, Southern, Eastern, Western, Central and North-Eastern Regions. Thus one finds that a host of options have been suggested starting with vertical merger (with sponsor banks), horizontal merger (amongst RRBs operating in a particular region) to liquidation by different committees that have gone into the issue of financial viability and restructuring strategies for the RRBs. More recently, a committee under the Chairmanship of A.V. Sardesai revisited the issue of restructuring the RRBs (Sardesai Committee, 2005). The Sardesai committee held that 'to improve the operational viability of RRBs and take advantage of the economies of scale, the route of merger/ amalgamation of RRBs may be considered taking into account the views of the various stakeholders'.

Merger of RRBs with the sponsor bank is not provided in the RRB Act, 1976. Mergers, even if allowed, would not be a desirable way of restructuring. The Committee was of the view that merging a RRB with its sponsor bank would go against the very spirit of setting up of RRBs as local entities and for providing credit primarily to weaker sections. Having discussed various options for restructuring, the Committee was of the view that 'a change in sponsor banks may, in some cases help in improving the performance of RRBs. A change in sponsorship may, *inter alia*; improve the competitiveness, work culture, management and efficiency of the concerned RRBs'. Against this backdrop, a number of issues need empirical probing. Such as, which are the RRBs that need focus and whether for them the sponsor bank has really to be made accountable. All these issues fall under the broader questions of what factors drive the performance of RRBs? And do the sponsor banks have a role to play?

PERFORMANCE OF REGIONAL RURAL BANKS

The RRBs, over the years have made impressive strides on various business indicators. For instance, deposits of RRBs have grown by 18 times and advances by 13 times between 1980 and

1990. Between 1990 and 2004, deposits and advances grew by 14 times and 7 times, respectively. Between the year 2000 and 2004, loans disbursed by RRBs more than doubled reflecting the efforts taken by the banks to improve credit flow to the rural sector. The average per branch advances also increased from Rs. 25 lakh in March 1990 to Rs. 154 lakh in March 2003. When one considers the deployment of credit relative to the mobilization of resources, the credit-deposit (C-D) ratio of RRBs were more than 100 per cent during the first decade of their operations up to 1987. Though the C-D ratio subsequently became lower, of late, it has shown an improvement and went up from around 39 per cent in March 2000 to 44.5 per cent in March 2004.

The presence of RRBs shows wide variation both across States and sponsor banks. Although RRBs are spread over twenty-six States, they have most of their presence in seven States, i.e., Andhra Pradesh, Bihar, Karnataka, Madhya Pradesh, Maharashtra, Rajasthan and Uttar Pradesh. Uttar Pradesh has the highest number of RRBs, i.e., thirty-six and Kerala has got only two amongst the major States of the country. The north-eastern States like Manipur, Meghalya, Mizoram and Nagaland have got only one RRB. Likewise, seven sponsor banks amongst twenty-eight, viz., Bank of Baroda, Bank of India, Central Bank of India, Punjab National Bank, State Bank of India, United Bank of India and UCO bank account for more than three-fifths of the RRBs. More than 160 RRBs earned profit in March 2004 while 150 RRBs were found to be earning profits for three consecutive years beginning with the year 2000-01. More than half of these loss-making RRBs are found to be operating in four States, i.e., Bihar, Madhya Pradesh, Maharashtra and Orissa. Seen at the level of sponsor banks, three banks, i.e., Bank of India, Central Bank of India and State Bank of India accounted for more than half of the loss-making regional rural banks. As a number of sponsor banks have promoted RRBs in more than one State, it becomes natural to ask whether the presence of RRBs sponsored by a few banks whose area of operation is confined to some specific States is camouflaging the performance of better run RRBs. There can be three possibilities in such a situation. One, irrespective of the State, the RRBs sponsored by some banks are incurring losses; second, irrespective of sponsor banks, certain States are simply not conducive to better performance for RRBs; and third, there is nothing inherent either with a sponsor bank or a particular State in which the RRBs operate to contribute towards the performance of RRBs and it is a combination of some other factors. To answer these possibilities, one needs to assess the presence of RRBs sponsored by different banks across the States and their performance. Such an attempt is made where performance of sponsor banks across regions is depicted. Seen from the perspective of the State in which they are operating, five out of the eight loss-making RRBs in Bihar are sponsored by the Central Bank of India and one each by the Punjab National Bank, SBI and the UCO bank. Of the five loss-making RRBs found in Madhya Pradesh, two are sponsored by Bank of Baroda and one each by the Bank of India, the Central Bank of India and the UCO Bank. Likewise, of the five loss-making RRBs found in Maharashtra, three are sponsored by Bank of India and two by Bank of Maharastra. From the sponsor banks' perspective one finds that the RRBs in which they have a stake and which are not earning profits, are not confined to a single State. It is spread across the States in which they have a presence. For instance, the eight loss-making RRBs for which the Central Bank of India is the sponsor bank, are spread over Bihar, Madhya Pradesh, Uttar Pradesh and West Bengal. Similarly, the twelve loss-making RRBs sponsored by the SBI are spread across Andhra Pradesh, Arunachal Pradesh, Assam, Bihar, Chhattisgarh, Jharkhand, Nagaland and Orissa. The same is the case with the RRBs sponsored by Bank of India and UCO bank. Hence, one finds no strong systematic pattern so as to infer whether or not the peculiarities of any particular sponsor bank or a specific State in which they operate drives the performance of RRBs. In such a situation, financial performance of the RRBs has been modeled based on balance sheet information of the RRBs for a ten-year period to decipher, what all factors that contribute to their financial health.

CONCLUSION

The study made an attempt to examine whether the problems associated with the RRBs are specific to certain sponsor banks or States in which they operate. To get a deeper insight, all the RRBs were categorized either as profit-making or loss-making ones. Regional rural banks earning profits consecutively for the past three years from the terminal year of the study have been classified as profit-making and the rest as loss-making. Such a classification led to 150 RRBs falling in the profit-making category and rest 46 as loss-making. The exploratory analysis revealed that the problem of the loss-making RRBs is neither confined to some specific States nor to a group of sponsor banks. In the absence of any strong systematic pattern so as to suggest that the performance of RRBs is driven by the peculiarities of any particular sponsor Bank or a specific State in which they operate, econometric estimation was employed so as to decipher the factors that contribute to their financial health. Based on the balance sheet information on individual RRBs for the past ten years, this study has approached the issue primarily form the asset side of the RRB's balance sheet. Given the linkage between the RRBs and their sponsor bank, an attempt was also made to infer whether or not the umbilical cord hypothesis is operational.

Both fixed effect and panel GMM estimations were carried out. The more appropriate GMM estimation results indicated that the loan portfolio management for the profit-making RRBs is an area of concern. Investments contribute positively to the financial performance of the profit-making RRBs. Advances while had a positive impact, investments, however, turned out to be inconsequential for the performance of loss-making RRBs. The results further indicated that the umbilical cord hypothesis is operational. The sponsor bank contributes positively to the financial health of the profit-making regional rural banks. For the loss-making RRBs, the sponsor bank acts as a drag on their performance. The income from investments coupled with synergy from the sponsor bank's association could mitigate the negative impact flowing from the loan portfolio for the profit-making RRBs. The loss-making RRBs on the other hand, could have done better had the sponsor banks played a proactive role, especially in their investment portfolio management. The loss-making RRBs need focused attention of all the stakeholders, in general, and of the sponsor bank, in particular, so as to transform them into profitable ventures. In view of the intricacies involved, some critical thinking is called for at the policy level in restructuring the loss-making RRBs are concerned. The sponsor bank for the loss-making RRBs could be given a time frame and if within this period, significant improvement is not made; the possibility of changing the sponsor bank as suggested by the Sardesai Committee may be a worthwhile option.

REFERENCES

Akhavein, J.D., Berger, A.N., Humphrey, D.B. (1997): "The Effects of Megamergers on Efficiency and Prices: Evidence from a Bank Profit Function," *Finance and Economic Discussion Series 9*, Board of Governors of the Federal Reserve System.

Arellano, M., and Bover, O. (1995): "Another Look at the Instrumental Variables Estimation of Error Components Models," *Journal of Econometrics*, 68, pp. 29-51.

Athanasoglou Panayiotis, P., Brissimis Sophocles, N. and Delis Matthaios, D. (2005): "Bank-Specific, Industry-Specific and Macroeconomic Determinants of Bank Profitability," *Bank of Greece Working Paper No. 25*.

Balachandher, K.G., John Staunton and Balashanmugam (2004): "Determinants of Commercial Bank Profitability in Malaysia," Papers presented at the 12th Annual Australian Conference on Finance and Banking.

Barth, J.R., Caprio, G., Levine, R. (2004): "Bank supervision and regulation: What Works Best?" *Journal of Financial Intermediation*, 13 (2), pp. 205-48.

Bell Frederick W. and Nell Mushy (1969): "Impact of Market Structure on the Price of a Commercial Banking Service," *The Review of Economics and Statistics*, May.

Benston, George J., Gerald A. Hanweck and David B. Humphrey (1982): "Scale Economies in Banking," *Journal of Money, Credit, and Banking*, Vol. XIV, No. 4, Part 1, November.

Bikker, J.A., Hu, H. (2002): "Cyclical Patterns in Profits, Provisioning and Lending of Banks and Procyclicality of the New Basel Capital Requirements," *BNL Quarterly Review*, 221, pp. 143-75.

Bose, Sukanya (2005): "Regional Rural Banks: The Past and the Present Debate," Macro Scan, URL: http://www.macroscan.com/fet/jul05/fet200705RRB_Debate.htm.

Bourke, P. (1989): "Concentration and other Determinants of Bank Profitability in Europe, North America and Australia," *Journal of Banking and Finance*, Vol. 13, pp. 65-79.

Consideration of the Regional Rural Banks (Amendment) Bill, 2004, Proceedings other than Questions and Answers, XIV Lok Sabh, 114, Reserve Bank of India Occasional Papers.

Das, Prasant (2000): "Sustainability Through Outreach—The Malbar Lighthouse Shows the Way," National Seminar on Best Practices in RRBs, BIRD, Lucknow.

Debate in the XV Lok Sabha on Regional Rural Banks (Amendment Bill, 2004).

Demirguc-Kunt, A., Huizinga, H. (2000): "Financial Structure and Bank Profitability," World Bank, Mimeo.

Demirguc-Kunt, A., Maksimovic, V. (1998): "Law, Finance and Firm Growth," *Journal of Finance*, 53(6), pp. 2107-37.

Edwards, Franklin R. (1977): "Managerial Objectives, in Regulated Industries: Expense Preference Behavior in Banking," *Journal of Political Economy*, February.

Following the recommendations of the Narasimham Committee (1991), there have been gradual relaxations in their choice of clientele and area of operations.

Goddard, J., Molyneux, P., Wilson, J.O.S. (2004): "The Profitability of European Banks: A Cross-Sectional and Dynamic Panel Analysis," *Manchester School*, 72 (3), pp. 363-81.

Haslem, John (1968): "A Statistical Analysis of the Relative Profitability of Commercial Banks," *Journal of Finance*, Vol. 23, pp.167-76.

Hausman, Jerry A. (1978): "Specification Tests in Econometrics," *Econometrica*, 46, pp. 1251-72.

Joshi, V.C. and Joshi, V.V. (2002): "Managing Indian Banks," Response Books, New Delhi.

Kannan, R. (2004): "Regional Rural Banks," URL: http://www.geocities.com/learning/banking2/rrb.html

Kwast, Myron L. and John T. Rose (1982): "Pricing, Operating Efficiency and Profitability Among Large Commercial Banks," *Journal of Banking and Finance*, Vol. 6.

Lack of a single owner with clear ownership and control, and no prospects for profits, diffused accountability and weakened oversight of the RRBs.

Malhotra, Rakesh (2002): "Performance of India's Regional Rural Banks (RRBs): Effect of the Umbilical Cord". URL: http://www.alternativefinance. org.uk/rtf/rrbsmalhotra.rtf.

Miller, S.M., Noulas, A.G. (1997): "Portfolio Mix and Large-bank Profitability in the USA," *Applied Economics*, 29 (4), pp. 505-12.

Mohan, Jagan (2004): "Regional Rural Banks Need a Shot in the Arm," *Financial Daily* from The Hindu Group of Publications, March 19th Edition.

Molyneux, P., Thornton, J. (1992): "Determinants of European Bank Profitability: A Note," *Journal of Banking and Finance*, Vol. 16, pp. 1173-78. The Performance of RRBs in India, 115.

Neely, M.C., Wheelock, D.C. (1997): "Why Does Bank Performance Vary Across States? Review," *Federal Reserve Bank of St. Louis*, Vol. 79, No. 2, pp. 27-40.

Net Income has been defined as the excess of total income over total expenditure.

Nitin Bhatt and Thorat, Y.S.P. (2004): "India's Regional Rural Banks: The Institutional Dimension of Reforms," *National Bank News Review*, NABARD, April-September.

Perry, P. (1992): "Do Banks Gain or Lose from Inflation," *Journal of Retail Banking*, 14(2), pp. 25-30.

Reddy, Y.V. (2000): "Future of Rural Banking." Address at Prof. G. Rama Reddy's Third Endowment Lecture, Hyderabad, *Reserve Bank of India Bulletin*, January.

Reddy, Y.V. (2000): "Rural Credit: Status and Agenda," *Reserve Bank of India Bulletin*, November.

Report on Trends and Progress of Banking in India (Various Issues), Reserve Bank of India, Mumbai, URL: (www.rbi.org.in).

Reserve Bank of India (2002): "Annual Accounts of Scheduled Commercial Banks in India (1989-2001)," Mumbai. URL: (www.rbi.org.in).

Reserve Bank of India (2004): "Report of the Advisory Committee on Flow of Credit to Agriculture and Related Activities From the Banking System," URL: (www.rbi.org.in).

Reserve Bank of India (2005): "Report of the Internal Working Group on RRBs," Chairman: A.V. Sardesai, Mumbai, URL: (www.rbi.org.in).

Revell, J. (1979): "Inflation and Financial Institutions," *Financial Times*, London.

Rhoades, Stephen A. 1977): "Structure and Performance Studies in Banking: A Summary and Evaluation," Staff Economics Studies, 92, Federal Reserve Board, Washington, DC.

RRBs alone have organized roughly 12 lakh self-help groups, 45 per cent of the total self-help groups in the country. RRBs have also issued over 40 lakh Kisan Credit Cards to the farmers and organized over 5,000 out of 11,000 farmers' clubs under NABARD scheme.

RRBs were established "with a view to developing the rural economy by providing, for the purpose of development of agriculture, trade, commerce, industry and other productive activities in the rural areas, credit and other facilities, particularly to small and marginal farmers, agricultural laborers, artisans and small entrepreneurs, and for matters connected therewith and incidental thereto" (RRBs Act, 1976).

Schuster, Leo (1984): "Profitability and Market Share of Banks," *Journal of Bank Research*, Spring.

Shaffer, S. (1994): "Bank Competition in Concentrated Markets," *Federal Reserve Bank of Philadelphia Business Review*, March/April, pp.3-16.

Shaffer, S. (2004): Comment on "What Drives Bank Competition? Some International Evidence" by Stijn Claessens and Luc Laeven, *Journal of Money, Credit, and Banking*, Vol. 36, pp. 585-92. Reserve Bank of India Occasional Papers.

Sharma, K.C.; Josh, P.; Mishra, J.C.; Kumar Sanjay; Amalorpavanathan, R. and Bhaskran, R. (2001): "Recovery Management in Rural Credit," Occasional Paper, No. 21, NABARD, Mumbai.

Short, B.K. (1979): "The Relation Between Commercial Bank Profit Rates and Banking Concentration in Canada, Western Europe and Japan," *Journal of Banking and Finance*, Vol. 3, pp. 209-19.

Short, Brock (1977): "Bank Concentration, Market Size and Performance: Some Evidence from Outside the United States," Mimeo, IMF, Washington, DC.

Smirlock, M. (1985): "Evidence on the (non) Relationship Between Concentration and Profitability in Banking," *Journal of Money, Credit, and Banking*, Vol. 17, pp. 69-83.

Specifically, the sponsor bank contributes thirty-five per cent of issued capital of a RRB, appoints its chairman, advises on decisions regarding investments, monitor its progress and suggest corrective measures to be taken by the RRBs. More on the relationship between the sponsor bank and their RRBs is discussed in Annex 2.

Staikouras, C., Steliaros, M. (1999): "Factors That Determine the Profitability of the Greek Financial Institutions," Helle'nic Bank Association, 19, pp. 61-66.

Statistical Tables Relating to Banks in India (Various Issues), Reserve Bank of India, Mumbai, URL: (www.rbi.org.in)

The Government of India (Ministry of Finance), issued nine notifications on September 12, 2005 for amalgamation of 28 RRBs into nine new RRBs sponsored by nine banks in six States. These amalgamations have become effective from September 12, 2005.

The left out RRB is the Kshetryià Kisan Gramin Bank due to lack of information on the Sponsor Bank for the entire period of 1994-2003. This RRB is sponsored by U.P.S.C.B., a Cooperative Bank.

The p-values for the Saran test are 0.18, 0.10 and 0.08 for the profit-making, loss-making and all RRBs, respectively.

Thingalaya, N.K. (2000): "The Other Side of the Rural Banking," BIRD, Lucknow.

This in a way testifies the appropriateness of employing the extended dynamic model for estimation. Guided by statistical significance, two lags of the dependent variable have been used in the GMM estimation.

Though the growth in credit when seen in isolation gives an impression of the impressive strides made by RRBs in disbursing credit, they account for a very small proportion (around 3 per cent) of the total assets of the Indian banking sector, despite their significant branch network.

Tschoegi, Adrian E. (1982): "Concentration Among International Banks—A Note," *Journal of Banking and Finance*, Vol. 6.

Tschoegi, Adrian E. (1983): "Size, Growth and Transnationality Among the World's Largest Banks," *Journal of Business*, 56, No. 2.

Velayudham, T. K., and Sankaranarayanan, V. (1990): "Regional Rural Banks and Rural Credit: Some Issues," *Economic and Political Weekly*, September 22, pp. 2157-64.

While C-D ratio for 50 RRBs was more than 60 per cent that for 87 banks was less than 40 per cent in March 2004.

Agricultural Development, Urban Bias, Agricultural Policies and Foreign Aid

Dr. Hari Mohan Mittal and Ms. Bharti Chauhan

Throughout history, agriculture-led development strategies with state support programs have been essential to achieve rapid economy-wide growth, poverty reduction, and structural transformation. Yet over the last three decades, the domestic and international policy environments have continued to discriminate against agricultural development in the poorest countries. The paper studies the causes and manifestation of this "urban bias," including discrimination in domestic pricing policies and in the international trade regime, decreasing financial support from LDC governments and aid donors, and increasing neglect of agriculture in development theory and economic research. The authors conclude that urban bias remains a persistent and paramount obstacle to sustained growth and poverty reduction in the Least Developed Countries (LDC).

A large literature shows that investments made by developing countries in agriculture—but also in rural infrastructure, health and education—are both pro-growth and pro-poor. Yet over the last three decades, there has been an inefficient and systemic bias against agriculture and the rural economy in the allocation of developmental resources. The bias is inefficient because no currently advanced country of some size became advanced without the agriculture sector first achieving substantial productivity gains in the early stages of development. The bias is systemic because it has fundamental institutional causes grounded in the political economies of both the developing and the developed countries, and in the development profession itself. In this paper we argue that because the bias has systemic institutional causes it may rightly be labeled the contemporary manifestation of "urban bias."[1]

Economists have long been aware of urban biases. Biases against rural development were part of the "blackwash" effects identified in the 1950s by Myrdal (1958). In the 1970s, World Bank President Robert McNamara (1973) made special note of the insufficient resource allocation to agriculture on several occasions. Other classic works focus on trade-based discrimination against agriculture (Krueger, Schiff, & Valdes, 1991; Little, Scitovsky & Scott, 1970). Binswanger and Deininger (1997), provided an authoritative exploration of the domestic political economy determinates of the bias against agriculture and more recent works also note urban biases in contemporary development policy (Byerlee, Diao, & Jackson, 2005; Rola-rubzen, Hardker, & Dillon, 2001: World Bank, 2003).

The basic purpose of this paper is impact of agricultural growth on economic development and poverty reduction and to examine that despite agriculture's importance, it has been persistently neglected in recent decades due to urban bias.

The broad summary demonstrates numerous dimensions of urban bias. Within the least developed countries themselves, market failures and adverse colonial inheritances pose structural obstacles to market-led agricultural development. These structural disadvantages have typically been compounded by systemic political economy forces in the LDCs which bias policies against smallholders in particular. Urban biases originating within LDCs are compounded by protectionism in the international trade regime resulting from an ironic 'rural bias' in the political economy of OECD countries.

The pervasiveness of urban bias, its costs and its stubborn institutional and ideological roots lead us to suggest that Lipton (1977) strong conclusion is still valid today: urban biases are the largest institutional impediment to growth and poverty reduction in the world's poorest countries.

Despite agricultural development foreign aid agencies have sharply decreased agricultural aid levels as well as research efforts towards agriculture. Urban biases are closely linked to development theory itself, especially with regard to the role of the state and the manner in which industrialization is best achieved.

The Role of Agriculture in Development

Substantial government involvement in agriculture seems to be a necessary precursor to both agricultural development and overall economic progress. Therefore, any policy which discriminates against LDC agriculture is likely to hinder economic growth and poverty reduction.

There is overwhelming evidence from theory, history and contemporary analysis that agricultural growth is a precondition to broader growth. A further important point is that agricultural growth is quintessentially pro-poor growth. The reasons are now well known: agriculture is generally labour-intensive and skill-extensive, so that agricultural growth creates additional employment with low entry barriers. Increased agricultural productivity also lowers food prices for both the rural and the urban poor, who typically spend most of their household budgets on food. Especially productivity growth on small family farms is very pro-poor; Lipton (2005) argues that this has been driving worldwide poverty reduction from 1700 to the present day. And again the empirical evidence in this context is impressive. Numerous cross-country and country-specific studies conclude that agricultural productivity is a major source of poverty reduction and almost certainly the major source at lower levels of development. For extensive agricultural development the government's support is inevitable.

Domestic Urban Biases Emerge and Persist

Both low food prices and cheap rural labour can also be obtained in the short-run, at least—from urban-biased policies[2] so that investments in agriculture are always perceived as necessary, despite pervasive market failure in this sector (Binswanger & Deininger, 1997), such failures also explain why LDC agriculture will typically attract very few resources in a low-income *laissez faire* economy.

The relative research interest on the economies of agriculture in the World Bank declined by about the same proportion as World Bank IDA aid flows to agriculture over the 1990s, which decreased from 19.7% of total aid in the mid-1990s to 8.4% in 2000.

Conclusions

The aforesaid study makes it clear that agriculture still has a vital role to play in igniting growth and poverty reduction at early stages of development. As such any bias against LDC agriculture is likely to be very costly, especially given the pervasive nature of market failure in this sector and the consequently critical role of state assistance to agriculture. But urban biases were widely acknowledged in the late 1970s and early 1980s, and urban-biased price regimes significantly dismantled in late 1980s and 1990s, other very important forms of urban bias have persisted (i.e. the international trade regime), and even intensified (i.e. government expenditure and foreign aid). The persistence of these biases is explained by a combination of domestic historical and structural factors, political economy dynamics both domestically and in the ORCD dono countries and anti-state development theories adhered to in the development profession and especially, the international financial institutions.

Targeted investments in agriculture and active opposition to urban bias in its many forms remain critical to growth and poverty reduction in our time.

Notes and References

1. We use the term "urban bias" somewhat loosely. Unlike Lipton, we place rather more emphasis on discrimination against the agricultural

sector more so than the entire rural sector, although the heavy dependency of the non-farm sector on the agricultural sector renders these distinctions fairly superfluous. Urban bias largely refers to discrimination against smallholders much more so than large scale farms.

2. For example, discrimination against agriculture can push unskilled workers off the land and into the cities where they will be willing to work for low wages. Food prices can be kept low implicit and explicit taxes on agriculture and via food imports. And in countries with high rural inequality, a sufficient food supply at low prices can be obtained from the land-abundant, rural elite in exchange for targeted subsidies.

Role of Department of Rural Development in India (DRDI) and National Bank for Agriculture and Rural Development (NABARD) in the Development of Rural Economy

Dr. M.L. Agarwal and Dr. Krishna Saraswat

The Rural Economy in India is wholly agriculture-based and it is of tremendous importance because it has vital supply and demand links with the other Indian industries. In India, agriculture accounts for almost 19% of Indian Gross Domestic Products (GDP). This is the main reason that Ministry of Agriculture, the Ministry of Rural Infrastructure, and the Planning Commission of India are the main governing bodies that formulate and implements the policy related to agriculture and the rural economy in India and its subsequent development for the overall growth of the Indian economy. In fact, the development of the Indian Rural Economy can be credited to the liberal policy of the Ministry of Rural Development, Government of India and the Planning Commission of India. As the Rural Development in India is one of the most important factors for the growth of the Indian economy, the Government has planned several programs pertaining to Rural Development in India. The role of the Department of Rural Development in India (DRDI) and National Bank for Agriculture and Rural Development (NABARD) can be studied as below.

ROLE OF DEPARTMENT OF RURAL DEVELOPMENT IN INDIA (DRDI) IN THE DEVELOPMENT OF RURAL ECONOMY

The Department of Rural Development in India is under the Ministry of Rural Development in the Central Government of India. The Department facilitates the provision of several services such as training and research facilities, human resource development, institutes of Panchayati Raj, and at the same time provides functional assistance to the DRDA and oversees the execution of projects and schemes.

Department of Rural Development also executes the schemes for wage employment and self-employment generation and for providing small irrigation and housing facilities to the rural poor, it provides economic aid to the poor in rural areas.

This department functions according to the formulated schemes. The important schemes undertaken by the department are:

1. Pradhan Mantri Gram Sadak Yojana (PMGSY)

The transportation facility in the rural areas is one of the important factors for the economic growth of the rural sector. The construction of the transportation facilities would also help the rural unskilled labour, as construction work of this stature requires large work force. The Pradhan Mantri Gram Sadak Yojana (PMGSY) is a scheme launched and fully sponsored by the Central Government of India. The main objective of the scheme is to connect all the habitations with more than 500 individuals residing there, in the rural areas by the means of weatherproof metaled roads.

2. Swarnjayanti Gram Swarozgar Yojana (SGSY)

This program is a single self-employment program for the poor rural people. The Swarnjayanti Gram Swarozgar Yojana was put to effect in the year 1999. The program was implemented as a total package encompassing all the characteristics of self-employment such as proper training, development of infrastructure, planning of activities, financial aid by the means of credit from banks, organizing the poor people in the rural areas into Self Help Groups, marketing support and subsidies.

3. Sampoorna Gramin Rozgar Yojana (SGRY)

The scheme was put to effect in the year 2001 with the merger of the Jawahar Gram Smridhi Yojana and Employment Assurance Scheme. The Central and State Governments at 75:25 ratios are sharing the execution cost of the scheme. The scheme aims at increasing the food protection by the means of wage employment in the rural areas, which are affected by the calamities after the appraisal of the State Government, and the Ministry of Agriculture accepts the appraisal.

4. Indira Awaas Yojana (Rural Housing)

This scheme was put to effect in the year 1996. With the declaration of the new National Housing and Habitat policy by the Government of India in year 1998, which stated 'Housing for all the authorities are putting emphasis on providing housing benefits all over the rural areas in the country.'

Role of National Bank for Agriculture and Rural Development (NABARD) in the Development of Rural Economy

NABARD is an apex rural credit institution which plays an important role in the implementation of various rural development programmes which was designed in July, 1982 to take over the function of rural credit from the Reserve Bank of India and also the refinancing and development function from Agricultural Refinance and Development Corporation (ARDC). NABARD ensures that there is adequate flow of credit for seasonal agricultural operations to maintain agricultural production. Also it has to accelerate the flow of credit for long-term investment in agriculture sector.

The main purpose of National Bank for Agriculture and Rural Development is to provide credit for the development and publicity of small scaled industries, handicrafts, rural crafts, village industries, cottage industries, agriculture, etc. The NABARD also supports all other related economic operations in the rural sector, promotion of sustainable growth in the rural sector. The NABARD also plays the role of a contributor to the rural development by the means of promoting institutional development, facilitating refinance to loan providers in the rural sector, inspection, monitoring, and evaluation of client financial corporations. Thus National Bank for Agriculture and Rural Development (NABARD) has been established as the premier rural development bank.

NABARD's role and functions can be enumerated below:

(a) NABARD initiates measures toward institution building for improving absorptive capacity of the credit delivery system, including monitoring, formulation of rehabilitation schemes, restructuring of credit institutions, training of personnel, etc.

(b) It coordinates the rural financing activities of all the institutions engaged in developmental work at the field level and maintains liaison with the Government of India, State Governments, the Reserve Bank of India and other national level institutions concerned with policy formulation.

(c) It prepares, on annual basis, rural credit plans for all the districts in the country. These plans form the base for annual credit plans of all rural financial institutions.

(d) It undertakes monitoring and evaluation of projects refinanced by it.

(e) It promotes research in the field of rural banking, agriculture and rural development.

(f) It functions as a regulatory authority, supervising, monitoring and guiding cooperative banks and regional rural banks.

Concluding it can be said that The Department of Rural

Development in India (DRDI) and National Bank for Agriculture and Rural Development (NABARD) are playing their pivot role in the development of rural economy of the country. It can be expected that these two bodies would remain successful in improving per capita income of rural inhabitants and would prove helpful in improving their standard of living in the coming future.

Working of Regional Rural Banks for Rural Society

Dr. Anil Gupta and Mr. Atul Gupta

Growing needs of agricultural output in our country intend to mechanize and to modernize the agriculture with sophisticated advancing technology. The sophistication, thus requires a bulk of finance, that too in an organized fashion. The use of various fertilizers, plant protection chemicals, high yielding variety of seeds, various tools and equipments, etc. is increasing day-by-day.

Obviously, the paucity of private funds for having all such agricultural delicacies for improved higher output would obstruct the process. The situation thus calls for the need of institutional credit for using the effective variety of agricultural inputs for the sector-concerned as well for the overall development in the economy.

Such inherent objectives encourage to design an approach to analyse the working of the Regional Rural Banks in providing with agricultural-credit for fast development of the rural society in the western part of Uttar Pradesh. Moreover, the present 'observation' is confined to one prosperous district of western Uttar Pradesh, viz., Janpad Muzaffarnagar (District Muzaffarnagar). Punjab National Bank took the lead role in 1984 to set-up the Regional Rural Bank in the District area for the benefit of the rural society accordingly.

Economic thinking and considerations are striking to focus its attention to include rural development programmes across the world particularly in developing nations. The fact is gaining the prominence today but the concept is alive from the past.

Gruff rural economy of Janpad seems to gain from financial assistance for specified target groups provided by the Kshetriya Gramin Bank. The process of development in this regard dates back to 1984. The target groups mainly consists small and marginal farmers, rural artisans and other members of the weaker part of the society in rural segments of Janpad. Various schemes of the Gramin Bank daubs effectively the inherent objectives for the benefit of such target groups.

Consequent to it, agricultural development was assigned the top priority rather the only priority in the First Five Year Plan (1951-56) in 1951-52 in Indian economy. Similar kind of significance is visible in the Draft Tenth Five Year Plan in recent times.

Subsequent to it, development in the field of agricultural credit and finance gained due weightage. This resulted the formation and organization of many co-operative societies and financial institutions from the State level to the district level. Formation of Regional Rural Banks is the outcome of such meaningful efforts to raise agricultural productivity on one hand, whereas, these are also helping in providing with agricultural finance at district level.

Looking at such consideration, the present paper is an attempt to undertake the analysis of the functioning of the Regional Rural Banks in Muzaffarnagar District, named as Muzaffarnagar Kshetriya Gramin Bank.

Since its inception in mid-eighties (1984-85), the Gramin Bank in the region tries to cater the needs of landless and marginal farmers with key-attention on other down-trodden segments of the society. This is in fact to boost up the development programme of the rural society by helping in agricultural as well as non-agricultural activities therein.

The basic hypothesis may be stated in terms of the fact that the rural society may be benefited gainfully if agricultural and agricultural-related and such allied activities are supported by proper finance-friendly activities, since rural society mainly depends on such agricultural activities. The job seems to be fulfilled by the programmes of Regional Rural Banks.

The problem of credit-requirements in agriculture can well be taken up both at macro and micro-levels. The macro-approach may intend to analyse the overall supply of credit and demand for credit; while, the micro-approach may provide with an in-depth detailed account of credit aspects like its distribution pattern, utilization and the extent of requirements *et. al.* Further, this may also explain relatively in an effective manner regarding the suitability, desirability and profitability of such credit sources for the expansion and development of the agricultural sector, and hence the rural sector.

Seemingly, it implies that the job of Regional Rural Banks would mainly be to bridge up the gap between rural and urban unequals through supporting the rural economy by financial assistance in different ways.

The contribution of Regional Rural Banks for the benefit of rural society may be analysed in terms of different functions of the bank. These function may include the analyses of bank deposits, bank loans across targets and achievements, disbursement of loans, financial performance of the bank, other kinds of advances, re-finance activity, loan deposit ratio, financing for non-target groups, fund management and Deposit Insurance Credit Guarantee Corporation Claims (DICGCC). This looks somewhat less comfortable to include all such functions of the Regional Rural Banks within the parameters of the scope of present paper.

Summary Observations

It is difficult to doubt the utility of the Regional Rural Bank to the rural masses. By bringing credit facilities at the door steps of poor sections of the rural community, these banks can relieve them from the grip of problems and of moneylenders. Since, the lead bank has been the sponsoring bank for Regional Rural Bank, the establishment of Rural Bank should be considered as a step towards strengthening the institutional structure at the district level where the lead bank is expected to play a crucial role in financing the economic development in the region.

The Regional Rural Bank has a very bright future in terms of services at the door steps of the rural folk, reducing the cost of service and in terms of potential source of rural credit. In fact, it provides the effective credit supply to small and marginal farmers, rural artisans and landless labourers.

Agricultural growth alongwith its relating allied sectors is mutually inclusive of the nature and extent of agricultural credit. Its availability is smoothened through the efforts of Regional Rural Bank which is termed as Kshetriya Gramin Bank in Muzaffarnagar Janpad. Gramin Bank helps the local rural economy to grow fast which does undertakes the pioneering job of providing rural credit for the benefit of target and non-target beneficiaries since its inception in the year 1984. The target group consists of small, marginal farmers and rural artisans mainly besides others.

Punjab National Bank, as already explained earlier, took the command role in establishing Gramin Bank for the benefit of local economy of Janpad Muzaffarnagar. Present paper is an attempt to encourage the analyses of structural pattern of different banking activities of Gramin Bank for the benefit of rural economy and weaker sections of the area comprising entire Janpad.

The Regional Rural Bank adopted a few innovative activities since 1993-94. These relate to NTG (Non-Target Group) financing, Fund Management Schemes and DICGC (Deposits Insurance Credit Guarantee Corporation) Claims. These estimates help in analysing the structural pattern of the Bank alongwith its performance and progress over the years. Moreover, the empirical analysis would concede the pattern of deposits and advances. Further, the role of institutional finances through Gramin Bank is examined for agro-economic development as well for non-agricultural benefits.

The present analysis is a simple attempt to focus the attention on the working of Regional Rural Bank for agricultural development in Janpad.

Needless to stress again and again that institutional credit for the rural development has remained a persisting requirement of Indian economy in terms of its population and dis-aggregation of net domestic product sector-wise.

Looking at such state of the rural sector, there has been a continuous pressure on the planners and the policy framers that institutional credit be provided without any constraint. Consequently, different financial institutions are undertaking the job, but, the emergence of Regional Rural Bank indicates somewhat different state in this direction. The role of Regional Rural Bank seems to be in solidarity for agricultural development alongwith the development of other sectors.

Growing population always demands more and more food grains in general. On either count, the significance of agricultural sector cannot be overlooked in any economy or within the particular economy. Thus, more and more fresh issues are emerging continuously in agricultural sector including provision for organised finances which need a more careful and systematic treatment.

On summing up, it will not be out of context to mention that many complicated challenges are there in the context of institutional finances for agricultural development in rural economy. Therefore, the present analysis may not be a conclusive effort in this direction rather it only initiates the process which does require a substantial amount of exercise to be carried out in this context.

Complex challenges are there but these are to be tackled with utmost care in order to improve and to strengthen the rural economy of the country, which in turn support the entire economy in general.

REFERENCES

Agarwal, D.C. (1971), "Institutional Credit for Agriculture in Malwa," *Indian Journal of Agricultural Economics*, Vol. XXVI, p. 565.

Agarwal, G.D. and Foreman, W.J. (1959), "Farm Resource Productivity in West U.P.," *Indian Journal of AE*, 15 (4).

Athavale, M.C., *et. al.*, (1971), "Green Revolution and Short-Term Co-Operative Credit—A Study in Two Districts of Madhya Pradesh," *Indian Journal of Agricultural Economics*, Vol. XXVI, 4, pp. 519-23.

Bank of Baroda (1977, November), "Commercial Banks and Agricultural Advances," Bank of Baroda, *Weekly Review*, Vol. 15, Nos. 46, 47 and 48.

Bhatia, J.P. (1975), Problems of Small Farming—A Case Study of Tribal U.P., *Indian Journal of Agricultural Economics*, Vol. XXX, 3, p. 240.

Bhargave, V.K. and Shah, S.L. (1968), "Credit Needs of a Changing Agriculture: A Potential Area for Commercial Bank Finance," *Indian Journal of Agricultural Economics*, Vol. XXII, p. 38.

Dantwala, M.L. (1961), "Agrarian Structure And Economic Development," Presidential Address, *Indian Journal of Agricultural Economics*, 16 (1).

Desai, B.M., and, Desai, D.K. (1971), "Farm Production Credit Needs in Changing Agriculture," Indian Institute of Management.

Farrell, M.J. (1957), "The Measurement of Productive Efficiency," *Journal of Royal Statistical Society*, Series A, 120.

Government of India, (1976), Report of the National Commission on Agriculture, Ministry of Agriculture, New Delhi.

Johnston, J. (1960), "Econometric Methods," McGraw-Hill, Kogakusha Ltd., Tokyo, 2nd Edition, p. 433.

Muzaffarnagar Kshetriya Gramin Bank, (1999-2000), 16th Annual Report, Head Office, MKGB (Muzaffarnagar Regional Rural Bank), Muzaffarnagar.

——, (1984), Annual Report, HO, MKGB.

Nurkse, R. (1973), "Problems of Capital Formation In Under Developed Countries," Oxford University Press, Delhi, Chapter 1, pp. 4-31, Indian Reprint.

Rao, C.H.H. (1965), "Agricultural Production Functions, Costs and Returns In India," Asia Publishing House, Delhi.

Reserve Bank of India (1954), General Report of the Committee on Direction of All India Rural Credit Survey, Bombay.

Singh, J.P. (1986), "Role of Institutional Finance in Agriculture," Ashish Publishing House, New Delhi.

Syndicate Bank, (1994, May-July), An Innovative Institutional Framework for Rural Entrepreneurship Development, (B.L. Chadha), Pigmy Economic Review, *Quarterly Economic Journal of Syndicate Bank*, Vol. 38, No. 4, Manipal.

Role of the Regional Rural Banks in the Economic Upliftment of Weaker Sections of the Rural Society

Dr. Suman Lata and Ms. Lipi

Introduction

The Regional Rural Banks were established with a view to developing the rural economy by providing, for the purpose of development of agriculture, trade, commerce, industry and other productive activities to the rural areas, credit and other facilities, particularly to the small and marginal farmers, agricultural labourers and small entrepreneurs or we can also say that the RRB was created to meet the excess demand for institutional credit in the rural areas, particularly among the economically and socially marginalised sections.

In order to provide access to low-cost banking facilities to the poor, the Government, 26 Sept. (1975) proposed the establishment of Regional Rural Banks which "combine the local feel and familiarity with rural problems which the cooperatives possess, ability to mobilize deposit and modern outlook which the commercial banks have." On 2nd October 1975 five Regional

Banks were established in India.

Moradabad and Gorakhpur in Uttar Pradesh, Bhiwani in Haryana, Jaipur in Rajasthan and Malda in West Bengal. These Banks were opened by Syndicate Bank, United Commercial Bank and United Bank of India respectively. Each Regional rural bank had an authorised capital of Rs. 1 crore and issued and paid up capital of Rs. 25 lakhs. The Act, 1976 sums up this over all vision to sub-serve both the development and the redistribute objectives.

OBJECTIVES OF THE RRBs

Main objectives of the Regional Rural Banks are as follows:

1. To provide the financial facilities for the development of agriculture trade, commerce and other productive activities to the economically and socially marginalised sections and the rural society.
2. To Provide low-cost banking facilities to the poor.
3. To Provide Employment facilities to the poor by appointing them as the workers of RRBs.
4. To raise the standard of living for the socio-economic upliftment of the weaker sections of the rural society.

EXPANSION OF REGIONAL BANKS

	Dec. 1975	*Dec. 1980*	*Dec. 1985*	*Mar. 1990*
Banks	6	85	188	196
Branches	17	3279	12606	14443

Source: NABARD Reports.

By 1991, there were 196 RRBs with over 14,000 rural branches in 516 districts with an average covering three villages per branch. The year 1990 marks the end of the expansion phase of regional banking, beyond which there has been no growth in the number of Regional Rural Banks. Between 1980 and 1987, while the number of RRBs increased a little more than two-fold, the number of branches of RRBs increased more than four-fold. During the Seventies maximum number of RRBs were thus opened in the Central, Eastern and the Northern regions in the country that had the largest number of backward districts. It was not totally unexpected therefore that by the end of the 1980, Several of these banks were showing losses on their books. Since the early 1990, there was a complete freeze on recruitment of the new staff in the RRBs. As a part of Comprehensives restructuring programme, recapitalisation of RRBs was initiated in the year 1994-95 a process which continued till 1999-2000 and covered 187 RRBs with aggregate financial support of Rs. 2188.44 crore from stakeholders.

In short, we have seen the three phases of Regional Rural Banking in India, the expansion phase (1976-90) which saw the rapid growth of the RRBs, the reform phase (1991-2003) which raised the profitability of these banks and the last and recent phase of improvement of RRBs.

EVALUATION OF RRBS

The Question of Viability

It was understood that the RRBs to survive as credit institution could not remain unviable for a long time, though the RRBs might not become viable in the initial years. It was realized that the question of viability of the RRBs could not be same as other business ventures. A business unit has all the freedom to take decisions on many matters such as staff recruitment, deploying it resources, opening branches, and methods of services. But the RRBs could not be flexible in many of their affairs even their client was specific, remote and not assisted by any one. Keeping in view the nature of the operations of the RRBs, these institutions could not certainly not be evaluated on the basis of mere financial viability. The viability of the RRBs had to be assessed in terms of increase in business per branch, productivity of staff, debt recovery rate, socio-economic improvement of the weaken sections of the society.

Problem of Growing Overdues

The most significant problem of the RRBs is the low recovery rate and loan overdues. These had not only lead to capital erosion but more importantly had resulted in non-recycling of funds. There were certain factors of this problem. Some of the internal factors like weak monitoring, lack of supervision, untrained staff, etc. The external factors were political interference, under development, lack of administrative support from the government in the matter of recovery, etc. About 39 to 49 per cent debts were not returned. This possesses the opposite impact on the development of the Regional rural Banks.

Financial System of RRBs

The Committee on the Financial System 1991 (Narasimham Committee) stressed the poor financial health of the RRBs to the exclusion of every other performance indicator. 172 of the 196 RRBs were recorded unprofitable with an aggregate loan recovery performance of 40.8 per cent. The low equity base of these banks did not cover the loan losses of most RRBs. In case of a few RRBs, there had also been an erosion of public deposits, besides capital. In order to impart viability to the operations of RRBs, Narasimham Committee suggested that the RRBs should be merged with sponsor banks. This proposed readily accepted. The committee suggests that the objective of serving the weaker sections effectively could be achieved only by self-sustaining credit institutions. This step marked a major turning point in the functioning of RRBs. There were also certain organizational problems such as low capital base, multiple ownership, lack of trained staff, problem of debt recovery, lack of financial resources, etc.

Major Reform and Measures

Kelkar Committee, 1986 made comprehensive recommendations both the organizational and operational aspect as:

- Enhancement of authorized Capital of RRBs from 1 crore to 5 crore and paid up capital from 25 lakh to 1 crore.
- Appointment of Chairman of RRBs by the concerned sponsor Banks in consultation with NABARD.
- Giving financial assistance to RRBs in their first five year of their existence.
- Provision of amalgamation of RRBs in consultation with all the concerned parties.
- Provision for rationalization of branch network including relocation and merger of loss-making branches.
- Permission to land to others outside target groups and deregulation of interest rates.

- Rising investment in Bank's Portfolios in the monetary and credit policy 2002-03 it was announced that the RRBs should maintain their SLR holdings in the form of government and other approval securities by converting existing deposits with sponsor banks.
- "The committee recommends that the RRBs should take steps for compiling and maintaining data regarding credit facility extended to small and marginal farmers and other weaker sections of the society to monitor that credit facilities being provided by RRBs reach the targeted beneficiaries."

RRBs AND RURAL POOR

The potential and the need for diversification of economic activities in the rural areas had begun to recognize, and this was a sector where the RRBs could play a meaningful role in the economic upliftment of the weaker sections of the rural society. The main aim of the Regional Rural Banks was to meet the excess demand for institutional credit in the rural areas, particularly among the economically and socially marginalised sections. RRBs as part of the multi-agency approach to rural credit are eminently suitable to do the job envisaged for them, that as district level organisations, they can be trusted to take banking closer to rural household. 90 per cent of the RRBs branches opened in these rural areas where before there had no banking facilities. The RRBs adopted new innovations for credit delivery with lower risk of default such as self-help group linked lending, non-priority sector collateralized lending, kisan credit card scheme for landed agriculturists, etc. It was an attempt to minimize credit risk and made easy loans. Between 1995 to 2003, short-term agriculture credit under the priority sector increased at about 29 per cent per annum, term loans declined by 2.6 per cent a year. These Banks has disbursed over Rs. 3500 crore in credit and mobilized over Rs. 4100 crore in deposit. The most significant achievement of the RRBs was enabling the weaker sections of the rural community access to institutional credit. The bulk of loans from RRBs were given to the rural poor (priority sectors), which accounted for over 70% of the total. Agriculture and allied activities took up more then 50% of the total advances. In addition, the RRBs were instrumental in extending credit for poverty allevation schemes and development programmes.

Purpose-wise Advances of RRBs

(Rs. Crore)

1.	Crop Loan	615
2.	Term Loan and Agricultural Loan	669
3.	Allied Activities	555
4.	Rural Artisan and Cottage Industries	277
5.	Retail Trade and Self-Employed	1052
6.	Consumption Loan	54
7.	Other purpose	290
8.	Indirect Advances	43
	Total	3555

Source: Report on Trend and Progress of Banking in India, 1990-91.

Several purpose-wise advances and loans were given by RRBs to the marginal poors. About 615 crore for crop loan, 1052 crore for Retail Trade and about 555 crore for Allied activities were given.

Now, it became easy to rural poor to fulfil their needs connected with trade, commerce and other financial activities. By providing them low cost banking facilities RRBs helps in raising the standard of living for the social and economic growth. The step taken by the government to merge the regional rural banks with the sponsor banks is appreciable. The percentage of rural credit given by the RRBs in the rural area is more than 90 per cent.

The objective of serving the weaker sections effectively could be achieved only by self-sustaining credit institutions. Yet in the liberalized banking era, these banks had to become competitive, improve their profitability and conform to prudential regulation of asset classification and provisioning norms on equal footing. At last keeping in mind the above views it can be said that the Regional Rural Banks plays an important role in the economic upliftment of the weaker sections of the rural society.

REFRENCES

Report of the Advisory Committee on Flow of Credit to Agriculture and Related Activities from Banking System, RBI, June 2004.

Co-operative Banks and Market: The vicious link, by N.A. Majumdar.
RBI, Handbook of Statistics on the Indian Economy.
Reserve Bank of India (May 2005), "Report of the Internal working groups on RRBs."
Indian Economy: Rudra Dutt & K.P.M. Sundaram.
Indian Economy: Himalaya Publishing.

Internet Websites:

http://www.google.com
http://www.globalevision.org

Role of Vananchal Gramin Bank in the Economic Development of Jharkhand: A Review

Prof. R.N. Singh and Dr. A. Kumar

I. Introduction

Regional Rural Banks (RRBs) have been in existence for more than three decades in the Indian financial scene. The very inception of regional rural banks can be seen as a unique experiment as well as experience in improving the efficacy of rural credit delivery mechanism in India. The genesis of the RRBs can be traced to the need for a stronger institutional arrangement for providing rural credit. The Narasimham Committee Conceptualised the creation of RRBs in 1975 as a new set of regionally-oriented rural banks. Subsequently, the RRBs were set-up under the Regional Rural Banks Act, 1976 (Section 3 of Chapter II of RRB Act, 1976). The public Sector banks in India have been empowered to sponsor RRBs by participating thing in their capital and also organizing and staffing them in the initial stages. The areas of operation of the RRBs have been very carefully selected. The economic backwardness of some of the districts has been weighted favorably for locating the RRBs. The participation of the central government in the capital of the RRBs is to the tune of 50 per cent (through NABARD) the share of the State government is 15 per cent, the remaining 35 per cent is the share of the sponsoring public sector bank. RRBs were supposed to evolve as specialized rural financial institutions for developing the rural economy by providing credit to small and marginal farmers, agricultural laborers, artisans and small entrepreneurs.

II. Vananchal Gramin Bank

A. Background

The background of VGB is not old. It is quite new. Its genises dates back 30th June, 2006. Vananchal Gramin Bank, sponsored by State Bank of India came into existence on the 30th June 2006 with the amalgamation of erstwhile Santhal Parganans Gramin Bank and Palamau Kshetriya Gramin Bank vide Govt. of India Notification F.No. 1/4/2006-RRB III dated 30.06.2008. The Bank covers 9 districts situated in Santhal Pargana and Palamau divisions of Jharkhand state. The Head Office of bank is located at Dumka with two controlling Offices, one each at Dumka and Daltonganj. Santhal Pargana Division with a geographical area of 14,129 sq. kms., consists of six districts—Dumka, Deoghar, Jamtara, Godda, Sahibganj and Pakur. Similarly, Palamau division with a geographical area of 11,651 sq. kms. comprises 3 districts—Palamau, Latehar and Garhwa. Both the Divisions are having vast natural resources especially standard and other basic commercial and economic activities, which are forest and coal but these are economically backward.

The lack of basic infrastructural facilities, industrialization, Socio-economic standard and other basic commercial and economic activities, which are considered to be prerequisites for economic growth, are non-existent in the region. The half of the total geographical area of Palamau Division is covered with forests. The share of SC/ST Population in the overall population of both the Divisions is high. The main crops raised in the area are: paddy, maize, wheat, potato and pulses. The agriculture in the region is mainly dependent on monsoon. Against the above backdrop of economic backwardness and limited resources, the Bank has been established with the objective of providing considerable impetus to the development of rural economy by providing credit and other banking services to the rural areas of Santhal Pargana and Palamau Divisions of Jharkhand state. The Bank is making relentless efforts for realizing this objective.

B. Branch Network

The Bank has total network of 178 branches out of which 103 branches are operating in Santhal Pargana division and 75 branches are functioning in Palamau Division. Out of 103 branches situated in Santhal Pargana Division 7 branches situated in semi-urban centers and out of 75 branches operating in Palamau Division, 10 branches are located at semi-urban centers. The remaining 161 branches located at semi-urban centers to 17. The remaining 161 branches are situated in rural areas. Out of the 161 rural branches, 96 such branches are operating in Santhal Pargana Division and 65 branches in Palamau Division. License for opening 8 new branches have been received from RBI, which will be opened during 2008-09.

C. Share Capital

The authorized share capital of the Bank is Rs. 100,000 thousands only and paid up capital is Rs. 20,000 thousands, which has been subscribed by the Government of India, State Bank of India and Government of Jharkhand in the ratio of 50:35:15 respectively.

D. Share Capital Deposits

Consequent upon the identification of the erstwhile S.P.G.B. and P.K.G.B. (Since amalgamated into V.G.B.) for restructuring under Phase-II, the Government of India sanctioned an additional equity support of Rs. 3,25,366 thousand to the bank during 1995-96. Further our bank has been identified by the Govt. of India during 2007-08 for restructuring in phase III also and Govt. of Jharkhand has already released its 15% share amounting to Rs. 66,599 thousand to our bank on 29.03.08. The Government of India and the sponsoring Bank, i.e. S.B.I., have not released their proportionate shares of restructuring/recapitalization fund to the bank as yet.

E. Deposits

Deposit mobilization is one of the top priorities for the

profitable operations of the Bank. The total deposits of the Bank, which stood at Rs. 9,251,611 thousand as on 31.03.2007, have been increased to Rs, 10,602,979 thousand as on 31.03.2008 resulting in net growth of Rs. 1,351,368 thousand. In percentage term it comes to 14.60% as against the budgeted growth rate of 15.00%.

The percentage of low cost (CASA) deposits to total deposit stands at 72.67% as on 31.03.2008. The average cost of deposits worked out to 4.54% during the year under report.

F. Borrowings/Refinance

Under various schemes of refinance of RRBs, we have availed of refinance facility from NABARD to the tune of Rs. 1,90,526 thousand and from sponsor Bank (SBI) Rs. 361,800 thousand during 2007-08. The total amount of refinance availed by us is Rs. 552,326 thousand. The instalments and interest due on the refinance were repaid to NABARD in time.

G. Cash and Balance in Current Accounts with Banks

The Bank exercised utmost care to increase efficiency in Fund Management by maintaining minimum balance in current accounts with the Sponsor Bank. As a result, the average balance in Current Accounts with sponsor bank came down to Rs. 14.62 crore from Rs. 26.17 crore. However, to take care of efficient customer services and avoid frequent cash remittance to branches, the retention limits of cash balance of all the branches were reviewed and increased wherever, considered necessary resulting is increase in average cash holdings with the branches.

H. Investment

Total of the Bank as on 31.03.08 stood at Rs. 7,093,811 thousand, which comprises of SLR investment to the tune of Rs. 2,372,841 thousand and Non-SLR Investment (TDRs/STDRs with SBI/ICICI Bank, Mutual Funds, etc.) of Rs. 4,720,970 thousand. Thus, the portfolio recorded a growth of Rs. 826,626 thousand during the year. The interest earned on SLR and Non-SLR investment during the year was Rs. 159,420 thousand and Rs. 365,487 thousand respectively.

III. PERFORMANCES/ROLE OF VGB

The VGB has been playing a significant role in financing both the farm and non-farm sector, the role and performances of VGB can be made clear with the help of following tables:

TABLE 1

Position of A.C.P. as on 31st March'2008 vis-a-vis Annual Target 2007-08

(Rs. in thousand)

Sl. No.	District	Agriculture Target No.	Agriculture Target Amount	Agriculture Achievement No.	Agriculture Achievement Amount	% of Achievement	S.S.I. Target No.	S.S.I. Target Amount	S.S.I. Achievement No.	S.S.I. Achievement Amount	% of Achievement	O.P.S. Target No.	O.P.S. Target Amount	O.P.S. Achievement No.	O.P.S. Achievement Amount	% of Achievement
1.	Dumka	—	411019	9347	92938	22.61	—	34822	23	5112	14.68	—	98274	806	62031	83.12
2.	Jamtara	—	173893	3825	42989	2472	—	14733	1	1500	10.18	—	41577	313	13687	32.92
3.	Deoghar	—	284552	8492	104918	36.87	—	24108	26	2938	12.19	—	68036	503	60141	88.40
4.	Godda	—	316169	5214	91950	29.08	—	26786	10	1375	5.13	—	75595	764	37211	49.22
5.	Sahibganj	—	268743	3684	46453	17.29	—	22768	0	0	0.00	—	64256	481	18287	28.46
6.	Pakur	—	173893	2344	22879	13.16	—	14733	0	0	0.00	—	41578	456	24611	59.19
7.	Garhwa	—	379402	2846	59302	15.63	—	33302	52	2117	6.36	—	92759	593	112910	121.72
8.	Latehar	—	142276	957	19982	14.04	—	12488	8	266	2.13	—	34785	148	14116	40,58
9.	Palamau	—	663953	7084	132826	20.01	—	58279	94	5736	9.84	—	162327	814	90465	55.73
	Total	—	2813900	43793	614237	21.83	—	242019	214	19044	7.87		679187	4078	433469	63.82

TABLE 1 (*Contd.*)

Position of A.C.P. as on 31st March 2008 vis-a-vis Annual Target 2007-08

(Rs. in thousand)

Sl. No.	District	*Total Priority Sector*				% of Achievement	*Non-Priority Sector*				% of Achievement	*Grand Total*				% of Achievement
		Target		*Achievement*			*Target*		*Achievement*			*Target*		*Achievement*		
		No.	*Amount*	*No.*	*Amount*		*No.*	*Amount*	*No.*	*Amount*		*No.*	*Amount*	*No.*	*Amount*	
1.	Dumka	—	544115	10176	160081	29.42	—	124920	971	67836	54.30	—	669035	11147	227917	34.07
2.	Jamtara	—	230203	4139	58176	25.27	—	52851	468	47015	88.96	—	283054	4607	105191	37,16
3.	Deoghar	—	376696	9021	167997	44.60	—	86483	842	52881	61.15	—	463179	9863	220878	47.69
4.	Godda	—	418550	5988	130536	31.19	—	96092	549	37535	39,06	—	514642	6537	168071	32.66
5.	Sahibganj	—	355767	4165	64740	18.20	—	81678	540	37858	46.35	—	437445	4705	102598	23.45
6.	Pakur	—	230204	2800	47490	20.63	—	52850	250	24727	46,79	—	283054	3050	72217	25.51
7.	Garhwa	—	505463	3491	174329	34.49	—	119464	503	28714	24.04	—	624927	3994	203043	32,49
8.	Latehar	—	189549	1113	34364	18.13	—	44800	311	24412	54.49	—	234349	1424	58776	2508
9.	Palamau	—	884559	7992	229027	25.89	—	209062	1373	97711	46.74	—	1093621	9365	326738	29 88
	Total	—	3735106	48885	1066740	28.56	—	868200	5807	418689	48.22	—	4603306	54692	1485429	32.27

TABLE 1 (*Contd.*)

Out of Which

(*Rs. in thousand*)

Sl. No.	District	K.C.C				% of Achieve-ment	S.G.S.Y.				% of Achieve-ment	N.T.G. Loan				% of Achieve-ment
		Target		Achievement			Target		Achievement			Target		Achievement		
		No.	Amount	No.	Amount		No.	Amount	No.	Amount		No.	Amount	No.	Amount	
1.	Dumka	2847		9283	78992	326 06	—	38663	285	19882	5142	—	220602	653	90443	41.00
2.	Jamtara	1204		3528	38178	293 02	—	12441	285	5397	43.38	—	93331	409	51220	54 88
3.	Deoghar	1971		8207	97607	41639	—	34215	371	9037	2641	—	152725	919	102478	67.10
4.	Godda	2190		5051	82795	230.64	—	24688	476	10711	43.39	—	169694	227	40200	23 69
5.	Sahibganj	1863		3575	41051	191.89	—	43200	208	9028	2090	—	144240	191	30728	2130
6.	Pakur	1204		2334	21325	193 85	—	26113	86	9930	3803	—	93332	292	34928	37 42
7.	Garhwa	2723		2664	51114	97.83	—	33600	474	17381	51.73	—	210968	463	32145	15.24
8.	Latehar	1021		663	12318	64.94	—	8200	347	7964	97,12	—	79113	311	24412	30.86
9.	Palamau	4766		3880	85647	81 41	—	24900	555	12693	50 98	—	369195	1334	107142	29.02
	Total	9789		39185	509027	198.01	—	246020	3087	102023	41.47	—	1533200	4799	513696	33.50

TABLE 1 (*Contd.*)

Out of Which

(*Rs. in thousand*)

Sl. No.	District	SHG (NABARD Linkage)		SHG (SHPI)		SHG (SGSY)		SHG (Total)		No. of SHG Formed				KVIC	
		Achievement		Achievement		Achievement		Achievement		NABARD Linkage	SHPI	SGSY	Total	Achievement	
		No.	Amount	No.	Amount	No.	Amount	No.	Amount					No.	Amount
1.	Dumka	147	2637	0	0	96	15661	243	18298	51	0	53	104	2	1400
2.	Jamtara	9	468	0	0	15	450	24	918	18	0	19	37	0	0
3.	Deoghar	45	1355	2	85	44	2289	91	3729	99	0	63	162	3	1435
4.	Godda	32	623	0	0	56	2660	88	3283	14	0	48	62	2	1190
5.	Sahibganj	3	75	0	0	50	5896	53	5971	4	0	50	54	0	0
6.	Pakur	5	87	0	0	82	9878	87	9965	7	0	16	23	0	0
7.	Garhwa	17	640	3	400	69	5491	89	6531	5	14	92	111	1	3
8.	Latehar	53	1120	2	40	182	4900	237	6060	18	23	339	380	0	0
9.	Paiamau	26	484	10	250	191	10534	227	11268	1	103	67	171	4	1586
	Total	337	7489	17	775	785	57759	1139	66023	217	140	747	1104	12	5614

TABLE 1 (*Contd.*)

(Rs. in thousand)

Sl. No.	District	General Purpose Credit Card (GCC)		SCC		
		Achievement		Target No.	Achievement	
		No.	Amount		No.	Amount
1.	Dumka	56	1400	110	316	7828
2.	Jamtara	26	700	60	83	2576
3.	Deoghar	41	1000	75	93	2123
4.	Godda	43	1100	80	326	7160
5.	Sahibganj	38	1000	60	313	7805
6.	Pakur	26	700	45	199	3999
7.	Garhwa	65	100	73	226	5565
8.	Latehar	46	1200	36	26	611
9.	Palamau	83	2100	221	170	4293
	Total	364	9300	750	1754	41650

IV. PROBLEMS

- Location of some of the RRBs is not in keeping with the principles enunciated in this respect. Wrong location may create new problems of co-ordination.
- Around 29 out of the 196 RRBs are incurring losses and in a majority of case their net worth is wiped out.
- Problems relate to mobilization of deposits and profitability of the RRBs. In case loaning is confined to weaker sections, the more affluent sections of farmers may not come forward to deposit their savings with these banks. Hence, costlier funds will have to come from the sponsoring banks. Besides, the lower rate of lending will make it almost impossible to earn any profits. As a result, the long-run viability of the banks will be doubtful.
- The RRBs have followed, in main, the methods of operation they had borrowed from the sponsoring banks. It is no wonder that these procedures have failed to find favour with the rural masses.
- A State Bank of India Group, evaluating the performance of RRBs, has noted the following shortcomings.

- Credit appraisal in many branches has not been satisfactory. Certain advances were granted without proper assessment of needs of the borrowers, cash accruals and repaying capacity.
- In certain cases, there was nothing on record to indicate that the presentation inspections were conducted by the officials before sanctioning of advances.
- Disbursements were made in stages without verifying the progress of work.
- Documents executed by the borrowers were incomplete.
- Stock statement had not been obtained regularly from the borrowers and where advances were granted against hypothecation of vehicles, the vehicles were not inspected.
- The problems of effectively reaching the masses remain unsolved. In other word, RRBs as they are cannot be expected to become genuinely rural in their outlook and operations.

V. Prospects

The V.G.B. is a Regional Rural Bank functioning in the two most backward divisions of Jharkhand. The V.G.B. has both challenges and opportunities. It has many operational problems. One of the main problems is related to mobilisation of deposits and profitability. The main motto of establishment of V.G.B. is to finance the most weaker section. As a result, the more affluent sections of farmers do not come forward to deposit their savings with this bank. The weaker sections have nothing to deposit. They have only to take loans from the banks. So the banks have to face the problem of liquidity and profitability. It is the dark side of the picture and that is temporary. The Regional Rural Banks have ample opportunities. So long as weaker sections are not strengthened, the problem of profitability will remain there. Awareness and persuation will make them savers and then the problem of liquidity will end gradually. The Reserve Bank of India, the sponsoring Bank and the State Government should come forward to make the fund available to the RRBs. The V.G.B. has to cover the major portion of the population, round about 72 per cent. In a nutshell, V.G.B. is not a forgotten army as lightly quoted in financial circles. It is forborn fighters and need to be commissioned for active ware against poverty and unemployment. Thus, the prospects of Vananchal Gramin Bank is very shining.

VI. Conclusion

Jharkhand is a new state. It has been carved out from Bihar. Jharkhand economy is rural-based economy. The two divisions of Jharkhand namely—Santhal Parganas and Palamau are the most backward divisional segments of Jharkhand dominated by Schedule tribes. These regions are still traditional non-monetized regions. Poverty stricken people are in utmost need of financial help. The percentage of poverty striken people among tribals is 72 which is just double of national average percentage. Under such deplorable circumstances the VGB is seen as a ray of hope. Despite the problems in supplying credit to the farmers, labourers and artisans the VGB's role in the rural development praiseworthy.

References

All India Rural Credit Survey Report, Vol. 1, Part II, Bombay, 1953, 186.

Annual Report (2nd) of V.G.B. 2007-08.

Bose, Sukanya (2005), "Regional Rural Banks: The Past and The Present Debate," Macro Scan, URL: http// www.macroscan.com/fet/ii105/ fet200705 RRB Debate.htm.

Charlie Macdonald, Cooperative in Bihar, 1971.

Dhingra, Ishwarchand, "The Indian Economy; Environment and Policy," Sultaṇ Chand & Sons, New Delhi, 2006.

District Census Hand Book, 2007, Santhal Pargana.

Economic Outlook for 2007-08.

Malhotra, Rakesh (2002): "Performance of India's Regional Rural Banks (RRBs): Effect of The Umbilical Cord."

Role of the Regional Rural Banks for Economic and Social Upliftment of Rural Society

Ms. Meenakshi Sharma, Ms. Bhawana Tyagi and Mr. Tarun Sharma

Rural Banking in India started since the establishment of banking sector in India. Rural Banks in those days mainly focused upon the agro sector. Regional rural banks in India penetrated every corner of the country and extended a helping hand in the growth process of the country.

National Bank for Agriculture and Rural Development (NABARD) is a development bank in the sector of Regional Rural Banks in India. It provides and regulates credit and gives service for the promotion and development of rural sectors mainly agriculture, small-scale industries, cottage and village industries, handicrafts. It also finances rural crafts and other allied rural economic activities to promote integrated rural development. It helps in securing rural prosperity and its connected matters.

State Bank of India has 30 Regional Rural Banks in India known as RRBs. The rural banks of SBI are spread in 13 states extending from Kashmir to Karnataka and Himachal Pradesh to

North-East. The total number of SBI's Regional Rural Banks in India branches is 2349 (16%). Till date in rural banking in India, there are 14,475 rural banks in the country of which 2126 (91%) are located in remote rural areas.

The Government of India, in July 1975, appointed a Working Group to study in depth the problem of devising alternative agencies to provide institutional credit to the rural people in the context of steps then initiated under the 20 Point Economic Programme. The Working Group identified various weaknesses of the co-operative credit agencies and the commercial banks and felt that these institutions would not be able to fill the regional and functional gaps in the rural credit system within a reasonable period of time. The Group therefore recommended a new type of institution which combines. Firstly, Local feel and familiarity with rural (possess) problems which co-operative banks. Secondly, Degree of business organization ability to mobilise deposit, access to money market and modernised outlook which commercial banks have. Thus, it was envisaged to combine desirable qualities of co-operative banks and commercial banks in RRBs at the same time, it was emphasised that the role of RRBs would be to supplement and not supplant the other institutional agencies already existing in the field.

The Government of India promulgated the Regional Rural Banks Ordinance on 26th September 1975, which was later replaced by the Regional Rural Bank Act, 1976. The preamble to the Act states the objective to develop rural economy by providing credit and facilities for the development of agriculture, trade, commerce, industry and other productive activities in the rural areas, particularly to small and marginal farmers, agricultural labourers, artisans and small entrepreneurs. The RRB Act empowers the Central Government to open the banks from time to time at places where it may consider it necessary. A Regional Rural Bank is jointly owned by the Government of India, the Government of concerned state and public sector bank, which sponsored it. The authorised capital of each bank is Rs. 1 crores (subsequently raised 5 crores) with paid-up capital Rs. 25 lacs (subsequently increased to Rs. 1 crore) which is held by them in the proportion of 50, 15 and 35 per cent respectively. Each bank carries the banking business within the local limits specified by the Government notification. Every RRB may undertake some types of functions: Firstly, The granting of loans and advances particularly to small and marginal farmers and agricultural labourers individually or to a group, co-operative societies, agricultural processing societies, co-operative farming societies, etc. Secondly, the granting of loans and advances to artisans, small entrepreneurs and small traders, businessmen, etc.

The Reserve Bank of India has brought RRB's under the ambit of priority sector lending on par with the commercial banks. They have to ensure that forty per cent of their advances are accounted for the priority sector. Within the 40% priority target, 25% should go to weaker section or 10% of their total advances to go to weaker section.

From a modest beginning with 6 RRBs in 1975, as many as 196 RRBs were operating in 500 districts with a network of 14,313 branches as on 31 March, 2001 excluding satellite branches and extension counters. The branch network comprises 6 metropolitan, 348 urban, 1875 semi-urban and 12,084 rural branches. RRBs have a large branch network in the rural area, which forms nearly 37% of the total rural branch network of all scheduled commercial banks.

The rural banking system with 196 banks and 14,300 branches, employing 70,000 staff is catering to the remote villages. There are six crore account holders and the turnover is a whopping Rs. 70,000 crore. RRB's operate under the regulatory supervision of NABARD. NABARD has the responsibility of laying down the policies for RRBs, to oversee their operations, provide refinance facilities, to monitor their performance and attend to their problems. These banks, which at the outset adopted lower scales of compensation for their staff than their sponsor banks, were specially mandated to lend to weaker sections at rates of interest with a concessional element. They could initially manage to lend at concessional rates because of their access to subsidised refinance from their sponsor banks and NABARD. But the RRBs were crippled soon enough by several factors among which was a new compensation policy in pursuance of which they had to pay their employees on par with those of their sponsor banks. Their character as low cost institutions specially designed to serve rural areas was thus lost irretrievably. They were also adversely affected by the problems of mounting overdues and uneasy industrial relations.

Other Deficiencies of RRBs are as under:

1. According to Narasimham Committee, RRBs have low earning capacity. They have not been able to earn much profits in view of their policy of providing low cost loans.
2. According to RBI, recovery position of RRBs is not satisfactory. There are a large number of defaulters.
3. Their cost of operation has been high on account of the increase in the salary scales of the employees of these banks in line with the salary structure of the employees of commercial banks.
4. In most cases these banks followed the same methods of operation and procedures as followed by commercial banks. Therefore, these procedures have not found favour with the rural masses.
5. In many cases banks have not been located at the right place. For instance, the sponsoring banks are also running their branches in the same areas where RRBs are operating.

RRBs were set-up by an ordinance promulgated by the President of India. Why? Three decades have passed since five RRBs were set-up on 2nd October 1975. These five: The Government of India, at that point of time, thought that in order to provide credit to the agriculture sector, to provide credit to the rural artisans, to the marginal farmers, there should be a separate bank, a rural bank. The main object of setting up of rural banks in 1975 was to help the rural people and the farmers. Seventy per cent of the people are living in rural areas and majority of this population is depending on agriculture. We have the rural industries and traditional industries. We have lakhs and lakhs of rural artisans and weavers. The Government of India felt that there should be some institutional mechanism to help the people, particularly, who are in the agricultural sector and who are in the rural industrial sector.

A working group was constituted prior to promulgation of ordinance, prior to setting up of regional rural banks and that working group submitted its report on 31st July 1975. That working group recommended for setting up of State sponsored region-based rural-oriented commercial banks, which would lend the rural touch, local feeling and familiarity with the rural problems and low cost profile with the professional discipline, ability to mobilise deposits and access to central money markets and the modernised outlook of commercial banks. In a sense, it was an experiment to hybridize commercial banking culture with a rural ethos. This is the backbone, or this was the main object for which these rural banks were set-up in 1975, that is, commercial banking culture with rural ethos

Today, farmers are committing suicide. We have not seen five years ago instances of 10,000, 12,000, or 13,000 farmers committing suicide. The farmers of Andhra Pradesh, Maharashtra, Karnataka, and even in some districts of Kerala have committed suicide. Even in Punjab, farmers have committed suicide. This is because there has been deceleration in the activities and in the role which these institutions should have played. If we go through the figures of rural credit, we could see how gradually it has reduced. As a result of this, the farmers had fallen into debt trap. As the farmers were not getting remunerative prices or even fair prices, they were not in a position to repay the loans which they had taken from the moneylenders. So RRBs should take adequate steps to solve this problem.

They were forced to commit suicides. We will have to realise this situation. There is a change in the Government that means the change in the policy also. So, these institutions have to be strengthened. 'Strengthened' means the objects for which these institutions were set-up in 1975. If the commercial banks were capable to provide assistance to the people living in the rural areas, then there was no need for having a separate bank for these people. That need was felt at that time, some 30 years back. Today, we will have to discuss and we will have to see whether we have been able to achieve those objects or not or we will have to traverse faster to achieve those targets.

Our main object should be to raise the people above the poverty line. In that respect, the Regional Rural Banks can play a vital role. So, with restructuring its organisation, the experience that we have gathered during the last 30 years of its existence was that from five RRBs it has grown up to 196 RRBs. So, we have to see how the economic condition of those people can be better-off who are living below the poverty line. That should be the main object when restructure or reorganisation or strengthening of RRBs will be taken into consideration.

The problem that we are today facing with the existing structure of the RRBs is absence of the unity of command and unity of approach which is expected of the proposed State-level banks under independent, Shri Pranab Mukherjee was the Minister of Finance at that time. While moving the RRB Bill for consideration he said: "The sponsor banks are entrusted with the duty of aiding and assisting the RRBs not only by subscribing to the share capital of the bank but in the recruitment and training of the personnel during the first years of the functioning of the RRBs. The sponsor bank will also provide managerial and financial assistance to the RRB." It is only Rs. 500 crore. I do not know what is the managerial assistance that is being provided. That was the object of providing a sponsor bank for each RRB. But that object was not fulfilled.

Another committee was constituted by the Reserve Bank of India under the Chairmanship of Shri B.S. Vyas. He also recommended for restructuring of RRBs. He has also recommended continuation of RRBs and also retaining their regional character and rural focus. He has said that the mandate has to continue. What was the mandate? Even as they need to be restructured into viable financial institutions, simultaneously, their regional character and rural focus should be retained. The Tenth Plan target of four per cent growth in agriculture leads to a projected credit demand of Rs. 7 lakh crore. Even if their share in it is eight per cent to nine per cent, RRBs would have to deal with Rs. 66,000 crore or more during the Tenth Five Year Plan. Their role would be important because of their strong rural branch infrastructure of more than 14,000 branches and rural orientation of their staff. While moving the Bill, the then Finance Minister had stated that the staff also would be from the rural areas, having rural orientation.

A number of committees were appointed, and recommendations made by them since 1985. A large number of working groups were also appointed to go into this issue. The Reserve Bank of India (RBI) has also made recommendations on this issue, but the Government has not taken any positive decision with regard to the reorganisation and strengthening of the Regional Rural Banks (RRB). Now, there is a need to do it, as it is overdue. A delay of 30 years is not a small period. We have gathered enough experience in this area, and with this experience, today, the rural banks are playing a very vital role with regard to providing lending support to the rural areas. The economic condition of 70 per cent of the people to be raised.

As way back in 1975, five Regional Rural Banks were set-up; the objective behind setting up those RRBs was really very nice because always in this august House we have been talking about the development of rural economy and we are talking about the people residing in rural areas. So, setting up of RRBs in 1975 was really a milestone in our economy.

REVIEW OF LITERATURE

A number of studies related to regional rural banks and rural economy have been conducted by economists at micro and macro-level. Their main finding have been discussed in the following:

Menon (1969) Suggested a rural credit scheme for India. Various schemes started by the Reserve Bank of India equate rural credit with agricultural credit. A rural community may acquire an additional wealth only when its produce is sold outside itself and the conditions are, therefore, conducive to economic stagnation in the rural areas. He further suggested that a sound rural credit scheme for India may provide finance not only for agriculture, fishery, rural industry, rural trade, rural transport, and all other economic activities of the countryside.

Bisen (1971) Examined the role of cooperative movement in meeting the short-term and medium-term credit needs of the farmers. Despite the increasing role of cooperatives in providing rural household credit, moneylenders of both types—agriculturist and professional, still occupy the first rank in meeting the financial requirements of rural households. (28 per cent of the cooperative credit is diverted by farmers to non-productive purposes.) According to him in Uttar Pradesh agriculturist money-lenders provide 36 per cent of rural credit, professional money-lenders provide 20 per cent and cooperative provide 17 per cent of agricultural credit.

The study (1978) revealed that within a short span of time the Regional Rural Banks have demonstrated their capability to serve the purposes for which they were established. The superiority of these Banks is derived from their relatively lower cost of operation, simplicity and low profile, local participation in management, familiarity of local staff and close association of the district level agricultural and rural development agencies. The study concluded that the Regional Rural Banks with some modifications in their organizations and functions can become very useful component in the totality of the rural credit structure.

Charan Das Wadhwa (1980) makes an analysis of the working of RRBs in India with two case studies in 1980. The major portion of the field work for the study was undertaken in May 1977 immediately after the establishment of the new institution of the RRBs in 1975.

The study (1981) emphasized that the Regional Rural Banks so far have been able to achieve the main objective of helping the weaker sections in the rural areas, namely, small and marginal farmers, landless agricultural labourers and rural artisans by providing credit to suit their requirements despite the constraint of a limited area of operation. The study revealed that the working group on rural banks has suggested that the viability of Regional Rural Banks is to be judged not only in financial terms but also from the size of their area of operation, the scope for development which the area of operation promises, and the efforts made by Regional Rural Banks at expanding and extending the area of rural credit.

Tripathi (1984) analysed the socio-economic status of beneficiaries who fall under integrated Rural Development Programme (IRDP) and the efforts made by the banks in improving their standard of living. The farmers equipped with better financial resources derived most of the benefits of new development schemes. The shortage of finance has been identified as a major constraint in cases of marginal and small farmers to change over to innovative practices of cultivation. The landless labourers, rural artisans and other weaker sections of the rural population have been put in the most disadvantageous position due to financial scarcity and their participation in the rural development programme has been found almost negligible.

According to the **World Bank** (2003) point out that the most important move to face the agriculturists from the clutches of the money lenders was the expansion of institutional credit to agriculture. The government has helped the co-operatives in a number of ways to expand their operations. In an important move, 14 major commercial banks were nationalized in 1969 and this was followed by the nationalization of 6 more banks in 1980. There are more than 30,000 commercial bank branches, 14,000 regional rural banks and about 1,00,000 rural credit co-operatives. This translates to about 4,700 people served by each RFL outlet.

Selva Kumar (2005) observed that the economy of our nation is based on rural India because 70 per cent of the people are dependent upon agriculture. The institutional finance to agriculture which constituted 22 per cent of the GDP in 2003-04 is inadequate. The commercial banks are closing down their rural branches and are concentrating on profit. Organised lending by the government institutions is necessary so as to recover the villagers from debt and poverty and to improve the employment opportunities and productivity. In this context, the Regional Rural Banks are specially suited to monitor regional development by providing financial assistance to the weaker sections of the society.

P. Chidambaram, Finance Minister (2006) revealed that I am prepared to go the extra mile to come to the aid of our farmers. To begin with, I propose to grant some relief to the farmers who have availed of crop loans form scheduled commercial banks, RRBs and PACS for Rabi 2005-06. Accordingly, an amount equal to two percentage points of the borrower's interest liability on the principal amount up to Rs. 100,000 will be credited to his/her bank account before March 31, 2006, have provided a sum of Rs. 1,700 crore for this purpose. I hope the House will welcome this exceptional gesture of the Government.

Objective of the Study

The aim of the study is to evaluate the role of RRB's in economic upliftment of weaker sections of the rural society. The main object of the establishment of RRB's were to provide banking facilities of rural sector and to develop the rural economy by providing financial assistance particularly to small and marginal farmers, agricultural labourers, rural artisans, retail traders and other persons of small means. The chief objectives of the study are summarized as follows:

- To find out the credit requirement of the weaker sections of the rural society in the district.

- To identify the problem faced by borrowers in getting loans.
- To study the attitude of borrowers regarding repayment of loans.
- To mobilize rural savings and channelise them for supporting productive activities in the rural areas.

REFERENCES

Sharma, K.K., *Reserve Bank of India and Rural Credit*, Premier Publishing Co.

Shekhar, K.C., *Banking Theory and Practice*, Vikas Publishing House, New Delhi.

Singh, Ajit, *Rural Development and Banking in India*, Deep & Deep Publications, New Delhi.

Srivastava, A.K., *Integrated Rural Development Programme in India*, Deep & Deep Publications, New Delhi.

Srivastava, R.M., *Management of Banks*, Pragati Prakashan, Meerut.

Tyagi, B.P., *Agricultural Economics and Rural Development*, Jai Prakash Nath Publication, Meerut.

Upadhyaya, R., *Management of Commercial Banks in India*, Deep & Deep Publications, New Delhi, 1985.

Wadhwa, C.D., *Rural Banks for Rural Development*, The Macmillan Co. India Ltd., New Delhi, 1980.

Economic and Social Impact of Regional Rural Banks (RRBs)

Dr. Pratibha Kushwaha

INTRODUCTION

Regional Rural Banks were established on the 26th September 1975 and the RRB Act, 1976 with an objective to ensure sufficient institutional credit for agriculture and other rural sectors. The RRB mobilize financial resources from rural/semi-urban areas and grant loans and advances mostly to small and marginal farmers, agricultural labourers and rural artisans. The area of operation of RRBs is limited to the area as notified by GoI covering one or more districts in the State.

The Regional Rural Banks have been affecting Rural Society since decades. Various positive effects have been noticed on Rural Society in Social as well as Economic sector. Rural Society is much stronger and powerful in terms of getting facilities and giving better output as it was never before.

Some key points which can make it clear to understand the "upliftment of weaker sections with help of RRBs" are as follows:

1. Objective of Regional Rural Banks

The main objective of setting up of RRBs was to provide institutional credit to the weaker sections especially to the small and marginal farmers, agricultural labourers, artisans and small entrepreneurs in the rural areas and bring about growth with social justice to the rural poor. Regional Rural Bank in India was set-up with the purpose of facilitating the promotion of rural business in India. The Regional Rural Banks in India are spread all across the country and have been playing an important part in the development and growth of the rural business and economy. In the early 1970s, the Government observed that despite a wide banking network and developmental initiatives in the first 25 years since Independence, a critical gap still existed in meeting the credit needs of the rural poor. To find a solution, the Government appointed a working group on rural credit, the Narasimham Committee, in July 1975. The committee observed that the cost structure of commercial banks, the attitude of bank employees and the lack of a professional approach in the co-operative credit system were the main stumbling blocks to rural credit.

The committee also observed that the deposits collected by banks from rural areas were not totally deployed there. The panel, therefore, recommended the creation of a new set of regionally-oriented rural banks which would combine a co-operative's local feel and a commercial bank's business acumen.

The Government accepted these recommendations and, accordingly, the ordinance of Regional Rural Banks, 1975 was promulgated on September 26, 1975. This was replaced by the Regional Rural Banks Act, 1976 on February 9, 1976. The mandate of these rural financial institutions were to:

- take banking to the doorsteps of the rural masses, particularly in areas without banking facilities;
- make available cheaper institutional credit to the weaker sections of society, who were to be the only clients of these banks;
- mobilize rural savings and canalize them for supporting productive activities in rural areas;

- generate employment opportunities in the rural areas; and
- bring down the cost of providing credit in rural areas.

With partnerships with the Central Government (50 per cent), State governments (15 per cent) and commercial banks (35 per cent), the number of RRBs rose from just six in 1975 to 196 by 1987, covering 476 districts. They financed only the weaker sections of the rural community — small and marginal farmers, agricultural labourers, small traders, and so on.

2. Meaning and Definition of RRBs

A rural bank is a financial institution that helps rationalize the developing regions or developing country to finance their needs specially the projects regarding agricultural progress.

3. Root Cause for the Idea

The RRBs were established "with a view to developing the rural economy by providing, for the purpose of development of agriculture, trade, commerce, industry and other productive activities in the rural areas, credit and other facilities, particularly to small and marginal farmers, agricultural labourers, artisans and small entrepreneurs, and for matters connected therewith and incidental thereto."

Inception of Regional Rural Banks (RRBs) can be seen as a unique experiment as well as experience in improving the efficacy of rural credit delivery mechanism in India.

4. Establishment of Regional Rural Banks

The RRBs have been set-up under the Regional Rural Banks Act of 1976. The public sector banks in India have been empowered to sponsor RRBs by participating in their capital and also organizing and staffing them in the initial stages.

5. Regional Rural Banks as a Strong Pillar

Since their inception RRBs have been acting like a strong support to promote comparatively less healthy section of Indian community. RRBs participated enthusiastically in poverty alleviation schemes (IRDP, for example) and disadvantaged area (drought-prone regions and deserts) development programmes. They quickly became an important and integral part of the rural credit system. However, their financial viability was initially overstretched by policy rigidities coupled with a low capital base in an environment of inadequate infrastructure and deeper social and economic disparities.

As at end-March 2003, there were 196 RRBs spread over 23 States/Union Territories and with a network of 14,350 branches, accounting for 44.5 per cent of the total rural network of all scheduled commercial banks (including RRBs). The rural and semi-urban branches of RRBs constitute 98 per cent of their network. Their deposits and advances as on March 31, 2003, were Rs. 49,078 crore and Rs. 22,028 crore respectively.

Thus, RRBs have done well in mobilizing rural deposits and infusing the thrift habit in their clients. The bulk of the loans from RRBs have been to priority sectors, which accounted for over 70 per cent of the total. Agriculture alone took up 46 per cent of the priority sector advances. The involvement of RRBs in providing credit support to small and retail trade and other non-farm rural activities is better than that of co-operatives and commercial banks.

6. Past and Present of RRBs

Regional Rural Banking in India has entered its third phase, after the first two phases of rapid expansion and neo-liberal reforms, respectively. While the third phase is distinguished in terms of the few attempts to strike a balance in the conundrum of 'viability *versus* outreach', a decisive break from the policies aimed at liberalization of banking is indispensable to a 'bank-led equitable rural growth' strategy.

By 1991, there were 196 RRBs with over 14,000 predominantly rural branches in 476 districts with an average coverage of three villages per branch. These banks had disbursed over Rs. 3,500 crore in credit and mobilized over Rs. 4,100 crore in deposits. Perhaps the most significant achievement of the RRBs during this period was in enabling the weaker sections of the rural community access to institutional credit. The bulk of the loans from RRBs were to the priority sectors, which accounted for over 70 per cent of the total. Agriculture and allied activities took up more than 50 per cent of the total advances. In addition, the RRBs were instrumental in extending credit for poverty alleviation schemes

The year 1990 marks the end of the expansion phase of regional banking, beyond which there has been no growth in the number of Regional Rural Banks (including branches).

7. Impact on Social and Economic Factors of Comparatively Weaker Sections in India

The importance of the rural banking in the economic development of a country cannot be overlooked. As Gandhiji said "Real India lies in villages," and village economy is the backbone of Indian economy. Without the upliftment of the rural economy as well as the rural people of our country, the objectives of economic planning cannot be achieved. In fact, the real growth of Indian economy lied in the emancipation of rural masses from acute poverty, unemployment, and socio-economic backwardness. The development of the rural sector is important for the economic growth of India. As India is an agrarian economy, the growth of the rural sector and the promotion of agricultural sector would give the economy a boost. The State Bank of India is one of the major commercial banks having regional rural banks. There are 30 Regional Rural Banks in India, under the State Bank of India and it is spread in 13 states across India. The number of branches of the SBI Regional Rural Banks is more than 2000.

A. Impact on Economic Factor

The Indian economy grew at an estimated 3.7 per cent in 2002-03 against 5.6 per cent in the previous year. This was largely because of the negative growth of 4.4 per cent in the agriculture sector. This steep fall in GDP highlights the vulnerability of the Indian economy to the performance of the agricultural sector. This is despite other macroeconomic indicators and sectors gaining in strength.

The Tenth Plan (2002-07) has set an ambitious average GDP

growth of 8 per cent per annum. To achieve this, it is important to revitalize and revamp not only the agricultural sector but also rural financial institutions. An annual average growth of 7 per cent from this secton alone in the next five years is crucial for achieving the GDP target.

The Task Force on Rural Credit for the Tenth Plan has projected institutional credit flow to agriculture and allied activities at Rs. 7,36,570 crore for 2002-07, which is more than treble (320 per cent) the credit flow (Rs. 2,29,853 crore) during the Ninth Plan (1997-2002).

The agriculture sector is emerging as part of the new economic order arising out of globalization and implementation of the Agreement on Agriculture (AoA) under the World Trade Organization (WTO). If some agreement is reached at the WTO negotiations, the agriculture sector in the country would be poised for a radical transformation. To withstand the global competition, enhanced productivity and sustainability of the sector has become imperative.

B. Impact on Social Factor

Apart from the State Bank of India, several other banks also functions as the promoter of rural development in India. The Regional Rural Banks in India has affected Indian social factors also. For example:

Support to Art and Craft

RRBs have been acting like a promoting tool for Rural Art and Craft business. Rural people are being supported by these banks to continue their family business.

Support to Small Scale Industries

Rural people run small scale industries, as they are getting loans from Regional Rural Banks without many formalities to start and run these industries.

Support to Co-operative Societies

Co-operative societies are quite useful for women to get employed. Regional Rural Banks also help in running and maintain these societies.

Support to Agriculture

Agriculture is a social as well as an economic factor. Being in agriculture field is much easier than ever before. New machineries and new techniques are making it easier to grow in this sector.

House Loans

The proposals relating to housing loans on mortgage guarantee and reverse mortgage are positive from a long-term perspective. The government will put in place regulations for the creation of mortgage guarantee companies, which typically provide protection to the lenders. Lenders would therefore be able to offer mortgage loans with higher loan-to-value (LTV) or lower down payments, which we believe is a positive for the housing finance sector.

National Housing Bank (NHB) will shortly introduce 'reverse mortgage' for senior citizens. Reverse mortgage is similar to a housing loan except that in a home loan the borrower pays a fixed equated monthly instalment (EMI) to the lending institution, while in reverse mortgage, the lender pays the borrower a fixed sum of money on a monthly (or quarterly) basis, the total payment being equal to the value of the property and the interest on the loaned amount. After the death of the borrower and the borrower's spouse, the housing company sells the property to recover the amount paid out along with interest at a rate similar to interest on housing loans.

Human Resources

Much of the RRB staff was recruited during the initial stages and there has been a ban on fresh recruitment since 1992. The staff is getting older whereas the complexities and demands of rural banking now call for more dynamism and youthful talent. Rural banking has emerged as a niche, wherein special skills and sensitivity are required. Therefore, the imposed ban on fresh recruitment should be reviewed at the earliest to enhance and diversify the business of RRBs.

Also, RRBs should be permitted to recruit specialists in the technology and agriculture fields. Similarly, grants/soft loans may be provided for technology so as to enable RRBs to compete with commercial/private banks that invest heavily in technology projects. The technology induction in rural banking would facilitate handling low-value, high-volume business effectively in a more cost-effective manner.

8. An Overview

Regional Rural Banks have been producing good impact on Indian socio-economic factors. Rural conditions are better than ever before. The other Regional Rural Banks in India which are affecting Rural India in progressive way are as follows:

Haryana State Cooperative Apex Bank Limited

The main purpose of the Haryana State Cooperative Apex Bank Limited is to financially assist the artisans in the rural areas, farmers and agrarian unskilled labor, and the small rural entrepreneurs of Haryana. Haryana State Cooperative Apex Bank Limited also referred as the HARCOBANK, is one of the apex organizations in the state of Haryana.

National Bank for Agriculture and Rural Development

The main purpose of the National Bank for Agriculture and Rural Development is to provide credit for the development and publicity of small scaled industries, handicrafts, rural crafts, village industries, cottage industries, agriculture, etc. The NABARD also supports all other related economic operations in the rural sector, promotion of sustainable growth in the rural sector. The NABARD also plays the role of a contributor to the rural development by the means of promoting institutional development, facilitating refinance to loan providers in the rural sector, inspection, monitoring, and evaluation of client financial corporations. National Bank for Agriculture and Rural Development (NABARD) was established as the premiere rural development bank.

Sindhanur Urban Souharda Co-operative Bank

The main purpose of the Sindhanur Urban Souharda Co-operative Bank is to provide financial support to the rural sector. The Sindhanur Urban Souharda Co-operative Bank is more commonly known as the SUCO Bank.

United Bank of India

The role played by the United Bank of India (UBI) as one of the regional rural banks is phenomenal. The UBI has propagated the network of branches in order to actively take part in the rural improvement and development.

Syndicate Bank

The Syndicate Bank has its grass roots in the rural sector. The development of the Syndicate Bank was in accordance to the development of the banking sector in India. The Syndicate Bank has performed actively in the development of the rural sector in India.

9. CONCLUTION

Regional Rural Banks since they have started almost four decades now and they have been proved as pillars and helping hand for weaker section in India. Rural Societies can rely on these banks for their monetary needs at times. To sum up, the mandate for the Regional Rural Banks still is largely relevant. Even 27 years since being instituted, the socio-economic conditions of the majority of the rural population continue to be a cause of concern for policy-makers of the country, especially in the post-reforms, WTO-mandated era.

Therefore, the requirement for a strong and flexible structure for rural financial institutions like RRBs in rural and semi-urban segments cannot be overemphasized. Financial sector reforms without social and rural sensitivity would only aggravate the complexities of agrarian sector reforms, which are yet to take shape. The proposed Farmers' Commission and the Vyas Committee constituted by the RBI need to look into these issues comprehensively to strengthen the rural credit-delivery mechanism.

REFERENCES

Indian Economy, Ishwar C. Dhingra.
The State of Indian Economy, V.B. Jugale and Y.V. Jugale.
The Performance of RRBs in India, Biswa Swarup Misra.
Saving The RRBs, Jayati Ghosh.

RRBs: The Present and Past Debate, Sukanya Bose.
RRBs: Need a Shot in the Arm, V. Jagan Mohan.
http://www.economictimes.times of India.com
http://www.indiatoqether.org
http://www.indiastudycentre.com
http://www.thehindubusinessline.com
http://www.rediff.com/money
http://www.manaqementparadise.com
http://www.chanqemakers.net
http://www.atypon-link.com
http://www.baqchee.com

Regional Rural Banks—Role in Agricultural Sector

Ms. Preeti Chhabra and Ms. Priya Mittal

INTRODUCTION

India is mainly an agricultural country. Agriculture accounts for approximately 33 per cent of India's G.D.P. and employs nearly 62 per cent of the population. It accounts for 8.56% of India's export. About 43% of India's geographical area is used for agriculture activity.

The present agricultural growth rate is not sufficient to guarantee food security to the growing population, generate more employment and remove poverty, which is concentrated in the rural sector and create an export surplus to achieve balance in external payments (H.B. Shivamaggi, 2000).

Since the days of the Rural Credit Survey Committee (1954), India has come a long way in its search for an appropriate rural banking set-up. Since then one committee after another has examined this problem. In order overcome this situation. The Govt. of India, in July 1975, appointed a Working Group to study in depth the problem of devising alternative agencies to provide institutional credit to the rural people in the context of steps then initiated under the 20 Point Economic Programme. The Working Group identified various weaknesses of the co-operative credit agencies and the commercial banks and felt that these institutions would not be able to fill the regional and functional gaps in the rural credit system within a reasonable period of time.

Therefore, Government of India promulgated the Regional Rural Banks Ordinance on 26th September 1975, which was later replaced by the Regional Rural Bank Act, 1976. The Regional Rural Banks in India are the major investors in different types of operations in the rural areas. The concept of rural banking in India dates back to the time when the banking sector was set-up in India. Regional Rural Banks in India were set-up with the purpose of facilitating the promotion of rural business in India. The Regional Rural Banks in India are spread all across the country and have been playing an important part in the development and growth of the rural business and economy. The development of the rural sector is important for the economic growth of India. As India is an agrarian economy, the growth of the rural sector and the promotion of agricultural sector would give the economy a boost.

The State Bank of India is one of the major commercial banks having regional rural banks. There are 30 Regional Rural Banks in India, under the State Bank of India and it is spread in 13 states across India. The number of branches the SBI Regional Rural Banks is more than 2000.

Several other banks, apart from the State Bank of India also functions as the promoter of rural development in India. The other Regional Rural Banks in India are:

Haryana State Cooperative Apex Bank Limited

The main purpose of the Haryana State Cooperative Apex Bank Limited is to financially assist the artisans in the rural areas, farmers and agrarian unskilled labor, and the small rural entrepreneurs of Haryana.

National Bank for Agriculture and Rural Development

The main purpose of the National Bank for Agriculture and Rural Development is to provide credit for the development and publicity of small scale industries, handicrafts, rural crafts, village industries, cottage industries, agriculture, etc. The NABARD also supports all other related economic operations in the rural sector, promotion of sustainable growth in the rural sector.

Sindhanur Urban Souharda Co-operative Bank

The main purpose of the Sindhanur Urban Souharda Co-operative Bank is to provide financial support to the rural sector. The Sindhanur Urban Souharda Cooperative Bank is more commonly known as the SUCO Bank.

United Bank of India

The role played by the United Bank of India (UBI) as one of the regional rural banks is phenomenal. The UBI has propagated the network of branches in order to actively take part in the rural improvement and development.

Syndicate Bank

The Syndicate Bank has it grass roots in the rural sector. The development of the Syndicate Bank was in accordance to the development of the banking sector in India and the Syndicate Bank has performed actively in the development of the rural sector in India.

THE AGRICULTURAL SCENE

Indian agriculture is the largest private sector enterprise in the country of over 100 million farmers. It contributes 24% of the countries GDP and provides food to nearly 1 billion people of the country. The sector produces 51 major crops, provides raw material to the country's agro-base industries and contributes nearly 1/7th of its total export earnings.

ISSUES AND CHALLENGES

Although agriculture contributes only 21% of India's GDP, its importance in the country's economic, social and political fabric goes well beyond this indicator. The rural areas are still home to some 72% if the India's 1.1 billion people, a large number of whom are poor. Most of the rural poor depend on rain-fed agriculture and fragile forests for their livelihoods.

Despite its great progress in increasing agricultural production,

India's average yield of cereal crops is less than half that of China and the United States. However, production must be increased without destroying the basic resources of soil and water, if it is to be sustainable, some of the issues are as follows:

Slow Down in Agricultural and Rural Non-Farm Growth

Both the poorest as well as the more prosperous Green Revolution states of Punjab, Haryana and U.P. have recently witnessed a slow-down in agricultural growth. Some of the factors hampering the revival of growth are:

- *Poor composition of public expenditures:* Public spending on agricultural subsidies is crowding out productivity-enhancing investments such as agricultural research and extension, as well as investments in rural infrastructure, and the health and education of the rural people. In 1999/2000, agricultural subsidies amounted to 3 per cent of GDP and were over 7 times the public investments in the sector.
- *Over-regulation of domestic agricultural trade:* While economic and trade reforms in the 1990s helped to improve the incentive framework, over-regulation of domestic trade has increased costs, price risks and uncertainty, undermining the sector's competitiveness.
- *Government interventions in labor, land, and credit markets:* More rapid growth of the rural non-farm sector is constrained by government interventions in factor markets—labour, land, and credit—and in output markets, such as the small-scale reservation of enterprises.

Inadequate Infrastructure and Services in Rural Areas

Weak Framework for Sustainable Water Management and Irrigation: Inequitable allocation of water: Many states lack the incentives, policy, regulatory, and institutional framework for the efficient, sustainable, and equitable allocation of water.

- *Deteriorating irrigation infrastructure:* Public spending in irrigation is spread over many uncompleted projects. In addition, existing infrastructure has rapidly deteriorated as operations and maintenance is given lower priority.

Inadequate Access to Land and Finance

Stringent Land Regulations Discourage Rural Investments

While land distribution has become less skewed, land policy and regulations to increase security of tenure (including restrictions or bans on renting land or converting it to other uses) have had the unintended effect of reducing access by the landless and discouraging rural investments.

- *Computerization of land records has brought to light institutional weaknesses:* State government initiatives to computerize land records have reduced transaction costs and increased transparency, but also brought to light institutional weaknesses.
- *Rural poor have little access to credit:* While India has a wide network of rural finance institutions, many of the rural poor remain excluded, due to inefficiencies in the formal finance institutions, the weak regulatory framework, high transaction costs, and risks associated with lending to agriculture.

Weak Natural Resources Management

One quarter of India's population depends on forests for at least part of their livelihoods.

- *A purely conservation approach to forests is ineffective:* Experience in India shows that a purely conservation approach to natural resources management does not work effectively and does little to reduce poverty.
- *Weak resource rights for forest communities:* The forest sector is also faced with weak resource rights and economic incentives for communities, an inefficient legal framework and participatory management, and poor access to markets.

Weak Delivery of Basic Services in Rural Areas

Low Bureaucratic Accountability and Inefficient Use of Public Funds

Despite large expenditures in rural development, a highly centralized bureaucracy with low accountability and inefficient use of public funds limit their impact on poverty. In 1992, India amended its Constitution to create three tiers of democratically elected rural local governments bringing governance down to the villages. However, the transfer of authority, funds, and functionaries to these local bodies is progressing slowly, in part due to political vested interests. The poor are not empowered to contribute to shaping public programs or to hold local governments accountable.

REGIONAL RURAL BANKS AND AGRICULTURE SECTOR

On the whole, it has to be admitted that Indian policy-makers have not been able to arrive at a banking structure and operational system which suit the credit and savings needs of agriculturist and at same time promote modern agriculture. N.A. Majumdar goes to the extent of saying " the near total neglect of rural credit by policy-makers during the period 1991-96 is largely attributable to the adverse environment created by the financial sector reforms." (Majumdar, 1999).

M.S. Swaminathan asserts that we now need an "evergreen revolution" producing more on less land and less water. He also says that as anything you do for small farmers, the focus should be on assisting and guiding small farmers (*Frontline*, Jan. 7, 2000). It is in this context that the role of rural banking institutions has to be reconsidered. A series of initiatives have been taken to create a favourable economic environment for the growth of agriculture sector.

CROP INSURANCE

A pilot scheme on seed crop insurance has been launched by the government from the current financial year to provide financial security and income stability to breeders and seed growers. The scheme will help in strengthening confidence and stimulate participation of breeders and seed growers to undertake seed production of newly released hybrid and improver varieties. Breeders, foundation and certified seeds of paddy, wheat, maize, soybeans, sorghum, pearl millet, sunflower, groundnut, gram, red gram and cotton in 10 major states have been covered under the proposed scheme.

CREDIT

Timely and adequate availability of credit is crucial for sustaining the growth of agricultural sector.

Commercial banks have been advised to increase the flow of credit to agriculture, to set-up specialized agriculture branches to deal with high-tech agriculture advances and to extend cash credit facilities for meeting the composite credit requirements of farmers. The capital base of NABARD has been increased to strengthen its financial capability. The weak regional rural banks have been recapitalized.

Credit to agriculture and small scale industrial sector has always commanded special attention, both in terms of policy issues and institution building efforts in view of their recognized importance in our national economy and especially in relation to their employment potential, income redistribution and support to the balance of payments. Narasimham Committee (Committee on Banking Sector Reforms)

BUDGET 2007-08 AND NABARD

Allocation for agriculture and allied activities increased from Rs. 7280 crore in 2006-07 to Rs. 8389 crore in 2007-08.

- *Under Bharat Nirman Programme:* Additional irrigation potential of 24 lakh hectares including 9 lakh hectares under Accelerated Irrigation Benefit Programme with increased allocation of Rs. 11,000 crore for 2007-08 as against Rs. 7121 crore in 2006-07 will be created.
- A sum of Rs. 100 crore allocated for New Rain Fed Area Development Programme.
- *Restoring Water Bodies*: As a follow up of plot project (launched in March 2005) to renovate and restore water

bodies in 13 states, World Bank has signed a loan agreement with Tamil Nadu for Rs. 2182 crore to restore 5763 water bodies having a command area of 4 hectares.

- *Ground Water Recharge*: A sum of Rs. 100 crore will be transferred to NABARD to facilitate creation of 7 million rainwater harvesting structures and dugwells for recharging of ground water. The subsidy (1005 for small and marginal farmers, 50% for other farmers) to be routed to the beneficiaries by NABARD through Lead banks.
- *Training of Farmers*: ICAR and 32 state agri-universities to set-up one teaching-*cum*-demonstration model of water harvesting centers. For this purpose, an interest-free loan of Rs. 3 crore will be given to each institution to create a corpus fund to be used subsequent for farmer's training programme.
- *Agriculture Extension*: A revamped Training and Visit programme to be introduced by MoA in consultation with state governments.
- Rs. 100 crore allocated (Rs. 50 crore each for G.B. Pant Agricultural University, Pantnagar and TNAU, Coimbatore) recognizing excellence in the field of agricultural research.
- Allocation for fertilizer subsidy enhanced from Rs. 17,253 crore (2006-07) to Rs. 22,452 crore (2007-08). Fertilizer industry in consultation with the Department of Fertilizer to conduct a study to find an alternative method of delivering subsidy directly to the farmers.
- *Enhancing Pulse Production*: Focus on increasing the production of breeder, foundation in certified seeds. Indian institute of pulses research, Kanpur and agriculture universities, IFFCO, KRIBCO, NAFED and private companies will be invited to scale up production of such seeds for increasing output of pulses.
- *Plantation Sector*: A Special Purpose Tea Fund has been launched for re-plantation and rejuvenation of tea. A similar financial mechanism for coffee, rubber, spices, cashew and coconut to be put in place.
- *Agricultural Insurance*: Weather-based crop insurance scheme to be introduced by agricultural insurance

corporation on an actuarial bases with an element of subsidy. (Rs. 100 crore allocation for 2007-08)

- To give a flip to the Food Processing Sector customs duties reduced on food processing machinery from 7.5% to 5%. Similar reduction for sprinkler and drip irrigation systems used for agriculture and horticultural purposes.
- Customs duty reduced on crude sunflower oil from 65% to 50% and on refined sunflower oil from 75% to 60%.

Agricultural Credit

- NABARD allow to raise resources to the tune of 5000 crore by issuing Rural Bonds which shall be eligible for suitable tax exemptions.
- *Farm Credit*: Target for 2007-08 fixed at 2,25,000 crore.
- To bring 50 lakh new farmers into the banking fold.
- Continuation of 2% interest subvention for ST crop loans (provision of 1677 crore).
- *Special Plan*: Relating to farm credit is being implemented (a period of 3 years) in the 31 identified distressed districts in four states involving a sum of Rs. 16,979 crores. Of this Rs. 12,400 crores will be on water-related schemes. The plan includes a provision of Rs. 153 crores for induction of high yielding milch animals and related activities to augment subsidiary income to the farmers.
- *Regional Rural Banks*: Branch expansion programme with atleast one branch in 80 uncovered districts. Phased recapitalization of RRBs having negative net worth.
- *RIDF-XIII*: The corpus of the fund raised to 12,000 crore in 2007-08 from 10,000 crore in 2006-07. A separate window for rural roads to continue under RIDF-XIII with a corpus of Rs. 4000 crore.
- *Financial Inclusion Fund* (corpus of Rs. 500 crore) with NABARD for meeting the cost of developmental and promotional intervention.
- *Financial Inclusion Technology fund* (corpus of Rs. 500) to meet the cost of technology adoption. The initial funding for both these funds to be contributed by GOI, RBI and NABARD.

A New Role for RRBs

It is imperative to re-focus the RRBs as development finance entities devoted to rural credit needs. The All India Regional Rural Bank Employees' Associations call to amalgamate all Regional Rural Banks (RRBs) into a single entity is a variation on its suggestion last year to compress all the 196 RRBs into six zonal units presided over by an apex body. There is little doubt that the RRBs need reorganising now more than ever before because they appear to have succeeded in bridging two apparently unbridgeable goals—efficient working with target focusing. That is a good sign; but it also poses a major problem.

Data from the Reserve Bank of India suggest that the RRBs are profitable units after decades of being in the red. In 2004-05, of the 196 units, 167 earned net profits of Rs. 904 crore while 29 incurred losses of Rs. 154 crore. This is in sharp contrast to 1993 when 172 units were in the red. This performance may be credited to the sponsor banks for inculcating a business instinct into the RRBs. Over the years RRBs have turned increasingly to investing; the RBI notes an increase in their investment-deposit ratio from 25 per cent in 2003 to 37 per cent in 2005. But the credit-deposit ratio has been higher, though skewed towards the non-agriculture sector; from 45 per cent in 2003 it has risen to 51 per cent in 2005. A blend of loans to non-agriculture sector and income from investments has brought a number of RRBs into the black. Judged by prudential norms, the RRBs are doing fairly well; they are also catering to the needs of agriculture credit.

PRIORITY AREAS FOR THE WORLD BANK SUPPORT

1. Enhancing Agricultural Productivity, Competitiveness, and Rural Growth

Enhancing productivity: Creating a more productive, internationally competitive and diversified agricultural sector would require a shift in public expenditures away from subsidies towards productivity enhancing investments. Second, it will require removing the restrictions on domestic private trade to improve the investment climate and meet expanding market opportunities. Third, the agricultural research and extension systems need to be strengthened to improve access to productivity enhancing technologies. The diverse conditions across India suggests the importance of regionally differentiated strategies, with a strong focus on the lagging states.

Improving Water Resource and Irrigation/Drainage Management: Increase in multi-sectoral competition for water highlights the need to formulate water policies and unbundle water resources management from irrigation service delivery. Other key priorities include:

(i) modernizing Irrigation and Drainage Departments to integrate the participation of farmers and other agencies in irrigation management;
(ii) improving cost recovery;
(iii) rationalizing public expenditures, with priority to completing schemes with the highest returns; and
(iv) allocating sufficient resources for operations and maintenance for the sustainability of investments.

Strengthening rural non-farm sector growth: Rising incomes are fueling demand for higher-value fresh and processed agricultural products in domestic markets and globally, which open new opportunities for agricultural diversification to higher value products (e.g. horticulture, livestock), agro-processing and related services. The government needs to shift its role from direct intervention and over-regulation to creating the enabling environment for private sector participation and competition for agribusiness and more broadly, the rural non-farm sector growth. Improving the rural investment climate includes removing trade controls, rationalizing labor regulations and the tax regime (i.e. adoption of the value-added tax system), and improving access to credit and key infrastructure (e.g. roads, electricity, ports, markets).

2. Improving Access to Assets and Sustainable Natural Resource Use

Balancing poverty reduction and conservation priorities: Finding win-win combinations for conservation and poverty reduction will be critical to sustainable natural resource management. This will involve addressing legal, policy and institutional constraints to devolving resource rights, and transferring responsibilities to local communities.

Improving access to land: States can build on the growing consensus to reform land policy, particularly land tenancy policy and land administration system. States that do not have tenancy restrictions can provide useful lessons in this regard. Over the longer-term, a more holistic approach to land administration policies, regulations and institutions is necessary to ensure tenure security, reduce costs, and ensure fairness and sustainability of the system.

Improving access to rural finance: It would require improving the performance of regional rural banks and rural credit cooperatives by enhancing regulatory oversight, removing government control and ownership, and strengthening the legal framework for loan recovery and the use of land as collateral. It would also involve creating an enabling environment for the development of micro-finance institutions in rural areas.

3. Strengthening Institutions for the Poor and Promoting Rural Livelihood

Promoting Community-based Rural Development: State Government efforts in scaling up livelihood and community-driven development approaches will be critical to build social capital in the poorest areas as well as to expand savings mobilization, promote productive investments, income generating opportunities and sustainable natural resource management. Direct support to self-help groups, village committees, user's associations, savings and loans groups and others can provide the initial 'push' to move organizations to higher level and access to new economic opportunities. Moreover, social mobilization and particularly the empowerment of women's groups, through increased capacity for collective action will provide communities with greater "voice" and bargaining power in dealing with the private sector, markets and financial services.

Strengthening Accountability for Service Delivery: As decentralization efforts are pursued and local governments are given more prominence in the basic service delivery, the establishment of accountability mechanisms becomes critical. Local governments' capacity to identify local priorities through participatory budgeting and planning needs to be strengthened. This, in turn, would improve the rural investment climate, facilitating the involvement of the private sector, creating employment opportunities and linkages between farm and non-farm sectors.

Rural Banking in India has made tremendous quantitative progress, but quality is a different matter. On the whole, it has to be admitted that the policy-makers have yet to arrive at a banking structure and operational system which suit agriculturists credit and saving needs and at the same time promote modern agriculture.

REFERENCES

N.A. Majumdar (1999), Reviving Rural Credit, *Economic and Political Weekly*, Vol. 34, pp. 1577-79.

H.B. Shivmaggi (2000), Reforms in Rural Banking: Need for Bolder Approach, *Economic and Political Weekly*, May 13, 2000.

Rural Development, Territorial Planning, Agriculture, Food Security, www.google.com.

Kaye Tasi (2006), Regional Rural Banks in Economic Development, www.google. com.

P. Eashavaraiah (2001), Liberalisation: The State and Agriculture in India, *Journal of Contemporary Asia*, Vol. 31.

Manish Ranjan Gupta and Sarabjeet Chaudhari, Formal Credit, Corruption and the Informal Credit Market in Agriculture in India: A Theoretical Analysis, www. google. com.

Role of Regional Rural Banks in Upliftment of Weaker Section of Indian Society

Mr. Anil Kumar Roy and Mr. Prabhat Kumar

Introduction

It is universally well established that in the process of economic development, banking sector plays a pivotal role. It is due to this factor that this factor occupied a central place in India's economic reforms agenda initiated Prime Minister Dr. Manmohan Singh in 1991 as the then Finance Minister. Since then the banking sector has performed exceedingly well by international standards and bringing in of private sector banks has brought high degree of competitiveness with increased efficiency, improved delivery system, enhanced level of banks net worth, asset valuation, profitability, and increased people's access to financial resources. Today, India's economic performance at 8-9% GDP growth could partly be attributed to expanded and diversified operations in the banking sector. Unfortunately, this record performance of banks has not been visible in Bihar. Thus, Bihar still remains confined to a very low level of economic growth. It is high time now for

Bihar to open and rejuvenate its exposure to the banking sector. There are a number of opportunities to seek benefits from the banking sector so that Bihar's economic growth process gathers momentum. How Bihar should move in that direction is the main theme of this Report: 1. Bank Operation in Bihar. 2. Available field survey and research reports reveal that Bihar's exposure to the banking sector has so far been limited. As a result, various sources of informal credit occupy the central place and farmer's ineffectiveness increases. Inadequacies in availability of credit from the banking sources have also led to low level of productive asset creation and entrepreneurship development. All these have had bearing on Bihar's economic growth. 3. Public sector banking operations still carry predominance.

Out of a total of 3989 branches of various banking entities, the branches of public sector and regional rural banks comprise almost 90% of the total branches operating in Bihar. Out of the total branches, 65% were in the rural areas. Bihar has a total of around 45,103 villages. This translates to one branch around the cluster of 13 villages, based on the total branch estimates of 2006. In terms of population, estimates suggest that the branch population per bank in Bihar is approximately 23,000 in comparison to the national average of 15,000. The rural-urban divide in Bihar is also very stark with each rural branch serving estimated 31,000 people as compared to 18,000 people in urban areas. 4. Given a rural area of about 94,000 square kilometers, this translates to a bank branch on an average of every 35 square kilometers (given a 1000 square kilometer urban area—the urban ratio is less than 1 square kilometer per branch). This suggests an inter-branch distance of at least 6 kilometers on an average in rural Bihar. However, there may be relatively higher density of branches near Block Headquarters and semi-urban centers. Outside these locations, the distance between bank branches may be as high as 18 to 20 kilometers. This may be disturbing for production centres being far away from banking hubs. Even to provide basic access to financial services, this is clearly insufficient and the target number of access points would need to be increased to at least 12,000 to give coverage of at least one financial service access point in every three to four villages. One immediate question that arises is that of the viability of such a banking infrastructure and how, considering that it has been difficult to manage the personnel challenges faced even by the existing low density of rural branches, these branches would be staffed.

In addition to the existing low density of branch presence, there is the added issue of the nature of services provided by the banking system as a whole, Regional Rural Banks (RRBs). The average deposit per individual is estimated at Rs. 55,000 (against the national average of Rs. 1,95,000), which is consistent with the low per capita average income of Rs. 5,700 per year. The situation on advances is even worse with Rs. 18,000 per capita, in which the effect of the low per capita deposit base is compounded by an unusually low credit-deposit ratio of 34.8% (in 2007) relative to the national average of over 70%. Interestingly, CBs had a very high credit-deposit ratio of 77% which, while below the national average of 100% for cooperatives, can still be considered very good relative to the banking sector average for Bihar. A very large part of this credit has turned out non-performing. The performance of Primary Agricultural Credit Societies (PACS) also reflects a similar state. While there are almost 6,000 PACS in Bihar, only 19% of them showed a profit in the year 2004-05 as compared to 43% nationally. The deposit base of Bihar is also very low. Overall, all the available information clearly reveals the following:

(i) There is a gross inadequacy in the density of financial services access in Bihar. However, it is possible that the cost and viability considerations may make it unviable to significantly expand the presence of branches in the State, (ii) The extreme poverty levels of the State are reflected in the aggregate deposit base. It is possible that this combined with the low branch density has led to a much larger base of non-financial assets such as gold jewellery and a few others. This means that at the State-wide level, there is improper allocation of financial resources taking place because of a wide-spread failure of financial intermediate, (iii) Problems of adverse selection and moral hazard seem extreme (as is reflected in the Non-Performing Asset Ratios of Cooperative Banks and PACS). The key challenge ahead then is to attempt to discover solutions to these seemingly intractable problems. The broad contours of the solutions explored in the following paragraphs include:

Development of a hybrid intermediate approach using new models of intermediation and new design principles, (i) *Back End:* Rapid improvement in the back-end infrastructure of cash handling, cash movement and clearing of cheques designed to support these new models of access and to address key drivers of high costs of financial intermediation, (ii) *Deep End:* A systematic attempt to eliminate the problems of information asymmetry and adverse selection throughout the State through the use of universal biometric identity cards and credit bureaus in which all financial services providers are mandatorily required to participate. Bihar, which has remained behind in banking services in all its aspects, requires comprehensive financial services to reach out to the vast poor segments of population. A strategy for universal access to financial services has thus to address two key challenges—ubiquity and comprehensiveness of range of financial services. Ubiquity refers to financial services that are easily accessible to individuals in terms of geographical proximity and the ease with which the services can be procured. For long, this was pursued in India through commercial banks opening branches in rural areas and Regional Rural Banks (RRBs).

Conclusion

Thus, a strategy for universal access to financial services has to address two key challenges—ubiquity and comprehensiveness of range of financial services. Ubiquity refers to financial services that are easily accessible to individuals in terms of geographical proximity and the ease with which the services can be procured. For long, this was pursued in India through commercial banks opening branches in rural areas and Regional Rural Banks (RRBs). However, this infrastructure was unable to address the demand for financial services in a comprehensive manner for a number of reasons, including high costs of services delivery and exclusive focus on credit. In order to achieve meaningful ubiquity, models of outreach must have ability to leverage local information while being cost-effective. A two-pronged strategy to deliver comprehensive financial services is proposed. These are:

(i) Delivering these services through high quality private sector (both for-profit and not-for-profit) local financial institutions, broadly referred to as Micro Finance Institutions (MFIs). (ii) Building technology enabled low cost direct service channels. These direct service channels would complement services provided by the MFIs. In order to meet this, a large number of micro-finance institutions (MFIs) set-ups could be formed. These could provide on leading to self-help groups and individuals.

REFERENCES

Desai, Bhupat M. and Namboodiri, N.V. (2001), Organization and Management of Rural Financial Sector: Test, Cases and Experiences, Oxford & IBH Publishing Co., New Delhi.

NABARD (2003), Progress of SHG-Bank Linkages in India, 2002-03, Mumbai.

RBI (1991), All India Debt and Investment Survey, Mumbai.

World Bank (2003), India Sustaining Reforms, Reducing Poverty, Oxford University, New Delhi.

Role of Regional Rural Banks in Rural Development—Problems and Suggestions

Dr. C.P. Gupta and Ms. Kamlesh Gupta

India is a rural country, about 70 per cent of the Indian population lives in rural areas. Agriculture is the main occupation of Indian rural population. The development of rural areas is obviously needed. Rural development can be defined as the integration and utilization of all the local resources, i.e. physical, biological, human, etc. and aims to improve the living conditions, productivity and employment opportunities, and develop potentials of rural resources.

The basic problem facing the rural poor is the insufficiency of their income to meet the minimum expenditure in production activities. Hence, credit plays pivotal role in their life. But the problem of credit for the rural poor is of course a complicated one. Rural credit in India did suffer from serious gaps and deficiencies. When commercial banks also failed to reach the small and marginal farmers, Regional Rural Banks were launched to fill the gap. RRBs were incorporated with a view to develop the rural economy by disbursing credit and extending banking facilities to the economically backward sector of rural community.

Problems faced by banks include the lack of awareness and banking habits in the people, location of villages in remote areas so difficulty of public transport system and Large scale non-recovery tendencies. Beneficiaries also face numerous problems like no tie-up arrangement of market, short supply of power, the length of procedure of getting loans, etc. along with so many others.

The responses obtained from the beneficiaries have brought to the following problems:

1. Agriculture inputs are not available in proper time.
2. Some beneficiaries face difficulty in giving margin money.
3. Non-availability of Raw material.
4. Short-supply of power.
5. Lack of repairing and infrastructure facilities.
6. The length of procedure and the involvement of number of persons in the process cause undue delays and all other complications. This delay has occurred in case of poorer persons more as compared to richer farmers.
7. The requirement of documents/papers, etc. for securing a loan from the bank is too much.

The bankers were facing liquidity crunch due to delay in the relief package and were unable to provide credit to farmers.

SUGGESTIONS

Following are some suggestions, which may be useful in fulfilling the gaps and in improving the banking services in discharging their responsibilities:

1. The banks should launch publicity drives and popularies their schemes of deposit mobilization in rural areas.
2. In order to enhance the credit absorption capacity concerted efforts should be made to popularies the credit schemes, formulate new schemes and activities in the area.

3. Systematic efforts should be made to provide infrastructure facilities in the villages like roads, communication systems, hospitals, veterinary aid, etc.
4. The subsidies to be given for various production purposes should be linked with repayment of loan so that an ideal credit climate can be created.
5. Initial investment of the farmer should be reimbursed by the bank while financing that activity.
6. There is an urgent need for revamping of rural lending of banks from the present target-oriented concept to result-oriented approach.
7. For bank organizations, such rules should be made that in this field, there is no undue interference of politics and these organizations are able to work freely without the economically, politically and socially forceful persons.
8. Most of the employees and officers should be appointed from the rural background so that they may take genuine interest in the rural development.
9. Banks should reduce their interest rates.
10. The loan should be provided in sufficient quantity. By it, the Scheme would succeed and the loan would be repaid also.
11. Use of Hindi should be made maximum while completing the work in rural and semi-urban branches.
12. Deployment of more technical personnel for handling technical work.
13. To increase the efficiency of the bank, computerization and mechanization to the full extent is very necessary.
14. As far as possible, banks should adopt the use of regional languages of dealings with beneficiaries.

Mr. Thorat has prepared a manpower road map upto 2015 for RRBs. The committee has observed, "There is a need to rationalize the promotion policy to ensure career progression in all employee categories. It would reward and motivate good performers and assert attrition." Interestingly, No RRB officers get promotion to the general manager level at present. Sponsor banks used to depute their officers to fill these slots. To consider setting up a rural national software for the proposed core banking solution in RRBs.

Setting up of a technology platform, reduction in non-performing assets, branch expansion, financial inclusion and recapitalisation support are some core issues.

Role of Regional Rural Banks in Demographic Transition of India

Dr. Sandeep Shandilya

1. Introduction

Demographic transitions must be considered while designing long-term economic policies of a nation. Demographic transition is concerned with economic developments when a country passes from a pre-industrial to an industrialized economy. India continues to be predominantly an agricultural nation but its industrial character also has its own enormousity. It has now been established by studies that when a country passes from pre-industrial to industrial form, the contribution of agriculture in Gross Domestic Product (GDP) continuously goes down. The same has happened with India. Developed nations which have fully matured as industrialized nations also witnessed such type of structural changes in their economies.

Growing urbanisation as a result of industrialization is a challenge which has its obvious demographic linkages. Regional Rural Banks (RRBs) play a significant role in seeing to it that credit flows to one of the most deprived sections of Indian society, i.e.

the weakest among the rural population. Proper management of credit creation through RRBs will infuse a sense of confidence among these sections thus strengthening the grass-root level of our economy, across the board.

2. Growing Urbanisation: An International Phenomena

Urbanisation or in other words migration of rural population to urban areas is a demographic phenomena which is taking place rapidly all over the world. "Ever since the emergence of the first urban centre on the world scene, the urban population has been growing more rapidly than the rural population. Consequently, the share of urban population in the total population of the world has been increasing. This increase in the share of urban population was only gradual until the industrial revolution. Since then the share of urban population has been increasing on an accelerated rate. The world's population is becoming increasingly urbanised. The rate has been rather rapid during the recent decades. While 29% of the world's population lived in urban areas in 1950, the corresponding figure for 1995 is around 45%. The proportion of urban population in the world is expected to reach 61% by 2025."[1]

Above information amply highlights the growing urbanisation all over the world. India is also not an exception. For India rampant urbanisation is a cruel reality which has its origin in economic development. A balanced development of rural and urban areas can help in checking this mindless urbanization. "Among the various continents, the continents of North and South America are the most urbanised continents with 79% of their population living in urban centres. It is closely followed by the continents of Europe (74%), Oceania (72%) and North and Central America (68%). The continent of Africa was the least urbanized continent with only 35% of its population having an urban residence. The situation in Asia was also not very different from the one prevailing in Africa. Only 39% of Asian population lived in urban centres."[2]

3. 1961 Census and Definition of 'Urban': Break-up Based on Agricultural and Non-agricultural Occupation

"The India censuses have been classifying areas with a

population of 5,000 or more and possessing certain urban characteristics as "Urban". But the 1961 census adopted more rigorous definition, and only those areas where three-fourth of the population was dependent on non-agricultural occupation were called Urban."[3] It is quite interesting to note that the definition of urban place as mentioned in 1961 census is based on the proporation of the population engaged in agricultural or non-agricultural occupation. This simple observation has high implications on the nature and pattern of demographic transition of India. Too much urbanization may help in boosting quantitative growth of Indian economy but its growth in qualitative terms will suffer a severe beating. Growing population in urban areas is a menance which must be checked as early as possible. Life in some Indian cities has already become havoc for the residents living there.

Regional Rural Banks can play a vital role in reversing the trend of rampant urbanisation by giving a boost to the growth of rural economy particularly agricultural sector. Spatial distribution of RRBs all over the country and their well spread network can contribute immensely to the growth of Indian economy in general and rural economy in particular. It is true that complete check on migration from rural to urban areas when a country is transforming herself into industrialized nation is not practically feasible but there is a saturation limit to such type of migration. Urban areas of India have begin to feel the heat of urbanisation.

4. Industrial Composition of India vs. State-wise Working Results of RRBs: A Demographic Analysis

Before attempting to analyse the correlation between RRBs and demographic transition of India let us elaborate on following information. "The Government is committed to increase credit flow to rural masses and all necessary steps will be taken to strengthen Regional Rural Banks (RRBs) assured the Finance Minister Shri P. Chidambaram while addressing the members of Parliamentary Consultative Committee attached to his Ministry in a meeting held on 25th April 2007. The Finance Minister informed the members that the process for structural consolidation of RRBs by amalgamating RRBs, sponsored by the same bank within a State, started two years back, has been completed in March 2007 (target was June 2007) with number of RRBs reduced to 96 from 196."[4] Infact the seeds of mergers of RRBs and thus reduction in their numerical figure were sawn with the recommendation of Khusro Committee of 1989 which argued that these banks have no justifiable cause for continuance and recommended their mergers with sponsor banks. However, to include a broader spatial distribution of RRBs all over India so as to draw a meaningful correlation of RRBs with demography of India, the RRBs data of 31 March, 2003 as taken from annual report of NABARD (2002-03) has been included for the purpose of study in this paper. Wide regional variations can be noticed in the industrial composition of India as reflected in 1991-2001 census (Table 1). On one hand there are states like Chhattisgarh where 76.4% of the work force (i.e. 44.5% in cultivation and 31.9% Agricultural labour) was engaged in agricultural sector and on the other hand we have states like Goa where only 9.6% of the work force was engaged in cultivation while agricultural labour accounted for 6.8% of the total workers. Similarly, wide regional varitations can be noticed in state-wise working results of RRBs. "All RRBs in Haryana and Tamil Nadu had recovery performance of above 80% and all RRBs in Punjab and Rajasthan, 15 RRBs (out of 16) in Andhra Pradesh, 12 RRBs (out of 13) in Karnataka had recovery levels above 60%. The recovery performance of RRBs in Uttranchal also stood just below 80% (79.3%). 1 RRB (out of 4) in Uttranchal had recovery between 40% to 60% and 2 RRBs had recovery level above 80%."[5] This is quite interesting to note that both Haryana (51.3%) and Tamil Nadu (49.4%) were having almost equal percentage of labourers in cultivation and agriculture put together. Moreover, recovery performance of RRBs in these states is also quite satisfactory, i.e. above 80%. Migration to big cities is fast eroding the quality of life in these cities. RRBs can play a significant role by infusing growth and energy to rural economy and thus keeping a sizeable chunk of population intact in villages thus enabling the rural population to enjoy the benefits of economic development without migrating to cities.

TABLE 1

India: Industrial Composition, 1991-2001

State/UT	*Cultivators*		*Agricultural Labourers*		*Household Industry Workers*		*Other Workers*	
	2001	*1991*	*2001*	*1991*	*2001*	*1991*	*2001*	*1991*
1	*2*	*3*	*4*	*5*	*6*	*7*	*8*	*9*
INDIA	31.7	39.7	26.5	27.4	4.2	2.4	37.6	30.5
States								
Himachal Pradesh	65.3	69.4	3.1	3.4	1.8	1.2	29.8	26.0
Nagaland	64.7	72.6	3.6	1.6	2.6	0.4	29.0	25.3
Arunachal Pradesh	57.8	60.8	3.9	5.4	1.3	0.2	37.0	33.7
Rajasthan	55.3	61.1	10.6	12.9	2.9	1.8	31.2	24.3
Mizoram	54.9	62.3	5.7	5.4	1.5	1.1	37.9	31.2
Uttaranchal	50.1	58.1	8.3	9.0	2.3	1.0	39.3	31.8
Sikkim	49.9	58.0	6.5	8.2	1.6	0.8	42.0	33.1
Meghalaya	48.1	56.3	17.7	13.0	2.2	0.4	32.0	30.3
Chhattisgarh	44.5	56.6	31.9	25.1	2.1	1.4	21.5	16.8
Madhya Pradesh	42.8	50.3	28.7	25.3	4.0	2.9	24.5	21.5
Jammu & Kashmir	42.4	NA	6.6	NA	6.2	NA	44.8	NA
Uttar Pradesh	41.1	53.4	24.8	20.8	5.6	2.5	28.5	23.3
Manipur	40.2	59.9	12.0	10.3	10.3	6.0	37.6	23.8
Assam	39.1	54.8	13.2	12.6	3.6	1.0	44.0	31.7
Jharkhand	38.5	50.8	28.2	24.1	4.3	2.2	29.1	23.0
Haryana	36.0	41.0	15.3	19.7	2.6	1.5	46.1	37.8

(Contd.)

TABLE 1 (*Contd.*)

1	2	3	4	5	6	7	8	9
Orissa	29.8	42.4	35.0	32.9	4.9	3.2	30.3	21.5
Bihar	29.3	41.1	48.0	43.7	3.9	1.5	18.8	13.6
Karnataka	29.2	35.4	26.5	29.9	4.1	1.9	40.2	32.8
Maharashtra	28.7	34.0	26.3	28.1	2.6	1.6	42.4	36.2
Gujarat	27.3	33.7	24.3	27.1	2.0	1.4	46.4	37.7
Tripura	27.0	39.0	23.8	24.2	3.0	1.6	46.1	35.2
Punjab	22.6	31.7	16.3	24.6	3.7	1.3	57.4	42.3
Andhra Pradesh	22.5	27.7	39.6	41.8	4.7	3.4	33.1	27.1
West Bengal	19.2	29.2	25.0	25.0	7.4	4.2	48.5	41.5
Tamil Nadu	18.4	25.0	31.0	36.2	5.4	3.6	45.3	35.2
Goa	9.6	16.6	6.8	10.8	2.8	2.4	80.7	70.1
Kerala	7.0	13.2	15.8	26.8	3.6	2.6	73.6	57.4
Union Territories								
Dadra & Nagra Haveli	34.6	62.1	12.9	12.7	0.7	0.3	51.8	25.0
Andaman & Nicobar Islands	15.8	17.9	3.8	6.7	5.2	7.1	75.3	68.3
Daman & Diu	5.5	17.0	1.8	5.9	1.6	1.6	91.0	75.5
Pondicherry	3.2	6.8	21.1	30.1	1.9	0.8	73.9	62.3
Delhi	0.8	1.2	0.3	0.9	3.1	1.4	95.7	96.5
Chandigarh	0.6	1.0	0.2	0.8	1.1	0.2	98.1	98.0
Lakshadweep	0.0	0.0	0.0	0.0	5.9	9.2	94.1	90.8

Source: Census of India, 2001: Primary Census Abstract, Total Population.

TABLE 2

State-wise Working Results of RRBs (As on 31 March 2003)

State	No. of RRBs	Profit Earning		Loss-making		Net Accumulated		Loans & Adv.	NPA Amt.	NPA %	Recovery %	
		No.	Amount	No.	Amount	Profits	Losses				June 2002	June 2003
1	2	3	4	5	6	7	8	9	10	11	12	13
Andhra Pradesh	16	15	90.65	1	-2.31	88.34	40.17	2953.54	272.55	9.23	70.19	70.96
Arunachal Pradesh	1	0	0	1	-11.19	-11.19	22.35	32.69	25.83	79.02	18.27	22.61
Assam	5	4	4.74	1	-3.25	1.48	103.83	468.18	83.91	17.92	50.73	58.86
Bihar	16	8	48.04	8	-60.66	-12.62	526.38	1143.86	232.09	20.29	56.35	60.17
Chhattisgarh	5	3	5.46	2	-5.6	-0.14	150.07	331.34	57.65	17.4	63.82	69.02
Gujarat	9	9	24.01	0	0	24	25.79	631.19	86.88	13.76	73.53	76.53
Haryana	4	4	46.89	0	0	46.89	17.09	676.22	48.98	7.24	83.17	84.73
Himachal Pradesh	2	2	4.11	0	0	4.11	0	196.32	12.79	6.51	78.07	80.79
J&K	3	1	9.92	2	-15.82	-5.9	99.68	161.13	20.79	12.9	59.75	63.85
Jharkhand	6	2	3.9	4	-23.6	-19.7	121.67	337.09	97.17	28.83	39.33	44.94
Karnataka	13	12	76.98	1	-0.96	76.02	0	2548.37	270.04	10.6	75.99	75.53
Kerala	2	2	29.84	0	0	29.84	0	1204.28	116.92	9.71	83.93	84.99
M.P.	19	16	16.99	3	-5.49	11.5	256.59	1323.44	187.68	14.18	70.06	72.49
Maharashtra	10	6	4.17	4	-18.52	-14.35	130.32	685.18	154.04	22.48	67.24	64.44

(Contd.)

TABLE 2 (*Contd.*)

1	*2*	*3*	*4*	*5*	*6*	*7*	*8*	*9*	*10*	*11*	*12*	*13*
Manipur	1	0	0	1	-2.15	-2.15	14.23	13.87	4.86	35.06	49.93	51.8
Meghalaya	1	1	13.1	0	0	3.1	0	40.62	13.63	33.56	51.16	54.3
Mizoram	1	1	0.29	0	0	0.29	5.58	33.73	10.33	30.64	50	61.23
Nagaland	1	0	0	1	-0.16	-0.16	1.58	4.33	0.62	14.41	50.72	61.17
Orissa	9	4	13.15	5	-43.97	-30.82	459.83	407.97	223.13	15.85	66.34	67.38
Punjab	15	15	35.44	0	0	35.44	0	350.71	18.39	5.24	91.35	92.71
Rajasthan	14	12	38.99	2	-7.29	31.7	196.72	1376.98	115.88	8.42	77.19	80.05
Tamil Nadu	3	3	18.33	0	0	18.33	0	529.24	23.05	4.36	88.11	89.28
Tripura	1	1	82.056	0	0	2.05	139.02	178.09	65.30	36.67	34.97	44.56
U.P.	36	34	240.75	2	-5.21	235.53	157.39	3985.91	813.96	20.42	66.99	70.04
Uttranchal	4	4	7.56	0	0	7.56	1.97	179.56	15.81	8.81	81.74	79.3
W. Bengal	9	7	8.6	2	-8.48	0.12	281.97	1364	227.4	16.67	65.15	69.33
All India	196	156	733.96	40	-214.66	519.29	2752.16	22157.8	3200	14.44	71.52	73.53

Source: Annual Report, NABARD (2002-03).

5. Proportion of Urban Population in Indian States vs. State-wise Working Results of RRBs: A Demographic Analysis

It can be seen from Table 3 that western India continues to be more urbanised than eastern India. Similarly, South India continues to be more urbanised than North India due to factors associated with resource potential of the concerned area and history of modern urbanisation. Himalayan region "in north and northeast constitutes the least urbanised part of India. Himachal Pradesh in the northern Himalaya had only 9.8% of its population living in urban areas. In another hill state Sikkim, this percentage is just 11.6%. Infact extremely low degree of urbanisation can be seen in the entire Himalayan belt from Kashmir to Arunachal Pradesh and Tripura. As in these areas urbanization is quite low, percentage of people living in rural areas is quite high and thus the role of RRBs becomes quite significant in these areas. It is quite interesting to note that the recovery percentage of RRBs in Arunachal Pradesh is poor 22.61% whereas in case of Tripura, it is 44.56%. These are among the poorest recovery performances of RRBs in India. There is an urgent need to revamp the overall management and functioning of RRBs in those areas where urbanisation is low and most of the proportion of the population resides in rural areas. In India urbanisation is not much in hill areas. Various factors can be attributed to it such as non-availability of developed means of transportation, limitation of physical resources, etc. In case of Himachal Pradesh, the urbanisation is least in the country, i.e. 9.8% in 2001 census. Himachal Pradesh has only two RRBs and their overall recovery percentage is around 80.79 percentage. A contrast can be seen in case of Arunachal Pradesh & Tripura and Himachal Pradesh. In case of Arunachal Pradesh proportion of urban population was 20.8% in the year 2001 whereas in case of Tripura, it was 17.0%. The same percentage in case of Himachal Pradesh was 9.8% as mentioned earlier. Considering the recovery percentage of RRBs in June, 2003, we find quite satisfactory position (80.79%) in case of Himachal Pradesh, while in case of Arunachal Pradesh (22.61%) and Tripura (44.56%). It is abysmal. It can thus be seen that RRBs can manage good recovery percentage irrespective of the degree of urbanization in their parent states.

TABLE 3

India: Proportion of Urban Population: 1981-2001

State/UT	*2001*	*1991*	*1981*
INDIA	27.8	26.1	23.3
States			
Goa	49.7	. 41	32
Mizoram	49.6	46.1	25.2
Tamil Nadu	44	34.2	33
Maharashtra	42.4	38.7	32
Gujarat	37.4	34.5	31.1
Karnataka	34	34.9	28.9
Punjab	33.9	29.6	27.7
Haryana	28.9	24.6	22
West Bengal	27.9	27.5	26.5
Andhra Pradesh	27.3	26.9	23.3
Manipur	26.6	27.5	26.4
Madhya Pradesh	26.5	23.2	20.3
Kerala	25.9	26.4	18.4
Uttranchal	25.7	NA	NA
Jammu & Kashmir	24.8	23.8	21
Rajasthan	23.4	22.8	20.9
Jharkhand	22.2	NA	NA
Utter Pradesh	20.8	19.8	18
Arunachal Pradesh	20.8	12.8	6.3
Chhattisgarh	20.1	NA	NA
Meghalaya	19.6	18.6	18
Nagaland	17.2	17.2	15.5
Tripura	17	15.3	11
Orissa	15	13.4	11.8
Assam	12.9	11.1	9.9
Sikkim	11.6	9.1	16.2
Bihar	10.5	13.1	12.5
Himachal Pradesh	9.8	8.7	7.7
Union Territories			
Delhi	93.2	89.9	92.8
Chandigarh	89.8	89.7	93.6
Pondicherry	66.6	64	52.3
Lakshadweep	44.5	56.3	46.3
Daman & Diu	36.2	46.8	36.8
Andaman & Nicobar Islands	32.6	26.7	26.4
Dadra & Nagar Haveli	26.9	8.5	6.7

Source: Census of India, 2001: Primary Census Abstract, Total Population, Table A-5.

6. Conclusion

Urbanisation and industrialisation is increasing at a rapid pace all over the world. According to an estimate by 2025, around 61% of the world population will reside in urban areas. Composition of contribution to GDP from various sectors of the economy in national income of different nations is also experiencing a sea change. Contribution of agriculture sector in GDP is decreasing in those nations where rate of industrialization is high. Growing urbanization is making life pathetic in urban areas. Proper attention and case of rural economy can provide answers to many such problems. Regional Rural Banks are the banks which provide credit to marginal farmers and the weakest among the weaker sections of rural sector. Strengthening of RRBs and subsequent modernization of rural economy will result in reducing incidences of migration from rural to urban areas thus leaving impact on demographic pattern of India.

Notes and References

1. R.C. Chandna, 'Geography of Population'; Kalyani Publication, Ludhiana, 2006, p. 392.
2. *Ibid.*, p. 393.
3. Thompson and Lawis, 'Population Problems'; McGraw-Hill, New York, 1967, pp. 123-25.
4. www.banknetindia.com/banking/70421
5. Anurag Agarwal, 'Regional Rural Banks (RRBs)'; *Kurukshetra*, a *Journal of Rural Development*, Ministry of Rural Development of India, Vol. 53, No. 9, July 2005, p. 23.

Working of Regional Rural Banks (Study Based on NABARD)

Mr. Rohit Mehra and Ms. Shruti Singh

The Idea of establishing Regional Rural Banks was mooted in the Twenty Point Economic Programme of July 1975 to cater credit needs of rural people. The Govt. of India appointed the Narasimham Committee in July 1975 to set-up the new institution in order: (i) to provide employment to the rural educated youth, (ii) to bring down the cost of rural banks by recruiting their staff on the same scale of pay and allowances.

NABARD

The National Bank for Agriculture and Rural Development (NABARD) was established on 12 July 1982 by the Govt. of India by merging the Agriculture Credit Deptt. of the RBI, the Agriculture Refinance and Development Corporation, the National Agriculture Credit Fund.

Objectives of the NABARD

The NABARD is an apex development bank which provides help for agricultural and rural development. It has been established with the following objectives:

1. To give undivided attention and purposeful direction to integrated rural development.
2. To act as a center piece for the entire rural credit system at the national level.
3. To act as a provider of supplemental funding to rural credit institution.
4. To arrange for investment credit to small industries, village, and cottage industries.
5. To provide refinance facilities to SLDBs, SCBs, RRBs and commercial banks for development purposes in rural areas.

Some of the Milestones in NABARD's Activities

- With its effects overseeing and monitoring of the implementation of the Govt. of India's programme to double the flow of credit to agriculture over a three year period from 2004-05, the total disbursement of credit reached Rs. 1,25,309 during 2004-05.
- Refinance disbursement to commercial banks, state cooperative banks, RRB's aggregated Rs. 8622.37 crore.
- As on 31 January 2007 through the Rural Infrastructure Development Fund (RDF) Rs. 59,795.35 crore have been sanctioned for 2,31,702 projects covering irrigation, rural roads, bridges, health and education, soil conservation, drinking water schemes, etc.
- Watershed development fund with cumulative sanctions of Rs. 578.95 crore for 427 projects in 124 districts of 14 states, has created a people's movement in rural India.
- Farmers now enjoy financial assess and security through 582.59 lakh kisan credit cards that have been issued through a vast rural banking network.

NABARD Today

- Initiates measures toward institution building for improving absorptive capacity of the credit delivery system, including monitoring, formulation of rehabilitation schemes, etc.
- Coordinates the rural financing activities of all the

institutions engaged in development work at the field level and maintains liaison with the Government of India.
- Prepares on annual basis, rural credit plans for all the districts in the country.
- Promotes research in the fields of rural banking, agriculture and rural development.
- Functions as a regulatory authority, supervising, monitoring and guiding cooperative banks and regional rural banks.

NABARD's Roles and Functions are Summarized below:

- Credit functions.
- Development and promotional functions.
- Supervisory functions.
- Institutional and capacity building.
- Role in trading.

Credit Functions

NABARD's credit functions cover planning, dispensation and monitoring of credit. These activities involves:

- Framing policy and guidelines for rural financial institutions.
- Providing credit facilities to issuing organizations.
- Preparation of potential linked credit plans.

Development and Promotional Functions

Credit is a critical factor in development of agriculture and rural sector as it enables investment in capital formation and technological upgradation. Various initiatives have been taken to strengthen the cooperative credit structure and the regional rural.

In order to reinforce the credit functions and to make credit more productive NABARD has been undertaking a number of development and promotional activities such as:

- Help cooperative banks and regional rural banks to prepare development action plans for themselves.
- Enter into MoU with State Govt. and cooperative banks specifying their respectives obligations to improve the affairs of the regional rural banks in a stipulated timeframe.

- Monitoring implementation of development action plans of banks and fulfilment of obligations under MoUs.
- Provide financial assistance to cooperative and RRBs for establishment of technical, monitoring and evaluation cells.
- Provide financial support for the training institutes of cooperative banks.
- Provide training for senior and middle level executives of commercial banks, RRBs and cooperative banks.
- Provide financial assistance to cooperative banks for building improved management information system.

Supervisory Functions

As an apex bank involved in refinancing credit needs of major financial institutions in the country, NABARD has been sharing with the RBI and RRBs.

As part of these functions: It

- Undertakes inspection of RRBs and cooperative banks under the provision of Banking Regulation Act, 1949.
- Undertakes inspection of state cooperative agriculture and rural development banks.
- Undertakes portfolio inspection, system study, besides off-site surveillance of cooperative banks and RRBs.
- Administering the credit monitoring arrangements in SCBs and CCBs.

Core Functions

NABARD has been entrusted with the statutory responsibility of conducting inspection of state cooperative banks, district central cooperative banks and RRBs under the provision of the Banking Regulation Act, 1949.

Objectives of Inspections

- To protect the interest of the present and future depositors.
- To ensure that the business conducted by these banks is in conformity with the provisions of the relevant acts/ rules, regulations.
- To examine the financial soundness of the banks.
- To suggest ways and means for strengthening the

institutions so as to enable them to pay more efficient role in rural credit.

Instruments of Supervision

- Periodic on-site inspection of 31 SCBs, 366 DCCBs, 20 SCARDBs and 102 RRBs and other apex level cooperative institutions.
- Supplementary appraisal.
- Off-site surveillance system.
- CMA returns.

The broad powers and functions of the board of supervision are:

- Giving directions and guidance in respect of policies.
- Reviewing the follow-up action taken by Deptt. of supervision on matters of frauds and internal checks and control.
- Suggesting necessary follow-up measures.
- Recommending appropriate training for inspecting officers of NABARD for imparting necessary skills and knowledge.
- Suggests measures for strengthening of DOS.
- Recommend issue of directions by RBI.
- Oversee the quality of inspections carried out and the reports issued.
- Undertake any other functions entrusted from time to time by the board of directors of NABARD.

The Board of supervision, since its formation on 20th November 1999, has held 31 meetings till 10 January 2007 and reviewed the financial position of cooperative banks and RRBs. Based on the observations of BOS, authority concerned have been apprised of the weaknesses.

Role of Regional Rural Banks and Micro Finance Institutions and Development of Society: With Special Reference of Andhra Pradesh

Dr. Prabha Singh

Before 1990's, credit schemes for rural women were almost negligible. The concept of women's credit was born on the insistence by women-oriented studies that highlighted the discrimination and struggle of women in having access to credit. However, there is a perceptible gap in financing genuine credit needs of the poor especially women in the rural sector. There are certain misconceptions about the poor people that they need loan at subsidized rates of interest on soft terms, they lack education, skills, capacity to save, credit-worthiness and therefore are not bankable. Nevertheless, the experiences of several SHGs (self-help groups) reveal that rural poor are actually efficient managers of credit and finance. Availability of timely and adequate credit is essential for them to undertake any economic activity rather than credit subsidy.

The Government measures have attempted to help the poor by implementing different poverty alleviation programmes but with little success. Since most of them are target-based involving lengthy procedures for loan disbursements, high transaction costs, and lack of supervision and monitoring. Banks often suffer from poor repayment leading to a high level of non-performing assets NPAs (non-performing assets).

Since the credit requirements of the rural poor can not be adopted on project lending approach as it is in the case of organized sector, there emerged the need for an informal credit supply through SHGs. The rural poor with the assistance from NGOs have demonstrated their potential for self-help to secure economic and financial strength. Various case studies show that there is a positive correlation between credit availability and women's empowerment.

Role of Development Banks

A. Small Industries Development Bank of India (SIDBI)

Promotional and Developmental Initiatives

The promotional and developmental activities carried out by SIDBI aims at boosting the small-scale sector growth, employment generation and upliftment of rural poor. The micro credit scheme received a major thrust in terms of policy changes and credit, which are inevitable for the growth potential of micro-finance sector. The Micro Credit Scheme (MCS) was formulated and put into operation in March 1994.

SIDBI plays an important role as an apex bank to provide financial services through an appropriate and responsive credit delivery system. Assistance is extended to well-managed NGOs for credit lending to rural poor with special emphasis on women to take up activities at a micro level. NGOs with good record of accomplishment are extended support services to improve their financial and managerial capabilities.

During the period 1998-99, under the MCS an assistance of Rs. 1413 lakh was sanctioned to 32 Micro Finance Institutions/ NGOs to benefit nearly 1.12 lakh poor mainly women for undertaking non-farm activities. Further the Government of India has sanctioned an aggregate assistance of Rs. 171 lakh and released an amount of Rs. 86 lakhs.

For channelling to 12 NGOs under SIDBI-GOl Trade Related Entrepreneurship Assistance and Development (TREAD) programme aimed at empowerment of women and capacity building requirements of MFIs. The MFIs may include NGOs and Community-Based Organizations (CBOs). So far, only three NGOs with a membership of over 8400 women have been assisted under the SIDBI-TREAD initiative.

MICRO FINANCE INSTITUTIONS

The SHG-Band Lineage Programme implemented through the formal banking system has not only gained momentum but has also taken rapid strides forward in recent years. As on 31 March 2005, 1.62 million SHGs comprising 24.25 million poor rural families have been credit-lined by the banks. During 2004-05, bank lending to SHGs was of the order of Rs. 2994.25 crore. With a view to further accelerate the availability of banking services in rural areas and leverage the existing Micro Finance Institutions, the Union Budget for 2005-06 contained the following measures as enunciated:

> "At present, micro finance institutions (MFLs) obtain finance from banks according to guidelines issued by RBI. MRLs seek to provide small scale credit and other financial services to low income households and small informal business. Government intends to promote MFLs in a big way. The way forward, I believe, is to identify MFLs, classify and rate such institutions, and empower them to intermediate between the lending banks and the beneficiaries. Commercial banks may appoint MFLs as "banking correspondents" to provide transaction services on their behalf. As MFIs require infusion of new capital, I propose to re-designate the existing Rs. 100 crore Micro Finance Development Fund as the "Micro Finance Development and Equity Fund". And increase the corpus to Rs. 200 crore. The fund will be managed by a Board consisting of representatives of NABARD, commercial banks and professionals with domain knowledge. The Board will be asked to suggest suitable legislation, and I expect to introduce a draft Bill in the next fiscal year".

Objective

The overall objective of the Scheme is to promote linkages between banks and MFIs so that the poor can have better access to financial services by MFLs. The specific objectives of the Scheme are: to provide capital/equity support to Micro Finance Institutions (MFLs) so as the enable them to leverage capital/equity for accessing commercial and other funds from banks, for providing financial services at an affordable cost to the poor, and to enable MFLs to achieve sustainability in their credit operations over a period of 3-5 years.

Definitions

(a) "Company" means a company as defined in section 3 of the Companies Act, 1956 (1 of 1956), and includes a foreign company within the meaning of section 591 of the Act and section 25 Company allowed to be registered without the addition of the words "Limited" of "Private Limited" at the end of its names;

(b) "Cooperative society" means a society as defined in the principal Act and includes cooperative societies registered under any State enactment for mutually aided or mutual benefit cooperatives or under the Multi-State Cooperative Societies Act, 2002;

(c) "Micro Finance Institution" means an entity whose principal object or principal business is the provision of micro-finance services to eligible clients and comprises micro finance organizations and MFI-NBFCs;

(d) "MFI-NBFCs" means a Non-Banking Financial Company as defined in the Reserve Bank of India Act, 1934 and regulated by Reserve Bank of India and whose principal object of principal business is the provision of micro finance services;

(e) "Micro Finance Organization" means an entity registered in any of the following legal forms whose principal object or principal business is the provision of micro finance services that are not regulated by Reserve Bank of India:

   (i) A society registered under the societies Registration Act, 1860;

   (ii) A Public Trust registered under the Indian Trust Act,

1880 or any state enactment governing religious or charitable public trusts;

(iii) A company registered under Section 25 of the Companies Act, 1956 and specifically exempted from registration by the Reserve Bank; and

(iv) A cooperative society registered under the provisions of the State Cooperative Societies Act or under the Mutually Aided or Mutual Benefit Cooperative Societies Act or Multi-State Cooperative Societies Act, 2002 or under any other law relating to Cooperative Societies in force in India.

Salient Features of the Scheme

(a) *Type of MFLs:* MFI-NBFC and MFOs comprising Societies, Trusts, Section 25 Companies, Co-operatives would be eligible for capital support from the Fund.

(b) *Mode of Support:* The mode of Capital/equity support to the MF is could be as under:

Sl. No.	*Type of MFI*	*Mode of Support*
1.	MFOs • Society • Trust • Sec. 25 companies • Cooperative Society	• Long-term debt • Soft loan
2.	MFI-NBFC	• Equity • Preference shares with a low coupon rate

(c) *Quantum of Capital/Quite Support:* The maximum capital support available for MFOs under the scheme is liked to the outreach and amount of loan outstanding as under: In the case of MFI-NBFCs, the equity support would be restricted upto 10 per cent of the total paid up capital of the entity support that would be considered would however be restricted to Rs. 2.0 crore.

(d) *General Criteria for Eligibility:* The broad eligibility norms for providing capital support to MFIs would be as under:

- The Memorandum of Association and bye-laws of the

MFI should have explicit powers to raise loans from banks and financial institutions to offer security for loans raised from banks and financial institutions in such form as may be required by the lender, and to carry on micro finance activities.

- MFI should have a track record of having undertaken micro finance operations at least for a minimum period of two years. The MFI should have achieved minimum outreach of 2500 poor individuals either through SHGs, Grameen groups, individual lending, etc.
- MFI should have been rated by an accredited rating agency under the NABARD's MFI rating scheme. Only the proposals above the cut-off level prescribed by NABARD would be considered eligible for capital/ equity support.

Outreach (No. of clients)	*Loan amount Outstanding*	*Capital Support*
Upto 10,000	Less than Rs. 2 crore	Maximum Rs. 25 lakh
10001-20,000	Less than Rs. 4 crore	Maximum Rs. 50 lakh
30001-50,000	Less than Rs. 10 crore	Maximum Rs. 1 crore

- MFI should have formulated a realistic business plan for the next 3-5 years demonstrating the financial sustainability of its operations.
- MFI possesses competent and adequate staff for proper appraisal and intensive supervision of its various operations.
- MFI should have string internal control systems and operating procedures. It should maintain a satisfactory and transparent accounting system, MIS<and appropriate internal and external audit systems.

Rating of MFIs

To facilitate the process of rating of MFIs, NABARD had introduced a scheme for financial assistance to banks for ratings of MFIs vide Circular No. NB.MCID/280/MFls/2005-06 dated 11 May 2005 addressed to all Scheduled Commercial Banks including Regional Rural Banks. This scheme has since been revised vide Circular No. NB.mCID/220/m/Fls/2006-07 dated 15 May 2006 and a copy has been sent to all Scheduled Commercial Banks including Regional Rural Banks.

Mahila Vikas Nidhi (MVN)

MVN is specially designed fund for economic empowerment of women. Training and employment opportunities are provided to them through creation of necessary infrastructure. Besides supply of improved inputs, production and technological improvements are also covered under the MVN scheme. The progress of this scheme has been noteworthy. By March 1997, 113 NGOs were supported benefiting over 14,000 women with an aggregate assistance of Rs. 499.69 lakhs.

B. National Bank for Agricultural and Rural Development (NABARD) and its Operation

A pilot project for linking SHGs with banks was launched by NABARD in 1992. The Reserve Bank of India (RBI) persuaded commercial banks, regional rural banks and cooperative banks to actively participate in the linkage programme. Under the RBI's guidelines, banks were given permission to open saving bank account in the name of SHGs and relaxation of security requirements. Thus, an informal credit system was evolved with assistance from formal financial institutions. The agencies involved in the schemes were NABARD, banks, NGOs and SHGs members. The main objectives were to provide the following:

Supplementary Credit to SHGs

- Reduction in transactions cost for both banks as well as SHGs by reducing paper work,
- To mobilize small savings among poor rural women,
- To build mutual trust and confidence between banks, NGOs and rural poor,
- To create healthy relations between SHGs members and the linking agencies, and
- Constant supervision and monitoring by banks through NGOs.

Case Study of Two Successful NGO's in Andhra Pradesh

The 'Padmavathy' Experience

The women in Tirupati were mostly migrants from nearby areas backed by illiteracy, poverty and lack of basic amenities. They were involved in odd activities with fluctuating incomes. Against this background, women had major responsibilities of maintaining their families. This necessitated the need for a regular source of credit. The efforts were to identify and promote income-generating activities among women through a credit delivery system. The banks were initially persuaded to provide loans at Differential Interest Scheme. Despite good repayments, banks could not meet the growing demands for credit on a continuous basis and there was no scope for repeat loans.

The Mahila Abyudaya Podupu Sangam is a self-managed group who generates financial resources through their own savings. Each sangam consists of 10 to 15 members belonging to a particular slum. The primary source of funds is from the savings of members and interest earned on loans extended. Each sangam creates a common fund in order to meet the operational cost. The repayment rate is 100 per cent because of individual responsibility of each member. Apart from financial functions, sangam is a platform for women to interact and address to many of their day-to-day problems. The interactions between sangams resulted in the formation of an association called 'Cluster Association'. Each sangam became a member of the same. The activities of the Association include; promotion of new sangams, resolution of conflicts within and between sangams, address to the common issues, etc.

The 'Padmavathy' which is a legal entity has certain objectives:

- To mobilize funds from formal financial institutions to meet the larger credit needs of its members.
- To promote formation of new sangams.
- To motivate the members to manage the financial requirements independently without external subsidies.
- To promote unity among women of different sangams to give them collective identity for collective action.
- Besides the above objectives, 'Padmavathy' functions as a forum for information and exchange of ideas among

different sangam members. It also has the responsibility of reaching out to more and more of poor women by expanding its activities.

Impact of 'Padmavathy'

'Padmavathy,' which started its operations a decade ago, had 221 sangams and 2647 members by July 1996. The sangams have mobilized Rs. 38.58 lakhs as savings and Rs. 8.31 lakhs as common fund after having met their operational costs. The sangam members with their own savings have a sense of security and confidence.

'Padmavathy' sangam is the first organization linked under the informal banking programme of SIDBI. Initially, it availed a soft loan of Rs. 4 lakhs from SIDBI with the purpose of promoting micro enterprises by women. This assistance had encouraged 200 women to start their own income generating activities. Because of a good repayment experience, SIDBI had sanctioned a second loan of Rs. 5 lakhs also a grant for training members for better credit utilization.

It is true that sustainability of any development initiative is possible only when the participants change their role from passive recipients to active own managers. The 'Padmavathy' experience has proved it through commitment to work sincere efforts to share the benefits of development, active involvement of several sangam members. The model further proves the fact that poor are bankable and the timely access to credit can bring about changes in the lives of thousands of poor women. The sangams have been successful in obtaining loans on reasonable terms with simple procedures. They have also been instrumental in motivating many members who were earlier idle, in taking up some economic activity. Thus, the experience of this model is a source of inspiration for many other poor women with the similar socio-economic conditions.

The Rashtriya Seva Samithi (RASS)

Background

The RASS was established in 1981 at Tirupati. The activities and programmes of RASS were designed for the development of poor in the drought prone Rayalaseema districts of Andhra

Pradesh. This region has a high percentage of population who belong to scheduled castes and the backward castes. The region does not have any major industries except a few agro-processing units. It also lags behind other regions of the State in terms of basic amenities. The rapid growth of population has aggravated poverty, unemployment and environmental degradation in the Rayalaseema region. Some of the anti-poverty programmes proved ineffective, as it was more on target achievement rather than human development. Moreover, the rural poor were not involved from the stage of planning to the stage of implementation and evaluation of programmes meant for their upliftment.

Objectives

The main objective of RASS was to adopt such a strategy, which would bring into fold the poor in the development process. The RASS, believes in the following:

- Involvement of poor in the entire process of development from planning to monitoring.
- Identification of priorities by the poor themselves.
- Empowerment of women as a key to self-sustained development of the poor.
- Provision of community infrastructure as an essential pre-condition for self-sustained growth.
- Development of agriculture and related activities using local knowledge and local resources apart from modern techniques to reduce the incidence of poverty and unemployment.
- The RASS considers the following four interventions as crucial for the poor to reach the stage of social consciousness and empowerment.

Human resource development (by way of massive education, skill upgradation, health services, safe drinking water, sanitation, etc. for the disadvantaged groups). Economic development (through propagation of modern agriculture and technology, family-based asset creating activities and waste land development), Attitudinal changes (to promote greater gender equality, self-reliance and environmental sensitivity).

Self-management and momentum (for the promotion of saving

and credit, community management of infrastructure, leadership and self-help).

Area of Operation and Growth

The core area of operation of RASS includes the districts of Cuddapah, Anantpur, Kurnool and Chittoor. The initial activities of RASS were concentrated in Chittoor district, which accounts for an estimated population of 4.3 million. Subsequently, these activities were spread to other districts of Rayalaseema.

Over a period of eighteen years, RASS has been successful in building up a large administrative infrastructure and reaching out to the rural poor in the backward areas within Andhra Pradesh and in the States of Orissa and Tamil Nadu. Because of its involvement in multi-faceted activities, several funding agencies at the national and international level have shown interest and confidence in RASS. Starting with three program activities in eight villages with 15 staff members, RASS has acquired the status of a national level organization. During 1997-98, RASS had 32 programme activities with 3695 programme staff in 3540 villages operating in three States. The budget of RASS which was Rs. 0.08 million in 1981 had gone up to Rs. 72.08 during the year 1998. Thus, RASS has recorded a phenomenal growth for the past eighteen years.

Women Centered Activities

To tap the potentialities and managerial capacities of rural women RASS has implemented several activities. RASS has been instrumental in organizing rural women to show their strength and defend themselves for their rights with the formation of Mahila Mandals. These Mandals work under the direct supervision and guidance of RASS and also, get regular information about Government programmes, bank financing, marketing trends, etc. The successful working of Mahila Mandals has resulted in the formation of a large number of Self-Help Groups (SHGs).

For women to get gainful employment especially belonging to SC, ST and BCs, RASS provides training facilities and generates innovative programmes. The vocational skills, thus acquired, help women to be self-reliant.

Growth and Performance of SHGs

The successful working of Mahila Mandals has resulted in the formation of a large number of Self-Help Groups (SHGs). In 1990 with the help from RASS, 30 SHGs were formed involving 10-15 women members. Within a year, there were 123 SHGs with a total membership of 1559 women. A significant feature of this system was that a large number of women shifted their borrowing from traditional moneylenders to SHGs at reasonable rates of interest. Moreover, RASS has linked with Rashtriya Mahila Kosh (RMK) and NABARD to mobilize funds. RASS has borrowed about Rs. 7 million from RMK and lent it to informal women groups. Along with the loan from RMK and their own savings, women groups have generated credit to the extent of Rs. 11 million. Some of the notable features of this scheme are a high percentage (96) of repayment, utilization of funds for income-creating activities and generation of saving by women members in the SHGs.

Criticized

1. Lack of support from male members (of the families) as well as banks.
2. Large magnitude of the target group of poor people Attitudinal rigidities.
3. Difficulty in creating awareness among people.
4. Limited resources with the NGOs.
5. Large requirements of training and sensitization of issues.
6. Limited number of experienced intervention agencies.
7. Diversities of situations due to wide coverage.

Overall Impression

- Use of resources (credit) for income-generating activities.
- Adoption of non-traditional activities.
- Improvement in the income levels of SHG members.
- Nearly 100% recovery of loans.
- Generation of small savings in the rural sector among women.
- Use of local knowledge and resources in productive activities.
- Reduction in transaction cost for both banks as well as SHGs.
- Maintenance of minimum records in the form of registers.

- Maintenance of proper accounts by the SHGs.
- Regular meetings of the SHG members to tackle problems among themselves.
- Healthy relation and coordination between SHGs, NGOs and banks.
- Grant assistance by banks to NGOs for capacity building (towards strengthening and monitoring of SHGs, training, computerization, etc.).
- Support services to NGOs by banks for networking with other smaller NGOs.

REFERENCES

NABARD, 1997, 'Micro-Finance Innovations and NABARD'.

RASS, 1998, 'Partners in Progress, Organizing Communities for Development'.

RASS, 1998, Awakening Gender Potential, The SHGs Way.

SIDBI, 1999, Annual Report, 1998-99.

SIDBI, 1997, Development Report, October 1997.

Sri Padmavathy Mahila Abyudaya Sangam, 1996, Community Banking—Our Gurthimpu.

Sri Padmavathy Mahila Abyudaya Sangam, 1996, Training Manual for Community Banking.

Role of the Regional Rural Banks in Economic Development in India

Dr. Anju pal, Dr. Upasna Sharma and
Dr. Sarita Jain

India is basically an agricultural country and agricultural development is important because it provides economic sustenance and builds up a strong industrial base. Indeed the importance of the rural banking in the economic development of a country can not be overlooked. As Gandhiji once said, "real India lies in village," and village economy is the back bone of Indian economy. Without the upliftment of the rural economy as well as the rural people of our country, the objectives of economic planning can not be achieved. In fact, the real growth of Indian economy lied in the emancipation of rural masses from acute poverty, unemployment and socio-economic backwardness.

The present study is a modest attempt to make an appraisal of the credit needs of the rural people of India. In this concern, the Regional Rural Banks in India are the major investors in different types of operations in the rural areas. Actually the concept of rural banking in India dates back to the time when the banking sector was set-up in India. Regional Rural Bank in India was set-up with the purpose of facilitating the promotion of rural business in India. Actually Regional Rural Bank (RRB) established under RRB Act, 1976 for the economic upliftment of the people living below poverty line. Regional Rural Banks in India are spread all across the country and have been playing an important part in the development and growth of the rural sector and the promotion of agricultural sector would definitely give the economy a boost.

The State Bank of India is one of the major commercial banks having regional rural banks. There are thirty Regional Rural banks in India, under the State Bank of India and it is spread in 13 States across India. The number of branches the SBI Regional Rural Banks is more than 2000. They are State sponsored, regionally-based and rural-oriented commercial banks. Apart from the State Bank of India several other banks are also functioning as the promoter of rural development in India. The other regional rural banks in India are as follows:

1. Harvana State Cooperative Apex Bank Limited

The Haryana State Cooperative Apex Bank Limited commonly called as HARCOBANK. It plays a vital role in rural banking. The main purpose of the Haryana State Cooperative Apex Bank limited is to financially assist the artisans in the rural areas, farmers and agrarian unskilled labor and the small rural entrepreneurs of Haryana. Haryana State Cooperative Apex Bank Ltd. also referred as the HARCOBANK, is one of the apex organizations in the State of Haryana. The HARCOBANK holds a special economic position in the State of Haryana. The Haryana State Cooperative Apex Bank limited offers several types of financial assistances to the individuals. The financial aids include credit for the promotion of agriculture, non-agrarian credit and bank deposit facilities. The HARCOBANK have been functioning as an investor for more than three decades.

2. National Bank for Agriculture and Rural Development (NABARD)

National Bank for agriculture and rural development (NABARD) is a development bank in the sector of Regional Rural Banks in India. It has been accredited with "matters concerning policy, planning and operations in the field of credit for agriculture and other economic activities in rural areas in India. NABARD was established by an act of parliament on 12th July 1982 to implement the National Bank for Agriculture and Rural Development Act, 1981. It replaced the Agricultural Credit Department (ACD) and Rural Planning and Credit Cell (RPCC) of Reserve Bank of India and Agricultural Refinance and Development Corporation (ARDC).

Functions of NABARD

The main functions of NABARD are as follows:

1. It works as an apex financing agency for the institutions providing investment and production credit for promoting the various developmental activities in rural areas.
2. It takes measures towards institution building for improving absorptive capacity of the credit delivery system, including monitoring, formulation of rehabilitation schemes, restructuring of credit institution, training of personnel, etc.
3. It provides short-term credit (up to 18 months) to State Cooperative Banks for seasonal agricultural operations (crop loans) marketing of crops, purchase and distribution of fertilizers and working capital requirements of cooperative sugar factories.
4. It provides medium-term credit (18 months to 7 years) to State Cooperative Banks and RRBs for approved agricultural purposes purchase of shares of processing societies and conversion of short-term crop loans into medium-term loans in areas affected by natural calamities.
5. It provides medium and long-term credit (not exceeding 25 years) for investments in agriculture under schematic lending to State Cooperative Banks, land development banks, RRBs and commercial banks.
6. It provides long-term assistance in the form of loans to state governments (not exceeding 20 years) for contribution to share capital of cooperative credit institutions.

7. It maintains a research and development fund to be used to promote research in agriculture and rural development so that projects and programmes can be formulated and designed to suit the requirements of the different areas.
8. It undertakes monitoring and evaluation of projects refinanced by it. NABARD's refinance is available to State Cooperative Agriculture and Rural Development Banks (SCARDBs), State Cooperative Banks (SCBs), Regional Rural Banks (RRBs), Commercial Banks (CBs) and other financial institutions approved by RBI. NABARD has its office at Mumbai. It operates throughout the country through its 28 regional offices and one sub-office located in the capitals of all the states/union territories. It has 336 district offices across the country, one sub-office at Port Blair and one special cell at Srinagar. NABARD is also known for its "SHG Bank Linkage Programme" which encourages India's banks to lend to self-help groups (SHGs). Because SHGs are composed mainly of poor women, this has evolved into an important Indian tool for microfinance.

3. Sindhanur Urban Souharda Co-operative Bank

Sindhanur Urban Souharda Cooperative Bank, popularly known as SUCO Bank. It is the first of its kind in rural banks of India. The main purpose of the Sindhanur Urban Souharda Cooperative Bank is to provide financial support to the rural sector. The impressive story of its inception is interesting and inspiring for all the youth of this country.

4. United Bank of India

United Bank of India also plays an important role in regional rural banks. It has expanded its branch network in a big way to actively participate in the development of the rural and semi-urban areas in conformity with objectives of nationalization.

5. Syndicate Bank

Syndicate bank firmly rooted in rural India as rural banking and has a clear vision of future. India by understanding the grassroots realities. Its progress has been abreast of the phase of progressive banking in India especially in rural banks. Syndicate Bank has its grass roots in the rural sector. The development of the Syndicate Bank was in accordance to the development of the banking sector in India. Syndicate bank has performed actively in the development of the rural sector in India.

The growth of the rural industries in India and the development of the rural business and economy have been dependent largely on the investment and financial aids provided by the regional rural banks in India. The government of India promulgated the regional rural banks ordinance on 26th September 1975, which was later replaced by the Regional Rural Bank Act, 1976. The preamble to the act states the objective to develop rural economy by providing credit and facilities for the development of agriculture, trade, commerce, industry and other productive activities in the rural areas, particularly to small and marginal farmers, agricultural laborers, artisans and small entrepreneurs.

The RRB act empowers the central government to open the banks from time to time at places where it may consider its necessity. A regional rural bank is jointly owned by the Government of India. Here we share the organizational structure of RRB in India:

Organizational Structure of RRB

The management of a RRB is vested in a nine member board of directors headed by chairman who is an officer deputed by a sponsor bank but appointed by the government of India—

- Three directors to be nominated the central government.
- Two directors to be nominated by the concerned state government.
- Three directors to be nominated by the sponsor bank.

The sponsor bank, besides subscribing to the capital and deputing one of its officials as chairman, provides assistance to RRB in several ways such as financial accommodation, deputing managerial and other staff and arranging the recruitment of staffs and their training.

Functions of RRB

RRB may undertake the following types of functions:

The granting of loans and advances particularly to small and marginal farmers and agricultural labors individually or to a group. Cooperative societies, agricultural processing societies, cooperative farming societies, etc. The granting of loans and advances to artisans, small entrepreneurs and small traders, businessmen, etc.

The Reserve Bank of India has brought RRB's under the ambit of priority sector lending on per with the commercial banks. They have to ensure that forty per cent of their advances are accounted for the priority sector within the 40% priority target 25% should go to weaker section or 10% of their total advances to go to weaker section.

The government is committed to increase credit flow to rural masses and all necessary steps will be taken to strengthen Regional Rural Banks assured the Finance Minister Shri P. Chidambaram while addressing the members of parliamentary consultative attached to his ministry in a meeting held on 25th April 2007. Speaking on this occastion the minister stated that the RRBs are playing an important role in developing the rural economy. RRBs have issued 69 lakh Kisan Credit Cards (KCCs) which is 11% of total KCCs and have been advised by the government to increase the number of KCCs. The RRBs have formed 7.4 lakh SHGs till 2005-06 making the access easier to the farmers. The finance minister told that the RRBs have been directed to lend more money to non-farming community also within the rural population.

Hence we can not deny the fact that the Regional Rural Banks has actively contributed to the growth of the rural sector. The growth of the rural industries in India and the development of the rural business and economy have been dependent largely on the investment and financial aids provided by the Regional Rural Banks in India. It is obvious that the number of rural branches should be increased rather than reduced. They should be encouraged to develop more sophisticated methods to meet the changing needs of farming and most of all there should be greater coordination between district planning authorities, panchayati raj institutions and the banks operating in rural areas. Only will the RRBs fulfil the promise that is so essential for rural development.

REFERENCES

B.S. Yadav and Archana Singhal, "Role of Regional Rural Banks in Rural Development," New Delhi, 2005.

Economic and Political Weekly, Vol. 3, No. 25, Mumbai, June 2007.

EDA and APMAS Self-help Groups in India: A study of the Lights and Shades, CARE, CRS,USAID and GTZ, 2006.

Frontline, Vol. 23, Issue 3, February 11-24, New Delhi, 2006.

Kaye Tasi, "Role of Regional Rural Banks in Economic Development," New Delhi, 2006.

Quoted in Alice Albin Morris and Sabastian Morris, "The Rural Infrastructure Development Fund: A Review," in India Infrastructure Report, 2003, New Delhi.

S.K. Misra and V.K. Puri, "Indian Economy—Its Development Experience, Himalaya Publishing House, Mumbai, 2007.

Yojana, Vol. 42, August, New Delhi, 2007.

Working of Regional Banks for Rural Society

Mrs. Anupa Singh

Agriculture plays a crucial role in the development of the Indian economy is still true. Agriculture is the most important sector of the Indian Economy from the perspective of poverty alleviation and employment generation. It accounts for about 25 per cent of India's national income at present. Agriculture is the foundation of our economy and is playing a key role in sustaining the economic growth of our country since independence. There is a structural lag in agriculture sector. This is reflected in low share of agriculture in national income but large share of work force dependency on agriculture.

The overwhelming majority of poor people in India are concentrated in rural area of the estimated 260 million Indians (or 26% of the population who live in poverty) some 193 million (or 74%) live in rural areas (Planning Commission of India's definition of poverty). The catalytic role played by credit for accelerating the economic development has been well recognized all over the world. Since the inception of Central Economic Planning in 1950, the government identified the credit needs of rural sector and framed policies conducive for the flow of institutional credit.[1]

Broadly, there are two sources of credit available to the farmers—institutional and private. Non-institutional or private sources include money-lenders, traders and commission agents, relatives and landlords; institutional sources consist of Government and Cooperatives, commercial banks including the Regional Rural Banks (RRBs). The non-institutional agencies dominated agricultural credit before the nationalization of major commercial banks. The share of institutional and non-institutional credit in the total agricultural credit in India is presented in Table 1.

TABLE 1

Source of Agriculture Credit in India (%)

Source	*1951-52*	*1960-61*	*1970-71*	*1980-81*	*1990-91*	*2001-02*
Non-Institutional	89.40	66.80	68.30	36.80	36.00	38.90
Institutional	10.60	33.20	31.70	63.20	64.00	61.10
Total	100.00	100.00	100.00	100.00	100.00	100.00

Sources: 1. Annual Report of NABARD, 2000 (Various issues, www.nabard.org.)
2. AIDIS, NSSO, 59th Round, 2003.

As can be seen from Table 1, in 1951-52, 89.4 per cent was non-institutional source and 10.6 per cent was institutional source. In pre-reform period 36.0 per cent was in non-institutional source and 64.0 per cent was in institutional source of credit and in the post-reform period there were 38.9 per cent in non-institutional source and 61.9 per cent is institutional source. It is observed that non-institutional source of credit has decreased highly from 1951 to 2002 and at the same time institutional source of credit has also continuously increased. There is found inverse relationship between non-institutional and institutional source of agricultural credit from 1951 to 2002. Since independence, a multi-agency approach consisting of co-operatives, commercial banks and regional rural banks has been adopted to provide cheaper and adequate credit to farmers. The major policy in the sphere of agricultural credit has been its progressive institutionalization for supplying agriculture and rural development programmes with adequate and timely flow of credit to assist weaker sections and less developed regions.[2]

The inadequacy of rural credit continued to engage the attention of the Reserve Bank and the Government of India throughout the 1950s and 1960s. The Agricultural Refinance Corporation (ARC) was set-up by the Reserve Bank in 1963 to provide funds by way of refinance, but credit co-operatives still did not function too well. Consequently the All India Rural Credit Review Committee was set-up in July 1966 to review the supply of rural credit in the context of the Fourth Five-year Plan in general, and the requirements of the intensive programmes of agricultural production in different parts of the country, in particular and to make recommendations for improving the flow of agricultural credit.

Despite all these efforts, the flow of credit to agricultural sectors failed to exhibit any appreciable improvement mainly due to the fact that commercial banks were not tuned to the needs and requirements of small and marginal farmers, while the co-operatives on the other hand, lacked resources to meet the expected demand. The solution that was found involved the establishment of a separate banking structure, capable of combining the local feel and familiarity of rural problems characteristic of cooperatives and the professionalism and large resource base of commercial banks. Following the recommendations of the working group on rural banks, headed by M. Narsimham as Chairman, Regional Rural Banks (RRBs) were set-up. Thus, by the end of 1977 there emerged three separate institutions for providing rural credit which is often described as "The multi-agency approach". Following the recommendations of the committee to review Arrangements for Institutional credit for Agriculture and Rural Development, the National Bank for Agriculture and Rural Development (NABARD) was set-up in 1982 to provide credit for the promotion of agriculture.

The extent of institutional credit for farmers in recent years is given in Table 2.

Table 2 shows that total agricultural credit from institutional sources had steadily increased from Rs. 6230 crores in 1984-85 to Rs. 1,80,480 crores in 2005-06. The contribution of cooperatives was 55 per cent of total institutional credit in 1984-85 but was only 22 per cent in 2005-06. Correspondingly commercial banks including RRBs have raised their share from 45 per cent to 70 per cent during this period. Table 2 shows that even though total institutional credit to agriculture, has been steadily rising, there has been steady decrease in percentage terms, in the contribution of cooperative banks in rural credit from 55% in 1984 to 22% in 2005-06. The share of RRBs is almost insignificant between 6 per cent and 8 per cent. The share of commercial banks has been steadily rising from 45 per cent to 70 per cent.[3]

TABLE 2

Institutional Credit to Agriculture

Year	*Cooperative Banks Amount*	*%*	*RRBs Amount*	*%*	*Commercial Banks Amount*	*%*	*Total Institutional Credit Amount*	*%*
1984-85	3,440	55	—	—	2,790	45	6,230	100
1997-98	14,090	44	2,040	6	15,830	50	31,960	100
2002-03	24,300	34	5,470	8	41,050	58	70,820	100
2005-06	39,400	22	15,220	8	1,25,860	70	1,80,480	100

Source: Economic Survey, 2006-07, p. 171.

One of the important points of the old 20-point economic programme of Mrs. Indira Gandhi during emergency was the liquidation of rural indebtedness by stages and provide institutional credit to farmers and artisans in rural areas. It was in pursuance of this aspect of the New Economic Programme that the Government of India set-up the Regional Rural Banks. The main objective of the regional rural banks is to provide credit and other facilities particularly to the small and marginal farmers, agricultural labourers, artisans and small entrepreneurs so as to develop agriculture, trade, commerce, industry and other productive activities in the rural areas. Regional Rural Banks (RRBs) were set-up under the Regional Rural Banks' Act, 1976. RRBs were expected to operate as state sponsored, region-based and rural-oriented commercial banks. RRBs were expected to mobilize resources from rural areas and play a significant role in developing agriculture and rural economy by deploying mobilized resources in rural sectors for the needy not covered by SCBS despite their large network. Keeping this objective in view, the capital of RRBs is held by the Central Government, concerned State Government and sponsor bank in the proportion of 50:15: 35. Initially, five regional rural banks were set-up on October 2,

1975 at Moradabad and Gorakhpur in Uttar Pradesh, Bhiwani in Haryana, Jaipur in Rajasthan and Malda in West Bengal. Each regional rural bank had an authorized capital of Rs. 1 crore, and issued and paid up capital of Rs. 25 lakhs. The sponsor banks have continued to provide managerial and financial assistance to RRBs and also other concessions such as lower rate of interest (8.5 per cent) on the latter's borrowings from sponsor banks. Further, the cost of staff deputed to RRBs and training expenses of RRB staff are borne by the sponsor banks. The Reserve Bank of India has been granting many concessions to RRBs such as they are allowed to maintain cash reserve ratio at 3 per cent and statutory liquidity ratio at 25 per cent and are provided refinance facilities through NABARD.

RRBs and NABARD

National bank has the responsibility to lay down policies for RRBs to over see their operations, provide refinance facilities and attend to problems faced by them. The National Bank undertakes all work relating to the establishment of RRBs, administration of refinance scheme, formulation of appropriate operational policies, monitor their performance and keep liaison with the Reserve Bank in regard to branch expansion and the statutory inspection of RRBs.

Progress of RRBs

RRBs have an important role to play in India's rural economy. In course of time, they are intended to eliminate moneylenders altogether. They have rendered service in the economic upliftment of the rural people, especially those living below poverty line. There are now 196 RRBs in 23 States with 14,500 branches. The rural and semi-urban branches of RRBs constitute 98 per cent of their network. Their deposits and advances as on March 31, 2003 were Rs. 49,078 crores and Rs. 22,028 crores respectively. Over 95 per cent of the loans of RRBs, were provided to the weaker sections. RRBs have done well in mobilizing rural deposits and infusing the thrift habit in their clients. The bulk of the loans from RRBs have been to priority sectors which accounted for 70 per cent of the total. Agriculture alone took up 46 per cent of the priority sector advances. The involvement of RRBs in providing credit support to small and retail trade and other non-farm rural activities is better than that of co-operatives and commercial banks. In the last 30 years, RRBs have been active participants in programmes designed to provide credit assistance to identified beneficiaries under the new 20-point programme, IRDP and other special programmes for scheduled castes and tribes. They are also implementing differential rate of interest (DRI) schemes for the weaker sections and physically handicapped persons.

As on March 31, 2002, the outreach of RRBs in terms of number of deposits and advances was 50.02 million and 11.94 million respectively. The per-employee accounts handled by RRBs were 885 against the national average of 464 in the banking industry. Similarly, the staff and branch network of RRBs, though respectively 6.7 per cent and 21.8 per cent of the national network, served 11.5 per cent of the total deposit accounts and 21.8 per cent of credit accounts of the banking industry.

During the first decade of their operations, RRBs concentrated on expanding credit services which were reflected in the credit-deposit ratio of more than 100 per cent upto 1987. Thereafter, the C-D ratio declined, reflecting a reorientation in their activities. However, the credit-deposit ratio improved to 55.7 per cent in 2005-06 from 41.3 per cent in 2000-01. This resulted in an increase in the share of income from advances from 34.7 per cent in 2000-01 to 53.8 per cent in 2005-06 (Table 3). The share of income from investment, in contrast, declined to 39.5 per cent in 2005-06 from 60.5 per cent in 2000-01.

In the wake of introduction of financial sector reforms in 1991-92, the commercial viability of RRB's emerged as the most crucial factor in deciding about their required role in the emerging economic scenario. The financial health of RRBs turned weak mainly due to its limited business flexibility with hardly any scope of expansion/diversification, smaller size of loans with higher exposure to risk-prone advances and professional inefficiency in financial deployment. To strength RRBs and improve their performance, the Reserve Bank allowed RRBs to lend to non-target groups, deregulated their deposit and lending rates, and permitted investment of their surplus funds in profitable avenues. These measures were supported with well-defined business plan preparation from the branches, time bound implementation for attaining profitability, human resource development programmes, and organizational development initiatives as an integrated tool for turnaround.

TABLE 3

Investment and Advances of RRBs

(Rs. crore)

Item	*2000-01*	*2004-05*	*2005-06*
1	2	3	4
(1) Share of Income from			
(i) Advances	34.8	49.7	53.8
(ii) Investment	60.5	42.9	39.5
(2) ID Ratio*	72.2	59.2	57.6
(3) CD Ratio	41.3	52.9	55.7

* ID (Investment-Deposit) Ratio = Investments including other bank balances and other investments to total deposits.
Source: NABARD.

The RRBs, which incurred losses of Rs. 426 crore in 1995-96, started posting profits after various reform measures were introduced. Net profits increased to Rs. 769 crores during 2003-04. Although net profits declined thereafter to Rs. 510 crore during 2005-06, mainly because of reduction is net margin and also payment of arrears, the overall health of RRBs has improved significantly over the years. The productivity of RRBs, both in terms of per branch and per employee, increased significantly during last 10 years.[4]

RESTRUCTURING OF RRBs

The Government has taken several measures for reconstruction/ recapitalization of the RRBs. The performance of RRBs improved in the years immediately following the first phase of recapitalization, i.e. in 1995-96 and 1996-97, but it was overshadowed due to the introduction of prudential norms of Asset Classification, Income Recognition and Provisioning for RRBs. The RRBs as a group made a profit of Rs. 73 crore for the first time during 1997-98 and improved further to Rs. 601 crore and to Rs. 608 crore during the last two years, i.e. 2000-01 and

2001-02, the viability-based categorization of RRBs as on 31st March 2002 shows that out of 196 RRBs, 86 RRBs have wiped-off their accumulated losses and in a way attained a sustainable viability whereas 89 other RRBs have achieved a turnaround and attained a current viability status leaving only 29 RRBs which continued to incur losses. The recovery performance of RRBs has shown a consistent improvement from around 40% in 1991-92 to 70% during the year 2001-02. The NPAS of RRBs have also been declining in percentage terms and stood at 16% as on 31st March 2002 as against 43% as on 31st March 1996 when the norms were first made applicable to the RRBs.

Since RRBs are important financial institutional in the rural credit structure, they continue to receive focused attention from NABARD. Government of India had set-up a working group under the chairmanship of Mr. M.V.S. Chalpathi Rao, Managing Director, NABARD in 2001 to examine various aspects of functioning of RRBs and to make recommendations for RRBs to become an effective instrument for development of the rural economy. To provide a thrust to agricultural lending, the Government of India announced a policy in 2004 to double the flow of credit by banks to the agriculture in three years. An internal working group as RRBs set-up by the RBI has suggested far reaching measures including mergers and acquisition of RRBs, change in sponsorship by involving private banks, appointment of chairman from the sector, minimum capital requirement and a host of new avenues of business to augment their fee-based incomes. The group has called for a change in sponsorship for which new banks, both from public as well as private sector, should be roped into improve competitiveness, work culture, management and efficiency of concerned RRBs. The committee has said that RRBs may be asked to maintain the capital to risk weighted assets ratio (CRAR) at 5% and overtime they may be expected to align themselves with Basel-I norms. To wipe out accumulated losses, provide for non-performing assets, and maintain a 5% CRAR, capital to the extent of around Rs. 3,050 crore would have to be infused in these banks with appropriate conditions. To increase their non-interest income, RRBs may be encouraged to actively consider distribution of products of mutual fund/insurance companies. They could also focus on other non-fund-based business like offering consultancy services to farmers and issuing drafts. In order to improve profitability and productivity, RRBs may rationalize their branch network.[5]

In order to reposition RRBs as an effective instrument of credit delivery in the Indian financial system, the Government of India after consultation with RRBs, the concerned State Governments and the sponsor banks initiated State-level amalgamation of RRBs, sponsor bank-wise in September 2005. Till October 31, 2006, 137 RRBs were amalgamated to form 43 new RRBs, sponsored by 18 commercial banks in 15 states, bringing down the total number of RRBs in the country to 102 from 196. The amalgamation process of phase I is in the process of being completed. NABARD is providing full guidance and support to smoothen the process of amalgamation. After amalgamation, RRBs would become bigger in size with a larger area of operation, which would enable them to function in a competitive environment more effectively by taking advantage of the economies of scale and reduction in transaction cost. The process of bringing down the number of RRBs would also make it more convenient for the sponsor banks to manage the affairs of RRBs. In view of amalgamation of RRBs, the number of both profit-making and loss-making RRBs declined to 111 and 22, respectively at end-March 2005. The sharper decline in income as compared with the expenditure resulted in lower net profits of Rs. 510 crore for RRBs during 2005-06 as compared with Rs. 748 crore during 2004-05. The ratio of gross and net NPAS declined sharply during the year to 7.3 per cent and 4.0 per cent, respectively, enabled by improved recovery to the extent of 80 per cent. RRBs issued loans to the extent of Rs. 32,871 crore during 2005-06, out of which the share of priority sector was 79.3 per cent. As at end-March 2006, the outstanding advances of RRBs were Rs. 39,713 crore, of which the share of priority sector was 81.7 per cent. The share of agricultural loans increased to 54.0 per cent at end March, 2005, while the share of non-agricultural loans declined to 46.0 per cent from 49.2 per cent during the period.

The time has come for the RRBs to come upon their own and play a greater role in agricultural credit under the overall guidance and advice of NABARD. To ensure this, the umbilical cord to their sponsor banks has to be severed.[6] The share of sponsoring institutions in the capital structure of RRBs need to be enlarged to make them a majority shareholder. By doing so the sponsor banks can convert them into vibrant and professional subsidiaries and area-specific Special Business Units (SBUs). In the long-run, RRBs may integrate all their agricultural and rural activities under the umbrella of these SBUs. Even Co-operative Banks can be merged with these SBUs at later stages. CRR and SLR requirements of RRB's need to be different from those applicable to other commercial banks which would make available more resources for rural credit deployment. Most of the RRB staff was recruited during the initial stages and there has been ban on fresh recruitment since 1992. The staff is getting older whereas the complexities and demands of rural banking now call for more dynamism and youthful talent. Rural banking has emerged as a niche, wherein special skill—set and sensitivity are required. Therefore, the imposed ban on fresh recruitment should be reviewed at the earliest to enhance and diversify the business of RRBs. The RRBs have to emerge as independent institutions and expand their operations and step-in into areas where cooperatives have weakened.

Notes and References

1. Manmohan, Geeta, Monika, Tushir and Sumita Chadha, "Rural Banking and Micro Finance," *Southern Economist*, May 15, 2008, p. 9.
2. Naidu, Vasudevulu C. and M. Rukmini Reddy, "Agricultural Credit in India: An Analysis," *Southern Economist*, February 15, 2007, pp. 11-13.
3. Dutta, Ruddar and K.P.M. Sundharam, "Organization of Rural Credit in India," *Indian Economy*, 58th Edition, 2008, Sultan Chand & Co. Ltd., pp. 557-58.
4. Report on Trend and Progress of Banking in India, 2005-06, Reserve Bank of India, Mumbai, pp. 102-05.
5. "Regional Rural Banks at Crossroads," *Southern Economist*, June 15, 2005.
6. Satish, P., "Agricultural Credit in the Post-Reform Era," *Economic and Political Weekly*, June 30, 2007, p. 2574.

Rural Sector Upliftment by Regional Rural Banks

Ms. Shikha Tyagi, Ms. Asha Bansal and Ms. Namrata Sharma

Introduction

Regional Rural Banks were established under the provisions of an Ordinance promulgated on the 26th September 1975 and the RRB Act, 1976 with an objective to ensure sufficient institutional credit for agriculture and other rural sectors. The RRBs mobilize financial resources from rural/semi-urban areas and grant loans and advances mostly to small and marginal farmers, agricultural labourers and rural artisans. The area of operation of RRBs is limited to the area as notified by Government of India covering one or more districts in the State.

RRBs are jointly owned by Government of India, the concerned State Government and Sponsor Banks (27 scheduled commercial banks and one State Cooperative Bank); the owners in the proportion of 50%, 15% and 35% share the issued capital of a RRB respectively. Regional Rural Banks have been in existence for around three decades in the Indian financial scene. Inception of regional rural banks (RRBs) can be seen as a unique experiment as well as experience in improving the efficacy of rural credit delivery mechanism in India. With joint share holding by Central Government, the concerned State Government and the sponsoring bank, an effort was made to integrate commercial banking within the broad policy thrust towards social banking keeping in view the local peculiarities. The genesis of the RRBs can be traced to the need for a stronger institutional arrangement for providing rural credit. The Narsimham Committee conceptualized the creation of RRBs in 1975 as a new set of regionally-oriented rural banks, which would combine the local feel and familiarity of rural problems characteristic of cooperatives with the professionalism and large resource base of commercial banks. Subsequently, the RRBs were set-up through the promulgation of RRB Act of 1976. Their equity is held by the Central Government, concerned State Government and the Sponsor Bank in the proportion of 50:15:35. RRBs were supposed to evolve as specialised rural financial institutions for developing the rural economy by providing credit to small and marginal farmers, agricultural labourers, artisans and small entrepreneurs. Over the years, the RRBs, which are often viewed as the small man's bank, have taken deep roots and have become a sort of inseparable part of the rural credit structure. They have played a key role in rural institutional financing in terms of geographical coverage, clientele outreach and business volume as also contribution to development of the rural economy. A remarkable feature of their performance over the past three decades has been the massive expansion of their retail network in rural areas. From a modest beginning of 6 RRBs with 17 branches covering 12 districts in December 1975, the numbers have grown into 196 RRBs with 14,446 branches working in 518 districts across the country in March 2004. RRBs have a large branch network in the rural area forming around 43 per cent of the total rural branches of commercial banks.

The rural orientation of RRBs is formidable with rural and semi-urban branches constituting over 97 per cent of their branch network. The growth in the branch network has enabled the RRBs to expand banking activities in the unbanked areas and mobilise rural savings. The mandate of promoting banking with a rural focus, however, would be an enduring phenomenon only when the financial health of the RRBs is sound. With built-in restrictions on their operations, it is common to expect that the financial health of the RRBs itself would be a matter of concern. As regards their financial status, during the year 2003-04, 163 RRBs earned profits amounting to Rs. 953 crore while 33 RRBs incurred losses to the tune of Rs. 184 crore. Ninety RRBs had accumulated losses as on March 31, 2004. Aggregate accumulated loss of RRBs amounted to Rs. 2,725 crore during the year 2003-04. Of the 90 RRBs having accumulated loss, 53 RRBs had eroded their entire owned funds as also a part of their deposits. Furthermore, non-performing assets (NPAs) of the RRBs in absolute terms stood at Rs. 3,299 crore as on March 31, 2004. The percentage of gross NPAs was 12.6 during the year ending March 31, 2004. While 103 RRBs had gross NPAs less than the national average, 93 had NPAs more than it.

Given the multi-agency share holding, this study makes an attempt to enquire into such factors that influence the performance of the RRBs and the role played by sponsor bank in a broader scenario. The problem has been approached in a deductive pattern. First, an attempt is made to identify the extent of the problem of loss-making RRBs and see if they are confined to some particular sponsor banks or States. If the problem banks and States could be identified that would help in focussing the attention for an enduring solution. Subsequently, a model-based approach has been pursued to identify the factors that are responsible for the problems faced by the RRBs. This study contributes to the literature on RRBs primarily in two ways. First, the issues concerning RRBs are an area that is less visited empirically (econometrically) compared to the vast literature on commercial banks.

District Coverage

RRBs covered 525 out of 605 districts as on 31 March 2006. After amalgamation, RRBs have become quite large covering most parts of the State in many cases. Assam Gramin Vikas Bank, an amalgamated RRB, covers 25 districts, the highest in the country, while five other amalgamated RRBs cover 10 or more districts each. However, 40 RRBs covered two districts and 16 RRBs covered a single district each in 2005-06. Increased coverage of districts by RRBs makes them an important segment of the Rural Financial Institutions (RFIs) for financial inclusion.

BRANCH NETWORK

The number of branches of RRBs increased to 14,494 as on 31 March 2006 from 13,920 branches as on 31 March 1989. The network of the 45 amalgamated RRBs (as on April 2007) was quite large and diverse varying from 85 to 680 branches. The Uttar Bihar KGB, an amalgamated RRB, has 680 branches, followed by Baroda Eastern UPGB with 539 branches. The branch network of stand-alone RRBs varied between 8 and 242 as on 31 March 2006.

KEY PERFORMANCE INDICATORS

Reforms introduced in RRBs by Government of India in consultation with RBI and NABARD have yielded positive results in respect of key performance indicators, as indicated under:

- 111 RRBs out of total 133 registered profit in the year 2005-06.
- CD Ratio has been increasing from 46% on 31 March 2004 to 53% on 31 March 2005 and further to 56% on 31 March 2006.
- Recovery percentage has been improving from 73% during 2003-04 to 80% during 2005-06.
- Consequently, net NPAs have declined from 8.55% on 31 March 2004 to 3.99% on 31 March 2006.
- Loans disbursement registered an impressive 35% annual growth in 2004-05 and 21% in 2005-06.
- Per branch productivity has increased from Rs. 5.71 crore on 31 March 2004 to Rs. 7.66 crore on 31 March 2006.
- Per staff productivity has increased from Rs. 1.19 crore on 31 March 2004 to Rs. 1.62 crore on 31 March 2006.
- There has been a decline in the total number of staff.

PERFORMANCE UNDER "DOUBLING OF AGRICULTURE CREDIT": RRBS

More importantly, the performance of RRBs under GoI's initiative on doubling of agriculture credit in three years (from base year 2003-04) and greater coverage of small and marginal farmers, have been impressive. They disbursed agriculture loans of the order of Rs. 12,404 crore during 2004-05 registering a phenomenal annual growth of 64% against the targeted 30%. During 2005-06, agriculture credit flow stood at Rs. 15,223 crore with a growth of 23%. Thus, RRBs have achieved the target of doubling of agriculture credit in 2 years. RRBs financed 18.58 lakh new farmers in 2004-05 and another 17.03 lakh new farmers in 2005-06.

RRB's Potential Role in Financial Inclusion

Post-merger RRBs represent a powerful instrument for financial inclusion. Their outreach *vis-a-vis* other scheduled commercial banks particularly in regions and across population groups facing the brunt of financial exclusion is impressive, as observed from an analysis of Basic Statistical Returns of the RBI and indicated in the following paragraphs. With merger infusing the much needed financial strength in RRBs coupled with the local feel and familiarity they command, RRBs are in a unique position to play a decisive role in financial inclusion.

Outreach

In rural areas, RRBs account for a substantial 37% of total offices of all scheduled commercial banks. In semi-urban areas, their share comes to 15%. It goes without saying that exclusion is more severe in rural areas.

Since their inception, regional rural banks (RRBs) have taken deep roots and have become a sort of inseparable part of the rural credit structure in India. The financial viability of the RRBs has, however, been a matter of concern since the 1980s, just five years after their existence. A number of committees have gone into the issue of their financial viability and possible restructuring. This study follows a deductive approach. First the extent of the problem of the loss-making RRBs has been studied to analyse if the problem is confined to some particular sponsor banks or States. Subsequently, an attempt is made to enquire as to factors that influence the performance of the RRBs and the role-played by the sponsor banks.

The empirical analysis has been couched in terms of profit and loss-making RRBs for a reasonably long (10-year) period to draw robust policy inferences.

Rural Banks in those days mainly focussed upon the agro-sector. Regional rural banks in India penetrated every corner of the country and extended a helping hand in the growth process of the country.

SBI has 30 Regional Rural Banks in India known as RRBs. The rural banks of SBI is spread in 13 states extending from Kashmir to Karnataka and Himachal Pradesh to North East. The total number of SBIs Regional Rural Banks in India branches is 2349 (16%). Till date in rural banking in India, there are 14,475 rural banks in the country of which 2126 (91%) are located in remote rural areas.

Apart from SBI, there are other few banks which functions for the development of the rural areas in India. Few of them are as follows:

1. Haryana State Cooperative Apex Bank Limited

The Haryana State Cooperative Apex Bank Ltd. commonly called as HARCOBANK plays a vital role in rural banking in the economy of Haryana State and has been providing aids and financing farmers, rural artisans, agricultural labourers, entrepreneurs, etc. in the state and giving service to its depositors.

2. NABARD

National Bank for Agriculture and Rural Development (NABARD) is a development bank in the sector of Regional Rural Banks in India. It provides and regulates credit and gives service for the promotion and development of rural sectors mainly agriculture, small scale industries, cottage and village industries, handicrafts. It also finance rural crafts and other allied rural economic activities to promote integrated rural development. It helps in securing rural prosperity and its connected matters.

NABARD's Roles and Functions are summarized below:

- Credit Functions
- Developmental and Promotional Functions
- Supervisory Functions
- Institutional and Capacity building
-

3. Sindhanur Urban Souharda Co-operative Bank

Sindhanur Urban Souharda Co-operative Bank, popularly known as SUCO Bank is the first of its kind in rural banks of India. The impressive story of its inception is interesting and inspiring for all the youth of this country.

4. United Bank of India

United Bank of India (UBI) also plays an important role in regional rural banks. It has expanded its branch network in a big way to actively participate in the development of the rural and semi-urban areas in conformity with the objectives of nationalisation.

Syndicate Bank was firmly rooted in rural India as rural banking and have a clear vision of future India by understanding the grassroot realities. Its progress has been abreast of the phase of progressive banking in India especially in rural banks.

REGIONAL RURAL BANKS

In the multiagency approach to provide credit to agriculture, Regional Rural Banks (RRB's) have special place. They are state sponsored, regionally based and rural-oriented commercial banks. The Govt. of India, in July 1975, appointed a Working Group to study in depth the problem of devising alternative agencies to provide institutional credit to the rural people in the context of steps then initiated under the 20 Point Economic Programme. The Working Group identified various weaknesses of the co-operative credit agencies and the commercial banks and felt that these institutions would not be able to fill the regional and functional gaps in the rural credit system within a reasonable period of time. The Group therefore recommended a new type of institutions which combines:

(a) Local feel and familiarity with rural possess problems which co-operative banks.
(b) Degree of business organization ability to mobilise deposit, access to money market and modernised outlook which commercial banks have.

Thus, it was envisaged to combine desirable qualities of cooperative banks and commercial banks in RRB's at the same time, it was emphasised that the role of RRB's would be to supplement and not supplant the other institutional agencies already existing in the field.

The Government of India promulgated the Regional Rural Bank's Ordinance on 26th September 1975, which was later replaced by the Regional Rural Bank Act, 1976. The preamble to the Act states the objective to develop rural economy by providing credit and facilities for the development of agriculture, trade, commerce, industry and other productive activities in the rural areas, particularly to small and marginal farmers, agricultural labourers, artisans and small entrepreneurs.

Capital Structure

The RRB Act empowers the Central Government to open the banks from time to time at places where it may consider it necessary. A Regional Rural Bank is jointly owned by the Govt. of India, the Government of concerned state and public sector bank, which sponsored it. The authorised capital of each bank is Rs. 1 crore and the issued capital is Rs. 25 lakhs; which is held by them in the proportion of 50, 15 and 35 per cent respectively. Each bank carries the banking business within the local limits specified by the Government notification.

Organisational Structure

The management of a RRB is vested in a nine-member Board of Directors headed by:

(i) Chairman who is an officer deputed by a sponsor bank but appointed by the Government of India.
(ii) Three directors to be nominated the Central Government.
(iii) Two directors to be nominated by the concerned State Government.
(iv) Three directors to be nominated by the sponsor bank.

The sponsor bank, besides subscribing to the capital and deputing one of its official as chairman, provides assistance to RRB in several ways such as financial accommodation, deputing managerial and other staff and arranging the recruitment of staff and their training.

Functions

Rural Bank in Farm Sector

NABARD has played a significant role in rural development. Over the period it has introduced several important schemes and innovative ideas to enhance the flow of rural and agricultural credit. NABARD provides policy support for various farm sector initiatives aimed at accelerating ground level credit flow by rural credit agencies for various farm-related activities under investment credit with a view to increasing agricultural production and productivity, generating rural employment, managing natural resources and alleviating rural poverty through credit and grant support. In addition, with the objective of facilitating development and ensuring prosperity in the rural sector, NABARD supports initiatives in Natural Resource Management and has developed unique models in the process which have become bench marks in their respective fields.

To this effect, the Development Policy Department—Farm Sector's Core Business is to provide policy and promotional support for various farm sector initiatives aimed at accelerating ground level credit flow by rural credit agencies for various farm-related activities under investment credit with a view to increasing agricultural production and productivity, generating rural employment, and raising the standard of living of rural poor through credit and grant. In addition, with the objective of facilitating sustainable and equitable development in the rural sector, the department supports initiatives in Natural Resource Management for implementation of development models.

Rural Bank in Handicrafts Industry

Handicrafts industry finance in India has increased in recent years. The industry of Handicrafts finance in India has helped in the growth of the industry. The Indian Handicrafts products reflect the rural cultural value and its richness of heritage.

The Indian Handicrafts industry is mainly based in the rural areas of the country. The majority of the production units of the industry of Handicrafts in India are based in rural and small towns. The Indian Handicrafts industry provides the second largest employment opportunities to the people in the country.

As the industry of Handicrafts in India is based mainly in rural areas it provides employment opportunities to the rural people mainly.

The majority of the people who work in the Handicrafts industry in India are women and those people who belong to the weaker sections of the society. The Handicrafts industry in India is a low capital investment industry for the products are prepared by using hands or with the use of simple tools.

The various reasons for the growth of Handicrafts industry finance in India are that the people in the rural areas do not have extra money to set-up business. As a result, they need financial help to start the handicrafts business. Further the Handicrafts industry in India has been on the rise for the amount of export in the industry has increased at a very rapid pace. The people in the rural areas thus in order to make money are setting up more and more Handicrafts-based businesses. This has also led to the growth of the finance in the industry of Handicrafts in India.

The various advantages of Handicrafts industry finance in India are that it has helped many rural people to become self-dependent. For if they had not got financial help then they would not have been able to set-up their own Handicrafts business. Further the advantages of the finance in the industry of Handicrafts in India are that as the number of business increased, the number of employment opportunities also increased. Thus Handicrafts industry finance in India helped to provide jobs to many people in the rural areas. Handicrafts industry finance in India advantages includes that it has given a major boost to the economy of the country. The National Bank for Agriculture and Rural Development is one such bank that provides Handicrafts industry finance in India.

Handicrafts industry finance in India has given a major boost to the industry. It has also helped the rural people to improve their financial condition a lot. This in its turn has improved the country's overall economy. Thus the Government of India as well as the various banks should make even more efforts to increase Handicrafts industry finance in India. This will help the Handicrafts industry in India to reach its heights.

As part of an initiative to bring a positive impact of globalisation to rural India, Exim Bank is looking for partners to take handicrafts made in rural Indian to markets abroad.

Speaking at a function organised by ITC at Cottage Industries in Kurumbapet near here on Monday, Exim Bank CMD T.C. Venkat Subramanian said that the bank was looking for partners who could form distribution houses to distribute handicraft products outside the country.

"Our role will be to interact with buying houses, finding design requirements, giving inputs on the pricing structure and logistics among other things. We have given a proposal to the Khadi and Village Industries Corporation (KVIC) to set-up a marketing and capacity building organisation."

"The bank can take an equity of 40 per cent, the KVIC could have 40 per cent, and the self-help groups that are benefited by this project could have a 20 per cent stake. But, KVIC is yet to reply," he added.

He said Exim Bank was interacting with rural industries, and had also sent 15 to 20 products for testing to their Singapore office.

"This includes chikan work from Lucknow and banana fibre shirts from Kerala. We have also spoken to the Confederation of Rural NGOs of India to link units that are working in similar products so that the SHGs or cottage industries could help consolidate their work and increase their income."

According to Manob Tagore of Cottage Industries, Exim Bank has partnered with ITC to provide international market access to their Mangaldeep range of incense sticks.

The partnership between Exim Bank and ITC has enabled ITC to export the products to Singapore, South Africa and USA.

Registrar of Cooperative Societies Sundaravadivelu said that a handicraft federation had been started by the Government recently.

The handicraft federation was started to increase the sale of handicrafts, make available raw materials, and provide space for units.

The bank's Chief General Manager Muthukumaran said that their rural initiatives included providing finance, facilities, and promoting products.

"'From 1987 to 1992 we have worked with 400 companies under a programme to take Indian products to developed countries," Mr. Muthukumaran said.

Banking as an Instrument of Social Change

Banking is the backbone of modern economy. No business, trade or commerce can be conducted on large-scale without an efficient banking system. Banking in some form or the other has always been there from the ancient times. When Jesus Christ turned the tables of money-changers outside the temple of Jerusalem, he was only protesting against the malpractices of the then existing banking system.

When Prophet Mohammed forbade usuary to his followers, he was only condemning the cruelty of bankers of those days, who used to suck the blood of their helpless victims in the form of exorbitant interest.

Before the nationalisation of banks in July 1969, the commercial banks of India had an urban and selective group outlook, responding mostly to the credit requirements of a few big industrialists and affluent businessmen. But the post-nationalisation era witnessed a radical change in banking policy. They have been vested with new social obligations, besides mobilising savings and credits with a view to gear up for a social and economic change in the country. Instead of becoming the banks of a 'particular section', they have become the banks of the 'general public'.

The new banking policy aims at ruralisation of banks. As a result there has been a phenomenal growth of bank branches. There has also been an astronomical rise in the number of employees. Further an ordinance called the Rural Banks Ordinance promulgated by the President on September 26, 1975, gave a momentum to the task of ruralising banks. As a consequence, the banking services are now available to the masses at their door-step, and the banking industry has entered the hinterlands and economically backward areas.

Fourteen major commercial banks were nationalised in July 1969. It was a new feather in the cap of the banking industry. The industry got a further impetus with the nationalisation of six more banks in 1980. The public sector banks account for about 90 per cent the total banking system in the country.

Before nationalisation banks were catering to the needs of only a small section of people belonging to the upper strata of society. That elitist approach of banks has since given way to an egalitarian one in the post-nationalisation period. The profit motive has been replaced by welfare motive. Before nationalisation, there was lack of banking facilities in rural areas. But after nationalisation, most of the branch expansion took place in rural areas. The proportion of rural branches has gone up many-fold. Before nationalisation, banks were financing large and medium scale industries while the priority sector namely agriculture, small-scale industries and exports was being neglected. After nationalisation this sector received greater attention. By March 1985, about 40 per cent of total credit was provided to priority sector.

The DIR (Different Rate of Interest) scheme was introduced in 1972 by the public sector banks for the upliftment of weaker sections of society. Under this scheme, banks are required to lend up to one per cent of their lending at a rate of 4% interest to specially disadvantaged classes. Landless labourers, small land-owners, rural artisans and members of scheduled castes and scheduled tribes are to benefit under this scheme. With a view to augment banking facility in rural areas, the Regional Rural Banks (RRBs) were established on October 2, 1975 on the recommendations of the working group set-up by the Government of India. The Regional Rural Banks have played a vital role in the development of rural economy by financing small farmers and petty entrepreneurs in villages.

The harassment caused to the people by the greedy and cruel money-lenders has now ended. Banks are offering loans to people on easy terms and with a low rate of interest. However, granting of such loans often results in non-repayment by the borrowers. Non-repayment adversely affects the profitability and viability of banks. Sometimes, such loans are written off on political considerations. The politics of loan melas and writing off of bank-loans have given a set-back to Indian Banking. So has the bank scams.

There is no wonder that there are allegations of misuse of public money for political purposes through loan melas and the like. All the same, the Union Government has initiated SEPUP (Self-Employment Programme for Urban Poor) to bring down the number of people living below the poverty line in urban areas. This scheme is being implemented by the banks. Of late, banking habit has also taken roots among the lower middle class people and this has resulted in an increase in savings. Increased saving is a positive feature in the economy of a country.

Banking is a major instrument for socio-economic transformation aiming at minimum rich-poor disparity. Our nationalised banks are, no doubt, playing their part effectively and they have helped a lot in the overall development of our country. However, nationalisation by itself cannot be a panacea for all the problems afflicting the banking system in the country. Much depends upon how these institutions are run and managed. If our nationalised banks are able to render more prompt and efficient service to masses, they would be able to make significant contribution to the country's economic development.

REFERENCE

NABARD, 1997, 'Micro-Finance Innovations and NABARD'.

Regional Rural Banks in India: A Quick Look

Ms. Shubhi Goel

In the early 1970s, the Government observed that despite a wide banking network and developmental initiatives in the first 25 years since Independence, a critical gap still existed in meeting the credit needs of the rural poor. There was a need to meet the excess demand for institutional credit in the rural areas, particularly among the economically and socially marginalized sections. Although the cooperative banks and the commercial banks had reasonable records in terms of geographical coverage and disbursement of credit, in terms of population groups the cooperative banks were dominated by the rural rich, while the commercial banks had a clear urban bias.

To find a solution, the Government appointed a working group on rural credit, the Narasimham Committee, in July 1975 which observed that the cost structure of commercial banks, the attitude of bank employees and the lack of a professional approach in the co-operative credit system were the main stumbling blocks to rural credit. The committee also observed that the deposits collected by banks from rural areas were not totally deployed there. The panel, therefore, recommended the creation of a new set of regionally-oriented rural banks which would combine a co-operative's local feel and a commercial bank's business acumen.

So finally, the ordinance of Regional Rural Banks, 1975 was promulgated on September 26, 1975 which was replaced by the Regional Rural Banks Act, 1976 on February 9, 1976. The RRBs were established with a view to develop the rural economy by providing; for the purpose of development of agriculture, trade, commerce, industry and other productive activities in the rural areas, credit and other facilities, particularly to small and marginal farmers, agricultural laborers, artisans and small entrepreneurs, and for matters connected therewith and incidental thereto.

Thus RRBs can be defined as institutions which "combine the local feel and the familiarity with rural problems which the cooperatives possess and the degree of business organization, ability to mobilize deposits, access to central money markets and modernized outlook which the commercial banks have". The multi-agency approach to rural credit was also to sub-serve the needs of the input-intensive agricultural strategy (Green Revolution) which had initially focused on "betting on the strong" but by the mid-seventies was ready to spread more widely through the Indian countryside. The RRBs Act, 1976 succinctly sums up this overall vision to sub-serve both the developmental and the redistributive objectives. The RRBs were established "with a view to developing the rural economy by providing, for the purpose of development of agriculture, trade, commerce, industry and other productive activities in the rural areas, credit and other facilities, particularly to small and marginal farmers, agricultural laborers, artisans and small entrepreneurs, and for matters connected therewith and incidental thereto."

The mandate of these rural financial institutions was to:

- Take banking to the doorsteps of the rural masses, particularly in areas without banking facilities;
- Take available cheaper institutional credit to the weaker sections of society, who were to be the only clients of these banks;
- Mobilize rural savings and canalize them for supporting productive activities in rural areas;
- Generate employment opportunities in the rural areas; and
- Bring down the cost of providing credit in rural areas.

The first RRBs were set-up on 2nd October 1975 on the basis of an ordinance which was replaced by the Regional Rural Banks Act on 1976. With partnerships with the Central Government (50 per cent), State governments (15 per cent) and commercial banks (35 per cent), the number of RRBs rose from just six in 1975 to 14,475 recently out of which 2126 (91%) are located in remote rural areas. The number of RRBs increased to 85 as at the end of 1980 and to 188 as at the end of 1985. The last RRB to be set-up was the Godavari Gramin Bank in April 1987 taking the total to 196. These 196 RRBs have 14,497 branches covering 427 districts and are spread over 23 states. Each RRB's area of operations extends over one to three districts with the exception of those in North-eastern states and a few other regions where the number ranges from four to nine districts. The number of branches per RRB also ranges from 8 to 223.

As a matter of policy, the RRBs were set-up mainly in the un-banked and under-banked regions of the country. An important aspect of the location policy was that the RRBs would cover a compact area of not more than two or three districts where the weaker sections of the population are predominant. During the seventies and the eighties, the maximum number of RRBs was thus opened in the Central, Eastern and the North-eastern regions in the country that had the largest number of backward districts.

Along with commercial banks, RRBs have participated enthusiastically in poverty alleviation schemes (IRDP, for example) and disadvantaged area (drought-prone regions and deserts) development programmes. They quickly became an important and integral part of the rural credit system. RRBs have done well in mobilizing rural deposits and infusing the thrift habit in their clients. The bulk of the loans from RRBs have been to priority sectors, which accounted for over 70 per cent of the total. Agriculture alone took up 46 per cent of the priority sector advances. The involvement of RRBs in providing credit support to small and retail trade and other non-farm rural activities is better than that of co-operatives and commercial banks.

However, RRBs faced some initial hiccups like low recovery and loan over dues. The internal factors which contributed to this were weak monitoring and supervision, apathy towards recovery, failure to link lending with development and to ensure end use of the loan. The external factors were political interference, wilful default, drought and floods, underdevelopment, lack of legal and administrative support from the state government in the matter of recovery, etc. Generally, recovery was low in respect of loans sanctioned under IRDP and other poverty alleviation programmes. Besides there were certain organizational problems such as low capital base, multiple ownership and divided responsibility, lack of adequate training for the RRB staff, etc. which called for intervention. So we can say that, their financial viability was initially overstretched by policy rigidities coupled with a low capital base in an environment of inadequate infrastructure and deeper social and economic disparities.

There have been three phases of Regional Rural Banking in India—the inception and expansion phase (1976-90) which saw rapid growth of the RRBs activities; the reform phase (1991-2002/3) which raised the profitability of these banks at the cost of massive rural disintermediation, particularly of the targeted borrower categories; and the most recent phase of stock taking and perhaps some repositioning to strike a balance in the conundrum of 'viability *versus* outreach'.

The advent of the financial sector reforms in the early 1990s emphasized the need for a self-supporting, 'stand-alone' viable institutional structure in the banking industry. RRBs were, therefore, permitted to finance the non-farm sector, and later, the non-target group to the extent of 40% in the first step and subsequently up to 60% so as to enhance the profitability and viability of these institutions, thus doing away with the emphasis on agricultural sector and the people with small means.

In current scenario, the regional rural banks are looking towards emerging business opportunities and taking a lead in financing both agricultural and non-agricultural sectors in rural areas. With mergers infusing the much-needed financial strength in these banks, coupled with the local feel which they command, the regional rural banks are in a unique position to play a decisive role in financial inclusion.

RRBs have emerged as the only surviving rural financial institution with a professional management culture to meet small-value, large-volume rural credit needs. Therefore, the time has come to revitalize/revamp the structure of RRBs along with co-operatives so that they play a critical role in achieving the developmental targets in the rural sector and emerge stronger. Rural banking has emerged as a niche, wherein special skill-set and sensitivity is required. Therefore, the imposed ban on fresh recruitment should be reviewed at the earliest to enhance and diversify the business of RRBs. Also, for further improvement and empowerment of RRBs, they should be permitted to recruit specialists in the technology and agriculture fields. Similarly, grants/soft loans may be provided for technology so as to enable RRBs to compete with commercial/private banks that invest heavily in technology projects. The technology induction in rural banking would facilitate handling low-value, high-volume business effectively in a more cost-effective manner..

The RRBs have succeeded in attaining financial viability; they need however to buttress this attainment. Financial strengthening and organizational development need to grow in tandem. The RRBs can forge mutually-beneficial relationships with other institutions operating in the rural economy. For instance, in the case of private banks unable to meet their agriculture lending targets, the RRBs can sell their attainments in the sector through securitization of debts, trading in agricultural loan credits or otherwise: thereby the RRBs can secure additional funds to raise lending volumes and agricultural lending will increase substantially.

The policies introduced during the reform period starting in the early 1990s have been instrumental in reorienting the RRBs toward financial viability. The new policies allowed relocation of branches, improved remuneration and incentives for RRBs staff and opened up lending and investment avenues.

Potentially, RRBs are a valuable tool for enhancing rural economic development particularly as they are point of entry for the bankable poor to the vast commercial banking system in India. Their importance derives from the fact they on account of local recruitment are familiar with the rural economy and have the ability to mobilize low cost deposits from a clientele that commercial banks are not able to reach adequately.

Some of the banks which functions for the development of the rural areas in India are:

- **State Bank of India:** SBI has around 30 Regional Rural Banks in India.

- **Haryana State Cooperative Apex Bank Limited:** The Haryana State Cooperative Apex Bank Ltd. commonly called as HARCOBANK plays a vital role in rural banking in the economy of Haryana State and has been providing aids and financing farmers, rural artisans, agricultural laborers, entrepreneurs, etc. in the state and giving service to its depositors.
- **NABARD:** National Bank for Agriculture and Rural Development (NABARD) is a development bank in the sector of Regional Rural Banks in India. It provides and regulates credit and gives service for the promotion and development of rural sectors mainly agriculture, small scale industries, cottage and village industries, handicrafts. It also finances rural crafts and other allied rural economic activities to promote integrated rural development. It helps in securing rural prosperity and its connected matters.
- **Sindhanur Urban Souharda Co-operative Bank:** Sindhanur Urban Souharda Co-operative Bank, popularly known as SUCO BANK is the first of its kind in rural banks of India.
- **United Bank of India:** United Bank of India (UBI) also plays an important role in regional rural banks. It has expanded its branch network in a big way to actively participate in the developmental of the rural and semi-urban areas in conformity with the objectives of nationalization.
- **Syndicate Bank:** It's firmly rooted in rural India as rural banking and has a clear vision of future India by understanding the grass-root realities. Its progress has been abreast of the phase of progressive banking in India especially in rural banks.

So we can conclude by saying that RRBs have taken deep roots and have become a sort of inseparable part of the rural credit structure in India and they play key role in rural institutional financing in terms of geographical coverage, clientele outreach and business volume and also contribution to development of the rural economy.

REFERENCES

Reserve Bank of India Occasional Papers, Vol. 27, Nos. 1 and 2, Summer and Monsoon, 2006, Biswa Swarup Misra.

The Ethical Value of Brand feelings in Rural Society—A micro-level study, P. Baba Gnanakumar Department of Commerce, Sri Krishna Arts and Science College, Coimbatore.

Part II, Co-operative, Rural & BOP Marketing, International Marketing Conference on Marketing & Society, April 2007, IIMK.

Regional Rural Banks: The Past and the Present Debate—Sukanya Bose.

Social Banking by Deepali Pant Joshi.

Working of Regional Rural Banks for Rural Society

Ms. Chandni Gupta and Ms. Aditi Tyagi

Regional Rural Banks were set-up to take banking services to the doorsteps of rural masses especially in remote rural areas with no access to banking service. These banks were originally intended to provide institution that credit to the weaker sections of the society called "target group". The Regional Rural Banks (RRBs) are conceived as institutions that combine the local feel and familiarity with rural problems, which the cooperatives possess and the degree of business organization as well as the ability to mobilise deposits, which the commercial banks possess.

Regional Rural Banks (RRBs) which appeared on the banking map of the country in 1975 have now become the main plank of the organized rural credit structure. Regional Rural Banks were established under the provisions of an Ordinance promulgated on the 26th September 1975 and the RRB Act, 1976 with an objective to ensure sufficient institutional credit for agriculture and other rural sectors. RRBs main target is rural development. Rural development means an "action-plan" for the social and economic upliftment of the rural areas. The action-plan is to focus on the lingering and emerging challenges in rural areas.

As Gandhiji said, "Real India lies in villages," and village economy is the backbone of Indian economy. Without the upliftment of the rural economy as well as the rural people of our country, the objectives of economic planning cannot be achieved.

India is basically an agricultural country and the study of rural development has attracted attention of the economist, planners and the social scientists in India.

Regional Rural Banks (RRBs) which appeared on the banking map of the country in 1975 have now become the main plank of the organized rural credit structure.

Regional Rural Banks were established under the provisions of an Ordinance promulgated on the 26th September 1975 and the RRB Act, 1976 with an objective to ensure sufficient institutional credit for agriculture and other rural sectors.

RRBs started their development process on 2nd October 1975 with the formation of a single bank (Prathama Grameen Bank). As on 31 March 2006, there were 133 RRBs (post-merger) covering 525 districts with a network of 14,494 branches. RRBs were originally conceived as low cost institutions having a rural ethos, local feel and pro-poor focus.

The RRBs mobilize financial resources from rural/semi-urban areas and grant loans and advances mostly to small and marginal farmers, agricultural labourers and rural artisans.

RURAL DEVELOPMENT

Rural development means an "action-plan" for the social and economic upliftment of the rural areas. The action-plan is to focus on the lingering and emerging challenges in rural areas. Lingering challenges like the challenge of rural credit and rural marketing. Emerging challenges, like the challenge of organic farming, and developing options of sustainable livelihood, other than farming.

RURAL CREDIT

Rural credit means credit for the farming families. Credit works as a lifeline for the farming families in rural India. Because: (i) most farming families on India are small and marginal holders, producing just enough for subsistence, not effecting any saving for further investment, and (ii) gestation period between crop-sowing and crop-sale is fairly long, hence, borrowing for the purchase of inputs (like seeds and fertilizers) becomes almost inevitable.

SOURCES OF RURAL CREDIT

Sources of agricultural credit are broadly classified as institutional and non-institutional. These are discussed as under:

Non-Institutional Sources

Traditionally, the credit requirement of farmers was met by non-institutional sources like the landlords, village traders and moneylenders. The farmers were always exploited by such sources.

Institutional Sources

The institutional sources include government and the regional rural bank. Regional rural bank, the co-operate credit institutions continue to be important institutional agencies for providing credit support and services for agricultural and rural development.

Regional Rural Banks

The main purpose of retting RRBs and land development Banks was to provide an adequate and cheaper rural wing to nationalized banks so that they could reach the remote rural areas in backward districts, and fulfil the objectives of the nationalization of banks. These banks operate at district level with local state, and are under obligation to provide credit largely to weaker section of the population.

SBI

SBI has 30 Regional Rural Banks in India known as RRBs. The rural banks of SBI is spread in 13 states extending from Kashmir to Karnataka and Himachal Pradesh to North-East, the total number of SBIs Regional Rural Banks in India branches is 2349 (16%). Till date in rural banking in India, there are 14,475 rural banks in the country (91%) are located in remote rural areas.

United Bank of India

United Bank of India (UBI) also plays an important role in

regional rural banks. It has expanded its branch network in a big way to actively participate in the developmental of the rural and semi-urban areas in conformity with the objectives of nationalisation.

Syndicate Bank

Syndicate Bank was firmly rooted in rural India as rural banking and have a clear vision of future India by understanding the grassroot realities. Its progress has been abreast of the phase of progressive banking in India especially in rural banks.

Sindhanur Urban Souharda Co-operative Bank

Sindhanur Urban Souharda Co-operative Bank popularly known as SUCO Bank is the first of its kind in rural banks in India. The impressive story of its inception is interesting and inspiring for all the youth of this country.

NABARD (National Bank for Agriculture and Rural Development)

NABARD was established by an Act of Parliament on 12 July 1982 to implement the national bank for agriculture and Rural Development Act, 1981, it replaced the Agriculture Credit Department (ACD) and Rural Planning and Credit Cell (RPCC) of Reserve Bank of India and Agriculture Refinance and Development Corporation (ARDC).

National Bank for Agriculture and Rural Development sectors mainly agriculture, small scale industries, cottage and village industries, handicrafts. It also finance rural crafts and other allied rural economic activities to (NABARD) is a development bank in the sector of Regional Rural Banks in India. It provides and regulates credit and gives service for the promotion and development of rural promote integrated rural development. It helps in securing rural prosperity and its connected matters.

NABARD is an apex institution entrusted with all matters concerning policy, planning and operations in the field of credit for agricultural and other economic activities in rural areas as well. Its main functions are:

- To serve as an apex refinancing agency for the institutions providing investment and production credit for promoting the various development activities in rural areas.

- To make measure towards institutional building for improving capacity of the credit delivery system including monitoring and formulating rehabilitation schemes, restructuring of credit institutions, training of personal, etc.
- Co-ordinate the rural financing activities of all the institutions engaged in developmental work at the field level and maintain liaison with government of India, State government, Reserve Bank, and other national level institutions concerned with policy formulations.
- Undertake monitoring and evaluation of projects refinanced by it.

NABARDs Role in Rural Development

NABARD supports the rural credit system by way of refinance for short-term, production/marketing activities, medium-term and long-term loans for technically feasible and financially viable projects in both Farm and Non-Farm sectors, through State Co-operative Banks (SCBs), and Regional Rural Banks (RRBs). The State Co-operative Agriculture and Rural Development Banks (SCARDBs) are supported for only term loans for investment credit. The Commercial banks are supported for short-term financing of primary weavers' societies and for term loans for investment credit.

NABARD provides finance to State Governments for completion of rural infrastructure development projects such as major and minor irrigation projects, soil conservation, rural roads and bridges, SHGs (Self Help Groups) through PRIs (Panchayati Raj Institutions), etc. from the "Rural Infrastructure Development Fund" (RIDF) created for the purpose. In the district of Birbhum, NABARD has sanctioned Rs. 13534.52 crores for Rural Roads, Rural Bridges, Flood Protection Structures, Minor Irrigation, Major Irrigation, Power Sector, Watershed Management and PHC (Anganwadi Centres). Out of the total sanction, Rs. 8715.23 crores has been drawn by the State Government. (Figures as obtaining on 10 January 2005)

NABARD also provides loans to State Governments to enable

them to contribute to the share capital of co-operative credit institutions. NABARD works in co-ordination with various central/state government agencies, and NGOs to implement projects like, watershed development, dry land farming, waste land development, forestry, Swarnjayanti Gram Swarozgar Yojana (SGSY) and other poverty alleviation programmes.

NABARD has raised a cadre of volunteers under its programme of Vikas Volunteer Vahini (VVV) to spread the message of "Development through Credit" to farmers and non-farm rural entrepreneurs.

NABARD has also been providing promotional grants to VAs/ NGOs for various programmes such as mother units, ancillarisation, common facility centres, training including skill up-gradation and entrepreneurship development, marketing, etc. under exclusive women and other schemes from its "Rural Promotion Corpus Fund". In the district of Birbhum, till date three Rural Entrepreneurship Development Programme (REDP) have been conducted and few more are in the pipeline. A one month long, special training programme to rural artisans (mostly women), engaged in Sola Pith and Kantha Stitch works have been conducted in collaboration with National Institute of Fashion Technology, Kolkata.

NABARD has established Research and Development (R&D) Fund to gain insights into the problems of agriculture and rural development through in-depth studies and applied research and experimenting innovative approaches backed by technical and economic studies. In Birbhum, to mention a few, studies on the functioning of Self Help Groups and Farmers' Clubs were undertaken. Also, an exclusive study on development of various loan products was conducted for obtaining an insight into the product requirement of the rural populace.

NABARD has set-up Soft Loan Assistance Fund for Margin Money to provide support to rural entrepreneurs with the required skills and aptitude but unable to provide margin money for availing bank loan.

NABARD has set-up Co-operative Development Fund (CDF) to improve management systems and skills in co-operative banks.

NABARD has constituted a "Credit and Financial Services Fund" to support credit innovations to improve the outreach of credit to the unreached rural poor. Till 30 November 2004, 4900

SHGs (56% thereof are women groups) were savings linked with 5 Commercial Banks, Mayurakshi Gramin Bank and Birbhum District Central Co-operative Bank. Out of the same 2368 groups (60% thereof are women groups) have been credit linked. The Mayurakshi Gramin Bank and seven NGOs in the district, has been identified as a Self Help Promoting Institution. This has helped in augmenting the flow of credit as well as in formation of more groups.

UP Rural Bank to get UK Award

Lucknow, May 28 while the think tank of the Mayawati government put their heads together to solve the problem of power shortage in the state, a divisional unit of the Regional Rural Bank (RRB) has won a British award for its endeavour in popularising non-conventional energy and thereby saving power.

The Lucknow division of RRB—Aryavart Gramin Bank—has been selected for the 2008 British Ashden Award. It is an internationally recognised yardstick for excellence in the field of sustainable energy or green energy.

Aryavart Bank's Deputy General Manager N.K. Joshi, who is the project leader and is also carrying out the responsibility of chairman on deputation, will receive the award in London during the Ashden awards week beginning June 14. The bank is among the seven finalists selected out of 77 participants.

It all began after Joshi came out with the idea to provide financial assistance for installation of Solar Home Lighting System (SHS). He started a scheme called Ghar Ghar me Ujala, which aimed "to improve living standard of people in the rural areas."

The Aryavart bank now gives a loan of Rs. 11,000 for one SHS set. This loan is repayable in 60 months and costs Rs. 245 per month to a family in the rural areas where a family spends Rs. 280 on kerosene on a monthly basis.

Banking Sector in Budget 2008

The Union Budget of India for the year 2008-09 was announced by the Indian Finance Minister, Mr. P. Chidambaram, on 29th February 2008. The policies and initiatives taken in the Union Budget of India 2008-09 on the Indian Banking sector were in tandem with the requirements of the Indian economy.

Small and marginal farmers have been relieved of all farm

loans, disbursed till March 2007 and also all loans, which are due till December 2007 and was unpaid till February 2008. These farm loan waivers would be facilitated by all the concerned Public Sector Banks and Regional Rural Banks of India. A total of Rs. 60,000 crores would be waived-off under such scheme. The settlement of these loan-waivers will be offered through special type of scheme. Further, the Public Sector Banks and Regional Rural Banks of India were also suggested, to bring within their fold, a minimum of 250 rural household accounts at every branch every year.

The Indira Awas Yojana was brought under the ambit of Public Sector Banks. Loan limit up to Rs. 20,000 per unit at 4% interest was fixed under differential rate of interest (DRI) scheme. The Finance Minister also advised the Indian PSU Banks to open 288 branches in minority districts of India. Further, he also asked the Indian banking industry to embrace total financial inclusion. In another landmark decision, the Finance Minister, Mr. P. Chidambaram said that the Ex-banking servicemen in India would be offered employment opportunities in the banking sector.

Another major announcement was that, the much talked-about 'Banking Cash Transaction Tax (BCTT)' would be withdrawn from the financial year 2009-10.

Experts believe the impact of the decisions and policies taken during the Union Budget of India 2008-09 on the Indian Banking sector would be mixed. It is expected that the Indian PSU banks will face pressure on their net interest margins due to the waiving-off of agricultural loans. Further, the cumulative cost that will be incurred for opening up of new Regional Rural Banks in India may substantially increase the operating cost for the banks. The inclusion of the Indira Awas Yojana houses under the differential rate of interest scheme and at 4% interest will increase the proportion of sub-PLR lending for the concerned banks.

The major Public Sector Banks of India like the State Bank of India, Bank of Baroda, Punjab National Bank may see their net interest margins shrinking till the subsidy for waiver of agricultural loans is being completely released. Moreover, experts are skeptical about the long-term benefit of such agricultural loan waiver as offered through the Union Budget of India 2008-09.

RURAL BANKING—A CRITICAL EVALUATION

Rural banking in India has expanded a great deal over time. The expansion has been significant particularly since nationalization of major commercial banks in the country in 1969. Nationalization of commercial banks marked the beginning of social banking in rural areas, implying provision of institutional credit at moderate rates of interest. Establishment of NABARD (as an apex body Coordinating activities of all financial institutions engaged in rural credit programmes) made a substantial difference. Rural financing became much more organized than ever before. It is not denying the fact that institutional credit has gone a long way in liberating the farmers from the debt-traps. Also, it is not denying the fact that institutional credit as facilitated commercialization of agriculture. But there is other side of the coin too. Certain deficiencies of rural banking are equally evident:

(i) Banking credit or institutional credit has invariably been linked with collateral, because of which small and marginal holders have not been the major beneficiary of it,
(ii) Owing to its policy of populism, the government has often been very lenient on the recovery of loans from the farmers, because of which there has been large number of overdue instalments, and
(iii) Apart from commercial banks, most financial institutions have failed to develop a culture of thrift among the farming families, mobilization of deposits, has never been encouraged.

Social banking in rural areas has certainly become dormant after economic reforms of 1991. Impact of debt on the farmers is generally becoming so huge that suicidal deaths are rising from hundreds to thousands, particularly in the states of Andhra Pradesh and Maharashtra. It is high time that the government considers rural banking as a social need rather than an activity to be left to the free play of the market forces.

Working of Regional Rural Banks (RRBs) for the Development of Rural Society

Ms. Priyanjana Maurya and Dr. Shailendra Bhushan Sharma

1. Introduction

India registered a GDP growth rate of 9% in 2007-08 which is reduced in comparison to GDP growth rate achieved for 2006-07 (9.6%). The GDP of industry and services sector were decreases to 8.5% and 10.5% respectively in 2007-08 as it was 10.6% and 11.2% respectively in the last financial year. A slight improvement in the GPD growth of agriculture has been achieved this year as it was 3.8% for 2006-07 and to date it is 4.5%. Developments in the agriculture contributes only 18% in to the total GDP which is very low in respect to the contribution from industrial and service sector that has 26% and 56% contribution respectively.

Many economists and policy-makers believe that the future growth of economy, to a large extent, will depend on the performance of the agricultural and rural sector. This is due to the fact that the manufacturing and service sectors cannot sustain the economy's growth if the rural sector underperforms. To improve the rural sector and its more contribution in the Indian economy, the government should more focus on funding to the rural peoples. Henceforth, it is the critical time to analyse the efforts taken by government for rural credit.

2. Efforts Toward Development of Rural Economy

Various attempts has been made by government as well as financial institutions to achieve the goals of improving rural financial demands and therefore to contribute towards national economy. The major developments in this respect are as follows:

1. Regional Rural Banks

In July 1975, the Government appointed the Narasimham Committee, which firstly recognized the importance of rural development to improve the economy and due to this recommended the creation of Regional Rural Banks (RRBs). The RRBs were established under the provision of ordinance promulgated on 26 September 1975. This was replaced by the Regional Rural Banks Act, 1976 on 9 February 1976. RRBs is owned by Government of India (50% shares), State Government (15% shares) and by Sponsoring Commercial Banks (35% shares). The objectives of RRBs is to built a backbone structure and develop the rural economy by providing, credit facility to small and marginal farmers, agro labours, agricultural processing societies, businessmen and small entrepreneurs.

2. Regional Rural Banks and NABARD Schemes

National Bank for Agricultural and Rural Development (NABARD) was set-up on July 1982 with the objective to framing, policy and guidelines for rural financial institutions providing credit facilities, preparation of credit plans, and inspection of Regional Rural Banks. NABARD running the various schemes for rural people, for example.

I. Investment Credit Schemes

Provides investment credit to eligible banks for manufacturing, processing and service sector activities in the SSI (Small Scale Industries) sector.

II. Production Credit Scheme

Provides short-term refinance for various production, marketing and procurements activities.

III. Rural Infrastructure Development Fund (RIDF)

Construction of Primary Schools, Primary Health Centres, Village Haats, Rain Water Harvesting, Fish Jetties, Rural Drinking Water Supply Scheme, Citizen Information Centres and Shishu Shiksha Kendras, etc.

IV. Swarojgar Credit Card Scheme

Provides adequate and timely credit to small artisans, handloom weavers, self-employed persons, rickshaw owners, other micro-entrepreneurs, etc.

V. Other Schemes

Besides the above schemes, NABARD also running Kisan Credit Card, Micro Finance Schemes, Generation of Rural Employment, Pilot Project for Integrated Development of Backward Blocs (PPID), Development of Bamboo Framing, Farm Mechanization, Financing Purchase for Land, Scheme for setting up of Agribusiness Centers and Credit Linked Capital Subsidy Scheme (CLCSS) for Upgradation of SSI

3. Evaluation of Performance of RRBs

The performance of RRBs from last fives year is given in table below.

Items	*March 2002*	*March 2007*
Number of RRBs	196	96
Number of offices covered	14664	14652
Deposit (Rs. in lakh)	4406312	8163050
Credit (Rs. in lakh)	1886876	4785511
Rural office	12041	11348
Rural office Deposit (Rs. in lakh)	3015459	5091397
Rural office Credit (Rs. in lakh)	1350902	3222620
Semi-urban office	2140	2575
Semi-urban office Deposit (Rs. in lakh)	1021822	2136113
Semi-urban office Credit (Rs. in lakh)	410531	1175979

(Contd.)

Items	*March 2002*	*March 2007*
Urban office	462	663
Urban office Deposit (Rs. in lakh)	358909	848990
Urban office Credit (Rs. in lakh)	121287	358175
Metros office	21	66
Metros office Deposit (Rs. in lakh)	10123	86550
Metros office Credit (Rs. in lakh)	4156	28738
Number of staff in RRBs	65481	63614

4. Challenges in Front of RRBs

Despite decades of efforts and experimentation in banking, the organized financial sector is still not able to meet the credit gap in the rural sector. The lower levels of per capita income, focus in the urban sector, lack of infrastructure and proper connectivity were the main hindrances for banks to venture into rural areas. Directed lending, cumbersome procedures, delay in sanctioning loans and lack of statutory backing for recoveries are other major impediment to the growth of banking in the rural sector.

5. Suggestions

- RRBs should be permitted to recruit specialists in the technology and agriculture fields and secondly grants/ soft loans should be provided for technology developments.
- The share of sponsoring institutions in the capital structure of RRBs needs to be enlarged to make them a majority shareholder. By acquiring the majority shareholding in RRBs, the sponsor banks/institutions can convert them into vibrant and professional subsidiaries and area-specific Special Business Units (SBUs). In the long-run, they may converge of all their agricultural and rural activities under the umbrella of these SBUs.
- The RBI needs to confine itself to a regulatory role for all financial institutions, including the rural ones for effective monitoring and control.

6. Conclusion

The RRBs has played its major role in rural development but

still not able to solve out the financing problem of rural peoples. Government should more focus on the restructuring of rural banking system. Nearly 75% population depends on the agriculture and the demand for food increasing at more than 2% per annum. In this context, productivity augmentation in agriculture and other allied sectors, expansion of rural credit, poverty eradication, infrastructure and development and export competitiveness of agricultural products should be considered high priority in the nation's development agenda.

Changing Patterns of Agricultural Credit in Indian Economy

Dr. Rajeev Tyagi and Dr. Rupesh Tyagi

Credit to agriculture is an essential input for farm development. Agricultural development can be contributed through various essential factors. Five essentials of agricultural development, they are: (i) market for farm product, (ii) constantly changing technology, (iii) local availability of supplies and equipment, (iv) production incentives, and (v) transportation. Five accelerators for agricultural development have been suggested *viz.* (a) education for production, (b) production credit, (c) group action by farmers, (d) improving and expanding agricultural land, and (e) national planning for agricultural development. Production credit is one of the essentials for agricultural development. Agricultural credit will help in making the existing areas of cultivable land under crops and help in making structural changes in relation to the available area of cultivable land. The common goal of credit is higher production; where higher production is not intended only for higher consumption purposes is supposed to be a source of funds for investment, i.e. capital stock. The vicious circle of low productivity will be broken through creating this kind of capital stock. In determining the nature of capital for agriculture, Bringer, G.K. includes not only the capital items in the balance sheet of agriculture but takes into consideration capital embodied in community facilities (such as schools, roads and dams) market facilities, technology and certain activities sub-serving the production. First, it is essential to take into consideration the current loans and similarly make an allowance for non-balance sheet items of a capital nature mentioned above. Credit for agriculture is required for efficient farm functioning because of following reasons:

(i) meagre resources of poor farmers whose number is very large,
(ii) purchase of major agricultural inputs outside the farm,
(iii) backwardness of farmers,
(iv) lengthy production period causing higher credit needs, and
(v) widespread rural indebtedness, Indian agriculturalists experience these difficulties. Agricultural credit is required to improve agricultural practices and purchase of input for growing yield. The role of agricultural credit in agricultural development is better explained by R.D. Sharma in the following manner:

"It consists in enlarging the net cultivable area by bringing waste and fallow land under cultivation, providing manure and chemical fertilizers, protection of land, the provision of irrigation, making large amounts of fixed and working capital available to agriculture, changing farm organisation, enlarging its share of gross national product and increasing labour return in agriculture. It has also some bearing on the problem of ensuring fair returns to agriculture. Adequate and times finance enhance the withholding capacity of the cultivators and their bargaining position with the increase in the holding capacity of the cultivators, the huge post-harvest market glut may be avoided which is the major factor in lowering the agricultural prices just after the harvest.... Right type of credit penetrates into agriculture and injects an element of healthy competition and concrete commercial calculations in farm operations. It turns agriculture into 'a way of living' as distinct from 'a way of life'. The subsistence farming gives way to commercial farming, the simply process of production makes room for mechanized operations and the attitudinal changes sweep the length and breadth of the countryside. Once the match-stick of credit ignites the flame, better managerial skills sustain it and a holy process of one inducing the other and covering all comes into effect. Thus the role of credit consists in laying the foundation stone of farm revolution and maintaining the structure built upon it."

Agricultural credit thus result into the commercialization of agriculture instead of subsistence farming. The Indian experience has shown this attitudinal performance: as and when agricultural credit is taken either from Government or financial institutions, the agriculture has changed into commercial purpose, mainly because of the compelling need for amortizing the loans taken. Moreover, it is profitable because both farmers and credit agencies gain. Agriculture requires credit for the purpose of capital formation on land and current expenditure, etc. Credit is needed for capital, current, family and other expenses. But only the provision of credit to agriculture will not solve the problem. The big-push with comprehensive socio-economic and socio-cultural efforts are essential. We can improve the economic efficiency by providing various inputs reasonable among which credit is the most important. However, this should not become full time work of Government. Credit is a bad master if it is mismanaged. It is like the French proverb, "credit supports the farmer as the hangman's rope supports the hanged. However, if it is used in proper and efficient manner, it can serve as an elevator".

The main purpose of credit borrowing is related to the economic development of a country is general, and the development of borrower in particular. Credit in banking is the actual or prospective debaters power or ability to obtain temporary money or goods or services in exchange by offering his promise of future payment with interest. It is the man's confidence expressed in another man which may bring economic and social change in rural areas.

A vast majority of our farms are very small in size. Out of 90 million, more than 80 million operational farm holding in the country are below 2 hectares in size. All such farmers are incapable to get even a daily bread from their size of holding. It, however, they are provided a credit either for their farm or for their subsidiary activities, they can improve their standard of living. Credit to such farmers should have a special character, because: (i) Agriculture is a complex industry, (ii) A considerable proportion of them have no assets neither sufficient land, nor any asset, (iii) Moreover, land is a shrinkage resource to them, and (iv) Difficult to forecast risks and uncertainties. This credit cannot be on the lines of industrial, trade and commercial credit. This should be so because the fate of our economy is dependent on such small and marginal farmers.

Agricultural capital is less mobile, and a farmer finds it difficult to divert his resources and shift from the cultivation of a particular set of crops to another set because of the presence of factors such as weather, suitability of soil and climate, etc. That is why subsidiary activities can be developed through adding further credit to the capital for example poultry, dairy, horticulture, sericulture, etc.

AGRICULTURAL FINANCE IN INDIA

Agricultural credit may be defined as the amount of investible funds made available for farm business, and farmer's family needs. In the past, agricultural credit was confined to a few needy farmers and a few elite lenders. During the drought conditions and scanty rainfalls, farmers used to get food grains from rich farmers (i.e. who have a surplus food grains all the time) on the condition that the same would be returned with interest after harvesting the next crop in the form of additional quantity of borrowed food grains.

The people engaged in such activities were village traders and feudal lords, which gradually moved towards the full-fledged job of money lending and were then called as money-lenders, who still hold their position in rural area. Security for the loans were precious ornaments and durable copper utensils, etc. for small amount of loans. If the amount was high, then farmers used to lease their land to the lender. There were two types of land leasing: (i) the ownership of whole land area to be retained by the lender until a borrower refund the borrowed amount. A lender manage to cultivate the leased land, and the whole yield went to the lender, (ii) in other form, a land area was leased for specific period, i.e. 3, 5, 7, 10 years, according to amount. The cultivation and yield remained with the lender for the said period. After completion of the period, the land was returned to the original owner (borrower). The cause and purpose of borrowing generally, relates to either drought or failure of crops or extravagant spending on cultural activities. The amount of debit differs according to various sections of peasantry.

The network of financial institutions in India may be categorized into two: (a) Unorganized (non-institutional); and (b) Organized (institutional), both of which are mainly related to money market. Capital market is not related to money market. Capital market is not related to the problems of agriculture. However, indirectly they come to the rescue of agriculture through money markets *via* central banks.

Agricultural credit may be direct or indirect. Direct credit is for the cultivators' farming operations and acquisition of assets. Indirect credit is for developing agricultural infrastructure like inputs distribution and co-operative marketing and processing units. This type of credit also include the credit to small farmers, landless labourers and other credit agencies, artisan, etc. Institutional (organized) and non-institutional (unorganized) agencies issue both direct and indirect credits to agriculture. One step further, non-institutional agencies supply credit even to cultural activities of borrowers.

Agricultural finance may be categorised into purpose or causes, because it is made available for various purposes. For example, agriculture, pisciculture, apiculture, sericulture, land development, farm mechanisation, drought animals, milk animals, forest development, piggery, poultry, plantations, bio-gas, gobar gas, market-hyard, dairy, service centres, godowns, cold storages, etc. Various credit agencies come forward to lend for these allied activities. Agricultural finance may be classified according to agro-business for which credit is essential. This may be hypothecation loans to farm business items. And other loans like cash credits are issued on economic status of the borrowers. Production credit is another way of borrowing which may be classified into settlement, development and equipment credit to agriculture.

EXPANSION OF INSTITUTIONAL CREDIT TO AGRICULTURE

There has been massive expansion of institutional credit to agriculture over the years. This would be clear from the fact that institutional credit to agriculture rose from Rs. 744 crore in 1970-71 to Rs. 9,830 crore in 1990-91 and Rs. 62,045 crore in 2001-02 (the last year of the Ninth Plan). The Tenth Plan (2002-07) has projected the total credit flow to agriculture and allied activities at Rs. 7,36,570 crore. However, in the first two years of the Plan, 2002-03 and 2003-04, the credit flow to agriculture from all formal sources was only Rs. 1,56,541 crore (Rs. 69,560 crore in 2002-03 and Rs. 86,981 crore in 2003-04). To fulfil the Tenth Plan target, major initiatives were, therefore, required to increase agricultural credit. To suggest measures to increase agricultural credit, the Reserve Bank constituted an **Advisory Committee on Flow of Credit to Agriculture and Related Activities from the Banking System** under the chairmanship of V.S. Vyas. This Committee submitted its final report in 2004. The Committee gave 99 recommendations of which 32 were accepted and implemented by the Reserve Bank. Some of the major recommendations were: (1) A review of mandatory lending to agriculture by commercial banks to enlarge direct lending programmes; (2) Public and private sector banks to increase their direct agricultural lending to 12 per cent of net bank credit in the next two years and to 13.5 per cent two years thereafter, within the overall limit of 18 per cent of total agricultural lending; (3) Banks to increase their disbursements to small and marginal farmers under Special Agricultural Credit Plan (SACP) by the end of the Tenth Plan Period (i.e. by end-March 2007) to 40 per cent; (4) Reduction in cost of agricultural credit by enhancing the cost effectiveness of agricultural loans; (5) Credit flow to small borrowers to be improved through reduction in cost of borrowing, revolving credit packages, procedural simplification, involvement of Panchayati Raj institutions and micro-finance, etc.

Relatives Shares of Different Financial Institutions

After nationalization of 14 major commercial banks in 1969, the commercial banks have consistently increased their share in institutional credit to agriculture from 38.4 per cent in 1980-81 to almost 70 per cent in 2005-06. As a result, the relative share of co-operative societies has declined from 61.6 per cent in 1980-81 to about 22.0 per cent in 2005-06. RRBs have contributed about 8 to 10 per cent of agricultural credit over the years.

TABLE 1

Relatives Shares of Different Financial Institutions

Year	*Co-Operative*	*Scheduled Commercial Banks*	*Regional Rural Banks*	*Total Credit to Agriculture*
1970-71	100.0	—	—	744
1980-81	61.6	38.4	—	3,292
1990-91	49.0	47.6	3.4	9,830
2000-01	39.4	52.6	8.0	52,827
2001-02	38.0	54.1	7.9	62,045
2002-03	34.1	57.2	8.7	69,560
2003-04	31.0	60.3	8.7	86,981
2004-05	25.0	65.0	10.0	1,25,309
2005-06	21.8	69.7	8.5	1,80,486

Sources: (1) Rakesh Mohan, "Agriculture Credit in India," *Economic and Political Weekly*, March 18, 2006, Table 1, p. 1016; and (2) Government of India, Economic Survey, 2006-07 (Delhi, 2007).

CONCLUSION

It, therefore follows that, the agricultural credit should be safe, cheap and it should educate the farmers in farm business. A credit institution should be structurally sound and should have the ability to generate its own profits, ability to take care of: (a) expenses for developing its business, (b) supervision of end-use of credit, (c) training and effective supervision of staff, and (d) other incidental liabilities including provisions for bad and doubtful debts.

REFERENCES

V.M. Dandekar and F.K. Wadia, "Development of Institutional Finance for Agriculture in India," *Journal of Indian School of Political Economy,* Volume 1, No. 2, July-December 1989, p. 201.

Government of India, *Economic Survey,* 2006-07 (Delhi, 2007), p. 172.

Hans P. Binswanger, *et. al.* "How Infrastructure and Financial Institutions Affect Agricultural Output and Investment in India," *Journal of Development Economics,* 41 (2), 1993, p. 355 and p. 361.

Reserve Bank of India, *Report on Currency and Finance,* 2001-02 (Mumbai, 2003), para 3.55.

Bringer, G.K., "Structure of Capital Market in Capital and Credit needs in Changing Agriculture (ed), Baum E.L. Harword G.D. and Heady E.O. The IOWA State University Press, IOWA, USA, 1961.

Sharma, R.D., "Agricultural Finance in India, pp. 16, 17.

Regional Rural Banks in India

Ms. Neetu Dubey, Ms. Renu Dubey and Mr. Mukesh Sharma

The latest policy pronouncements of the Government have been largely agriculture and rural centric. The constitution of a farmer's commission is one among them. Rural credit is emerging as a focal issue and this can be gleaned from the fact that the Government earmarked Rs. 15,000 crore in the Interim Budget to revitalise the co-operative structure. In this context Regional Rural Banks (RRBs), which operate in 476 districts of the country, too need further strengthening. The institution of Regional Rural Banks (RRBs) was created to meet the excess demand for institutional credit in the rural areas, particularly among the economically and socially marginalised sections, although the Co-operative banks and the commercial banks had a clear urban bias. In order to provide access to low-cost banking facilities to the poor, The Narasimham Working Group (1975) proposed the establishment of a new set of banks as institutions which "Combine the local feel and the familiarity with rural problems. Which the Co-operative possess and the degree of business organisation, ability to mobilize and Deposits, access to central money markets and modernised outlook which the Commercial banks have."

INTRODUCTION

After the adoption of the New Economic Policy in 1991, the Indian economy is becoming more and more mature with the passage of time of structural changes undertaken in different sectors and areas. The GDP growth rate has been much higher than the Neo-Hindu rate growth and it has averaged over eight per cent during the past three years. While there has been acceleration in the industrial sector, especially manufacturing and services sector, and the country is graduating from a low-income regime to a middle income regime, these has been deceleration in agricultural growth, which reflects as a broad-based slowdown in the productivity growth. Some of the poorest and most populous states have fallen behind. The economic census 2005, employment growth in the non-farm sector is much lower and average employment itself has declined during the 1990s as comported to the 1980s. While growth is important, it is also imperative that growth becomes more inclusive because if certain regions, sector or groups of people are denied economic opportunities for long periods, the spread and sustainability of growth itself is threatened. The Eleventh Five Year Plan, the Planning Commission has emphasised the need for faster and greater inclusive growth during the Eleventh period. The banking sector, as the most important financial intermediately to mobilise the savings leading to increase investments, facilitating growth would, thus play the most crucial role in attaining the stipulated economic objectives through expansion of the coverage of banking services by reaching the vast Unbanked and Underbanked population of the country.

The institution of Regional Rural Banks (RRBs) was created to meet the excess demand for institutional credit in the rural areas, particularly among the economically and socially marginalised sections. The RRBs Act, 1976 succinctly sums up this overall vision to sub-serve both the developmental and the redistributable objectives: The RRBs were established "with a view to developing the rural economy by providing for the purpose of development of agriculture, trade, commerce, industry and other productive activities in the rural areas, credit and other facilities, particularly to small and marginal farmers, agricultural labours, artisans and small entrepreneurs and for matters connected therewith and incidental thereto."

HISTORICAL PERSPECTIVE

In the early 1970s, the Government observed that despite a wide banking network and developmental initiatives in the first 25 years since Independence, a critical gap still existed in meeting the credit needs of the rural poor. To find a solution, the government appointed a working group on rural credit, the Narasimham Committee, in July 1975. The committee observed that the cost structure of commercial banks, the attitude of bank employees and the lack of a professional approach in the co-operative credit system were the main stumbling blocks rural credit.

The committee also observed that the deposits collected by banks from rural areas were not totally deployed there. The panel, therefore, recommended the creation of a new set of regionally-oriented rural banks which would combine a co-operative's local feel and a commercial bank's business acumen.

The Government accepted these recommendations and accordingly, the ordinance of Regional Rural Banks, 1975 was promulgated on September 26, 1975. This was replaced by the Regional Rural Banks Act, 1976. The mandates of these rural financial institutions were to:

- take banking to the doorsteps of the rural masses, particularly in areas without banking facilities;
- make available cheaper institutional credit to the weaker sections of society, who were to be the only clients of these banks;
- mobilise rural savings and canalise them for supporting productive activities in rural areas;
- generate employment opportunities in the rural areas; and
- bring down the cost of providing credit in rural areas.

With partnerships with the Central Government (50%), State Governments (15%) and commercial banks (35%), the number of RRBs rose from just six in 1975 to 196 by 1987, covering 476 districts. They financed only the weaker sections of the rural community small and marginal farmers, agricultural labourers, small traders, and so on.

Along with commercial banks, RRBs participated enthusiastically in poverty alleviation schemes (IRDP, for Example) and disadvantaged area (drought-prone regions and deserts) development programmes. They quickly became an important and integral part of the rural credit system. However, their financial viability was initially overstretched by policy rigidities coupled with a low capital base in an environment of inadequate infrastructure and deeper social and economic disparities.

As at end-March 2003, there were 196 RRBs spread over 23 states/Union Territories and with a network of 14,350 branches, accounting from 44.5% of the total rural network of all scheduled commercial banks (including RRBs) The rural and semi-urban branches of RRBs constitute 98% of their network. Their deposits and advances as on March 31, 2003, were Rs. 49,078 crore and Rs. 22,028 crore respectively.

Thus, RRBs have done well in mobilising rural deposits and infusing the thrift habit in their clients. The bulk of the loans from RRBs have been to priority sectors, which accounted for over 70% of the total. Agriculture alone took up 46% of the priority sector advances. The involvement of RRBs in providing credit support to small and retail trade and other non-farm rural activities is better than of co-operatives and commercial banks.

As on March 31, 2002, the outreach of RRBs in terms of number of deposits and advances was 50.02 million and 11.94 million respectively. The per-employee accounts handled by RRBs were 885 against the national average of 464 in the banking industry. Similarly, the staff and branch network of RRBs, though respectively 6.7% and 21.8% of the National network served 11.5% of the total deposit accounts and 21.8% of credit accounts of the banking industry.

The Challenges

The Indian economy grew at an estimated 3.7 per cent in 2002-03 against 5.6 per cent the previous year. This was largely because of the negative growth of 4.4 per cent in the agriculture sector. This step fall in GDP highlights the vulnerability of the Indian economy to the performance of the agricultural sector. This is despite other macro-economic indicators and sectors gaining in strengths.

The Tenth Plan (2002-07) has set an ambitious average GDP growth of 8 per cent per annum. To achieve this, it is important to revitalize and revamp not only the agricultural sector but also rural financial institutions. An annual average growth of 7 per cent from this sector alone in the next five years is crucial for achieving the GDP target.

The Task Force on Rural Credit for the Tenth plan has Projected institutional credit flow to agriculture and allied activities at Rs. 7,36,570 crore for 2002-07, which is more than treble (320 per cent) the credit flow (Rs. 2,29,853 crore) during the Ninth Plan (1997-2002).

The agriculture sector is emerging as part of the new economic order arising out of globalisation and implementation of the Agreement on Agriculture (AoA) under the World Trade Organization (WTO). If some agreement is reached at the WTO negotiations, the agriculture sector in the country would be poised for a radical transformation. To withstand the global competition, enhanced productivity and sustainability of the sector has become imperative.

With the demand for food increasing at more than 2% per annum, the financial, land and water resources in the rural sector have come under serve strain. At the same time, agriculture is a matter of livelihood and food security, with nearly 650 million people depending on it. In this context, productivity augmentation in agriculture and other allied sectors, expansion of rural agriculture products have assumed high priority in the nation's development agenda. It is in this context that the Rs. 50,000 crore outlay has been proposed by the Government to be implemented by NABARD.

The Rural Non-Farm Sector (RNFS) has emerged as a key focus area for creating employment in the rural sector and to enable migration from the over-stretched farm sector. The strategy of rural institutions would have to include strengthening the credit delivery system for increasing RNFS employment.

THE QUESTION OF OWNERSHIP

The approach of the Estimates Committee in looking at the

Regional Rural Banks was unique in that most other official Committees in the recent years even while noting the deteriorating patterns in credit activities by the RRBs have completely bypassed the subject while making policy recommendations. Instead attention is held by issues of ownership and capital requirements for the RRBs as necessary steps towards restructuring. At present there is no Capital to Risk weighted Asset Ratio (CRAR) prescription for RRBs. The internal Working Group on RRBs (RBI, 2005) has recommended that the RRBs be asked to maintain 5% to begin with, and over time they may align themselves to the Basle I standards. To wipe out the accumulated losses, provide for the NPAs, and maintain 5% CRAR for the RRBs in the existing scenario, the working Group's calculations show that capital to the extent of Rs. 3,050 crore would have to be infused. It is obvious that the RRBs are being restructured along the same lines as the commercial banks. Is the step necessary? We on the lines that the new freedom given to banks to determine their portfolio, including investments in stock markets might result in high levels of risk in the system, which the regulators believe can be contained through capital requirements, the same logic cannot be applied to RRBs simply because such portfolio choices can never be allowed for these institutions. On the other hand, given that the income recognition and asset classification norms have already caused these institutions to shy away from credit activities to an unacceptable extent, further prudential norms involving high risk-weight on most loaning business can only exacerbate these tendencies further. It is widely establish in the developing country contexts that the response of banks to hitting regulatory constraints on their capital ratio is mostly through cutting back loans or by switching from higher to lower risk weight assets, rather than by raising capital. At a time when most rural areas are starved of credit, it is difficult to comprehend the urgency to impose capital requirements on the RRBs.

The Subject of consolidation of the RRBs as a way of raising their viability and profitability has recurred several times since the beginning of the reform process but without any policy outcome. Various working group and committees have prescribed different measures as also models for restructuring the RRBs. We pick up the most recent threads in the debate. The Chalapathy Rao Committee (2002) had proposed that the Government reduce the number of RRBs to around 40 from the present 196. Option for mergers could be mergers of RRBs following 'one-sponsor bank approach' or they could be amalgamated with their sponsor banks, and thereafter the RRBs could operate as ' commercial entries'. The Vyas Committee II (June 2004), on the other hand, has forwarded a more logical solution. After weighing the various options for amalgamation, it decided that could not consider "the option of merger with sponsor bank, as it would go against the rationale of the third channel for rural credit with a clear rural focus and regional orientation." Instead, it recommended merger of RRBs so as to create a zonal bank for RRBs in the North-East and rural banks at state level for the rest of the country. These banks would work on a stand alone basis and the sponsor banks plus NABARD would contribute to the equity. In the latest document on the subject, the Internal Working Group on RRBs (RBI, 2005) has also proposed consolidation of the RRBs as the merged entities will have a larger area operation and the merger process will help in strengthening some of the weak RRBs. Eliminating the option of merger of RRBs with sponsor banks, the Group has forth two options: merger between RRBs of the same sponsor bank in the same state and merger of RRBs sponsored by different banks in the same state.

Independent of the officials' deliberations, the All Indian Regional Rural Banks Employees' Association (AIRRBEA) has proposed that the RRBs be amalgamated to form zonal or state-level RRBs. They have cited two strong reasons to make the case. "The RRBs must be restructured into zonal or state level RRBs under any public sector apex banking institution or NABARD, so as to ensure the unity of command and cross subsidisation. . . . As in any banking institution, if the central balance sheet is prepared at the apex level, the losses of the few RRBs (in the Eastern, North-Eastern and Central regions) . . . can easily be taken care of with the huge aggregate profit of a majority of the RRBs." Further, a National Body like that of NABARD should monitor the activities of such RRBs. Opposing the demands of All-India RRB Officers Federation for amalgamation of RRBs with the sponsor banks as the only route to sustainability, AIRRBEA has demanded delinking of the RRBs from the sponsor banks so as to ensure functional autonomy for the rural banks, and to relive the burden of 'sole' commercial orientation so that the rural activities can be pursued more freely. (emphasis ours).

The Roadmap

RRBs have emerged as the only surviving rural financial institutions with a professional management culture to meet small-value, large-volume rural credit needs. Therefore, the time has come to revitalise/revamp the structure of RRBs along with co-operatives so that they play a critical role in achieving the developmental targets in the rural sector under the Tenth Plan and emerge stronger.

In this context, the following initiatives are suggested:

> RRBs need to be adequate capital support to enable them have a net Capital Adequacy Ratio (CAR) of 5%. The issue of capital infusion by the owners assumes critical importance and needs immediate attention to enlarge the scope of RRB operations.

The share of sponsoring institutions in the capital structure of RRBs needs to be enlarged to make them a majority shareholder. By acquiring the majority shareholding in RRBs, the sponsor banks/institutions can convert them into vibrant and professionals' subsidiaries and area-specific Special Business Units (SBUs).

In the long-run, they may converge all their agricultural and rural activities under the umbrella of these SBUs. Even co-operative banks can be merged with these SBU at later stages.

Nabard has evolved over the past two decades into a strong and rural-sensitive developmental institution with complete grass-root level understanding of the complexities of the agricultural and rural sectors. Nabard has become a major shareholder in the proposed Agricultural Insurance Cooperation of India Ltd., which includes General Insurance Cooperation and four public sector insurance companies, extend crop insurance cover to all farmers. Similarly, Nabard has played a pioneering role in setting up and opertionalising the National Commodity and Derivatives.

Exchange (NCDX) with equity participation in associate with other national level institutions such as ICICI Bank, LIC and NSE (National Stock Exchange).

Similarly, they may acquire an equity stake in the grass-root level rural financial institutions such as RRBs from the central government and state government to enable them play a more direct and proactive role in rural credit. Nabard should thus become an apex development bank in the rural and agricultural sectors with direct equity participate in RRBs along with sponsoring institutions.

With District Development Managers (DDMs) in most of the districts and also on the boards of all RRBs and co-operatives, Nabard is now fully equipped organizationally and expertise-wise to emerge as a strong player in the rural credit system. A case in point is the promotion of Self-Help Group (SHG) movement by Nabard, Which reflects its immense capability in capacity building and nurturing the rural credit delivery system.

Similarly, the RBI, during the past two decades, has passed on the mantle of rural planning and credit to Nabard, its own subsidiary. Post-reforms and post-liberalization of trade and foreign exchange, the RBI is donning the role as super regulator of the monetary and financial system.

With increasing complexity of macro-economic management, the RBI needs to confine itself to a regulatory role for all financial institution, including the rural ones. The supervisory role of rural financial institutions needs to be restored to the RBI for effective monitoring and control. CRR and SLR requirement of RRBs and rural SBUs need to be different from the dispensation given to other commercial banks.

A different dispensation under CRR and SLR would make available more resources for rural credit deployment. The rate of interest paid on CRR balances held by these rural institutions might also be 100 basis points above what is paid to commercial banks. Similarly, the central Government and all state government need to park their rural development funds with RRBs to ensure cheaper flow of demand deposits. These simple measure, without any cross-subsidisation, would bring down the cost of credit to the rural/agricultural sector.

At the same time, the stipulated 18 per cent benchmark for leading to agricultural needs to be hiked to 25 per cent commensurate with contribution of this sector to GDP. Similarly, the minimum benchmark credit-deposit ratio of 60 per cent needs to be insisted upon for each bank/RRB in every rural districts of the country to ensure adequate credit flow to the rural and semi-urban sectors.

Much of the RRB staff was required during the initial stage and there has been ban on fresh recruitment since 1992. The staffs are getting older whereas the complexities and demands of rural banking now call for more dynamism and youthful talent. Rural banking has emerged as a niche, wherein special skill-set and sensitivity is required. Therefore, the imposed ban on fresh recruitment should be reviewed at the earliest to enhance and diversity the business of RRBs.

Also, RRBs should be permitted to recruit specialist in the technology and agriculture fields. Similarly, grants/soft loans may be provided for technologies so as to enable RRBs compete with commercial/private banks that invest heavily in technology projects. The technology induction in rural banking would facilitate handling low-value, high-volume business effectively in a more cost-effective manner.

In sum, the mandate for RRBs as envisaged in the Act of 1976 is still largely relevant, as the socio-economic conditions of a majority of rural population continue to be a cause of concern for policy-makers. Therefore, the requirement of a strong and flexible structure for RRBs in the rural segment cannot be overemphasised. The Proposed Farmers' Commission and the Dr. Vyas Committee constituted by the RBI need to look into these issues comprehensively to strengthen the rural credit-delivery mechanism.

References

Banerjee, A., Singh, S.K., Banking and Financial Sector Reforms in India, 2002, Deep & Deep Publications Pvt. Ltd., New Delhi.

Monga, G.S., Sinha, R.K., Nationalisation of Banks: Retrospect and Prospects, Deep & Deep Publication, New Delhi.

Singh, A., Rural Development and Banking in India, 1989.

Singh, Poonam, Gramin Nirbal Vargo Ke Utthan Mein Banko Ka Yogdan, 2002.

Thakur, D., Indian Banking and Money Market, 1997.

Tomar, A.K., Prakash, Jai, Role of Regional Rural Bank in Economic Development, 1996.

Magazine & Journals

Kurukshetra

Yojna
Vaarta
Southern Economist
Economic & Political Weekly
News Paper
Times of India
Economic Today
Hindustan Times
Amar Ujala
Danik Jagran

Websites

www.org.com
www.yahoo.com
www.mainstreamweekly.net
www.nabard.org
www.rural.nic.in
www.ari.nic.in

Index